Case Studies in Leadership and Adult Development

This book serves as an instructional tool for development of skills related to the organizational leadership of adults. The text offers teaching cases that explicitly partner the leadership and adult development literature bases so readers can work to apply leadership for adult development to real-world scenarios.

Case Studies in Leadership and Adult Development: Applying Theoretical Perspectives to Real World Challenges consists of 19 chapters, organized into three parts. Part I has four chapters drawn from business and industry leaders' experiences encompassing cases from nonprofit, for-profit, and non-governmental agencies. Part II has three chapters that focus on the challenges of leading through crisis, including how the Covid-19 pandemic shapes decision making and impacts leadership in both K–12 and higher education environments. Part III offers a comprehensive view of education through 12 chapters, four of which are drawn from higher education settings. Part III's balance includes cases from elementary, middle, and secondary schools and district-level leadership.

Written for graduate level courses in adult education, each case focuses on at least one major theory from both the leadership and adult development domains. With questions for discussion and reflection, the book allows students to explore the linkages between leadership theories and adult development theories within the context of real-world scenarios.

Kristina N. LaVenia teaches and researches leadership for improved organizational outcomes with a special focus on leadership for adult development. Her background as a school counselor informs her educational research and leadership preparation work.

Judy Jackson May is an associate professor of educational administration and leadership, whose research focuses on factors impacting the academic, emotional, and social success of students of color. This lens is strongly informed by her experiences as a former special education teacher, district curriculum coordinator, and urban school principal.

Case Studies in Leadership and Adult Development
Applying Theoretical Perspectives to Real World Challenges

Kristina N. LaVenia and
Judy Jackson May

NEW YORK AND LONDON

First published 2022
by Routledge
605 Third Avenue, New York, NY 10158

and by Routledge
2 Park Square, Milton Park, Abingdon, Oxon OX14 4RN

Routledge is an imprint of the Taylor & Francis Group, an informa business

© 2022 Taylor & Francis

The right of Kristina N. LaVenia and Judy Jackson May to be identified as
the authors of the editorial material, and of the authors for their individual
chapters, has been asserted in accordance with sections 77 and 78 of the
Copyright, Designs and Patents Act 1988.

All rights reserved. No part of this book may be reprinted or reproduced or
utilised in any form or by any electronic, mechanical, or other means, now
known or hereafter invented, including photocopying and recording, or in
any information storage or retrieval system, without permission in writing
from the publishers.

Trademark notice: Product or corporate names may be trademarks or
registered trademarks, and are used only for identification and explanation
without intent to infringe.

Library of Congress Cataloging-in-Publication Data
Names: LaVenia, Kristina N., 1970- editor. | Jackson May, Judy, 1959-
editor.
Title: Case studies in leadership and adult development : applying
theoretical perspectives to real world challenges / edited by Kristina N.
LaVenia and Judy Jackson May.
Description: New York, NY : Routledge, 2022. | Includes bibliographical
references and index.
Identifiers: LCCN 2021019532 (print) | LCCN 2021019533 (ebook) |
ISBN 9780367354596 (hardback) | ISBN 9780367354589 (paperback) |
ISBN 9780429331503 (ebook)
Subjects: LCSH: Adult learning--Case studies. | Adult education--Case
studies. | Adulthood--Psychological aspects--Case studies. | Leadership--
Case studies.
Classification: LCC LC5225.L42 C38 2022 (print) | LCC LC5225.L42
(ebook) | DDC 374.001/9--dc23
LC record available at https://lccn.loc.gov/2021019532
LC ebook record available at https://lccn.loc.gov/2021019533

ISBN: 978-0-367-35459-6 (hbk)
ISBN: 978-0-367-35458-9 (pbk)
ISBN: 978-0-429-33150-3 (ebk)

DOI: 10.4324/9780429331503

Typeset in Baskerville
by Taylor & Francis Books

Contents

List of illustrations	viii
Dedication	ix
Endorsements	x
Foreword	xii
Reviewers	xv
List of contributors	xvi
Introduction	xxii

JUDY JACKSON MAY AND KRISTINA N. LAVENIA

PART I
Introduction to Part I   1

1 Adult Development and Nonprofit Board Leadership: The Clash
   of Self-Authoring Minds   5
   JENNIFER A. JONES

2 Helping a Nonprofit CEO Pivot Her Leadership Style   14
   DENISE M. CUMBERLAND AND GREGORY NIELSEN

3 Exploring the Role of Emotion and Perceptions of Risk When
   "Leading From the Middle"   23
   DEIDRE M. LE FEVRE

4 It's Time for Transformation! Using Transformational Leadership to
   Support Transformational Learning and Attract Emerging Leaders   31
   JILL FOX BERNACIAK

PART II
Introduction to Part II   41

5 Responding to School Crises through Compassionate Leadership:
   A District Leader's Journey with Covid-19   45
   KARA LASATER AND CLAY LASATER

vi *Contents*

6 Higher Education Leadership in an Unprecedented and Uncertain Environment: The Case of a Midwestern Private Institution   55
BRIGETTE S. GIBSON

7 Dr. Remote Instruction: Time Constraints and Critical Consciousness in Crisis Leadership   65
GUY L. PARMIGIAN

PART III
Introduction to Part III   75

8 Activating and Sustaining Motivation for Social Justice Leadership in Secondary Education   83
RACHEL ROEGMAN AND JASMINE D. COLLINS

9 Learning Transfer: The Missing Link to Leading the Successful Implementation of Professional Development in Schools   93
CORINNE BRION

10 Leading for Transformation? The Decisions of New Coaches Matter   103
LISA L. ORTMANN, KATHERINE BRODEUR AND SUSAN L. MASSEY

11 We Can Do This! Transformational Leadership for School Improvement   112
JEREMY D. VISONE

12 Because They Are Worth It: Utilizing Servant Leadership to Increase First Generation College Persistence   122
ALEXIS N. HARTLEY AND SONYA D. HAYES

13 Using a Feminist Approach to Leadership Education to Promote Coaction Among Women Collegiate Student-Athletes   131
JOANNA LINE

14 Visionary and Mission-Minded School Leadership Grounded in Adult Learning Theory   140
TYRONE BYNOE

15 Curriculum and Pedagogy Considerations for Connecting Personal Growth and Leadership Development   148
RONALD S. GLICKMAN AND MAX H. GLICKMAN

Contents vii

16 Preparing Educators to Lead Professional Learning in P–12
Schools: Applying Research on Leadership Development and
Adult Learning 158
DUSTIN MILLER AND ANIKA BALL ANTHONY

17 The Gap between Theory and Practice: A Scenario from Higher
Education 167
VIKTOR WANG AND GERALDINE TORRISI-STEELE

18 "I Can't Hear You": Incorporating Developmentally Appropriate
Feedback for Adults in Balkor Elementary Charter School 176
PATRICIA M. VIRELLA

19 The Sharpie Incident: Coloring in the Lines and School Policing
of Black Hair 185
JENNIFER L. MARTIN

Index 195

Illustrations

Figures

8.1	Sample Slides from Principal Wells's Presentation	86
9.1	Multidimensional Model of Learning Transfer (MMLT)	99
11.1	Purpose Statement for the Teaching and Learning Team at SBA.	116
11.2	Team Relationship Organizer about School Improvement Planning	116
15.1	College Student Development Framework	154

Tables

8.1	Teacher Referrals, Disaggregated by Race and Offense	85
8.2	Discipline Consequences, Disaggregated by Race	85
17.1	Static Organizations Versus Learning Organizations	172

Dedication

This work is dedicated to my husband, Mark, as well as to my children David, Sophie, and Charlie. Your belief in me means more than I can say.

Kristina N. LaVenia

This publication is dedicated to my parents Carlos Anderson Jackson (1930–1974) and Dr. Faith Lilly Jackson (1936–2013), who gave of themselves to put the world at my feet. And to my blessed children Jennifer, Jacquelyn, and Alicia, without whose unconditional love I would cease to be.

Judy Jackson May

Endorsements

Challenges to 21st century organizational leadership are steeped in the culture of each institution. Facilitating learning for strong leadership requires that individuals experience realistic situations and practice making data-driven, equitable decisions. *Case studies in leadership and adult development: Applying theoretical perspectives to real world challenges* provides engaging scenarios with rich details for leaders to engage in self-reflection, role-playing, and data analysis. Organizational research within each scenario gives leaders a framework for discussion and decisions. This text is relevant and timely for 21st century school administrators, nonprofit and business managers, and for university programs providing coursework in organizational and educational leadership.

Jennifer Groman, PhD, Ashland University

Bravo to LaVenia and May for skillfully applying real world case stories to discover best practices in leading organizations from elementary school to non-governmental agencies, in their latest book, *Case studies in leadership and adult development: Applying theoretical perspectives to real world challenges.* Melding research and practice, the book provides opportunities to transform and grow adult leaders that promote emotional well-being, and compassionate and inclusive leadership through an equitable lens. Organizations can use the guided discussions and practical exercises as an easy-to-implement teaching tool.

Diana R. Patton
Speaker, Consultant, Social Justice Advocate and Attorney
Diana R. Patton Consulting, LLC
Author of *Inspiration in My Shoes* and *This Yogi's Journey*

Case studies in leadership and adult development: Applying theoretical perspectives to real world challenges is a refreshingly excellent read! As a district level urban school leader, we are facing unprecedented leadership challenges. Kristina LaVenia and Judy May present opportunities for adult leadership development in a diverse format. The book utilizes a variety of cases covering topics such as social justice, constructive conflict, pandemic crises response, racial bias and educational equity, and feminist leadership. A great way to discover best practices applicable to any leadership role!

Dr. Treva E. Jeffries
Assistant Transformational Leader of Equity, Diversity and Inclusion
Toledo Public Schools

Even those of us who have "conquered" global finance and tech markets on Wall Street should not lose focus on the need to understand our clients in environments that may be multigenerational and diverse. It is essential to be aware of the leadership challenges of potential stakeholders and *Case Studies in Leadership and Adult Development: Applying Theoretical Perspectives to Real World Challenges* offers a landscape of perspectives that can inform our daily work. In the fast-paced tech-based setting, leadership training is not always prioritized, and this book can serve as a valuable tool for adult leadership development.

Charles Stephen Thompson
Founder and CEO, Brooklyn Helpdesk, Inc. and
DevOps Software Engineer, Symbiont.io
New York, NY

Foreword

In *Case studies in leadership and adult development: Applying theoretical perspectives to real world challenges*, LaVenia and May blend theoretical perspectives with practicing professionals' rich experiences to provide authentic application in real time. This leadership preparation textbook's strength is that it allows leaders to embrace complex organizational and leadership challenges. The cases offer extensive engagement from various fields, which will challenge intellectual thought.

The book contains 19 chapters organized into three parts written by practitioners representing a myriad of experiences across interdisciplinary sectors. Ten chapters focus on public and charter schools in elementary, middle, and high school; five chapters focus on higher education; and four chapters focus on business entities. As a timely reflection of the current climate, the editors highlight the chapters exploring crisis leadership in the midst of the Covid-19 pandemic. The main parts of the text are introduced by an editor summary outlining chapter themes. Each chapter provides a real world scenario accompanied by theoretical perspectives, discussion questions, and activities. According to Patricia Gouthro (2019), "ensuring that adult education is a practice informed by theory enables educators to understand the complexity of the teaching and learning process" (p. 60).

Effective leadership is singularly the most significant element in the success of any organization. Some may opine that the term "effective leadership" is overused and lacks meaning. I strongly disagree. In reflection of over 40 years as an educator, 30 of which have been in complex organizational leadership roles, I believe the term can be uniquely defined. Effective leadership is the ability to draw, focus, maintain, and grow the attention, dedication, and spirit of a group's adult members, bringing their mindsets, ideas, aspirations, and experiences.

The challenges of effective leadership evident throughout the 20th century increased exponentially in the 21st century. And the pandemic served to exacerbate existing problems leaving few organizational structures untouched. From nonprofit to corporate ventures, from K–16 educational settings to post-secondary institutions, and from small to big business, the impact of the pandemic merely illustrates what we already knew; successful leadership is essential now more than ever.

Foreword xiii

LaVenia and May have tapped an avenue of learning that is tried and true; adults learn best from peers in realistic environments. The publication represents Malcolm Knowles' (1980) conceptualization of andragogy, which is the "art and science of helping adults learn" (p. 43). Knowles and other researchers have confirmed that adults enjoy control over their learning, learn best from timely and applicable experiences, and learn from problem-solving opportunities.

The case study instructional design is the most effective way to engage leaders and understand both the theory and practice of actual experiences that are substantive, detailed, perplexing, authentic, and powerful. The case study methodology provides leaders with an unbelievable opportunity to challenge leader beliefs and add significant knowledge to their ability to problem solve in their actual leadership experience. According to Sommer and Strong, "A useful theory is the residue of multiple experiences and an aid to interpret new instances" (2016, as cited in Gouthro, 2019, p. 62).

I appreciate this collection based on my leadership experiences. During my career, I have served as a lecturer, tenured faculty member, and program chair in higher education. In my eight years at Bowling Green State University, I enjoyed the distinction of visioning and creating the Leadership Studies Doctoral Program, an interdisciplinary doctorate for professional adult learners that remains a highly regarded and successful program after 25 years. It is rare to serve as a tenured professor and the Chief Executive of a large urban school district. This unique combination has increased my appreciation of the case study design.

My professional background allows me to strongly endorse this collection of chapters as valuable in the higher education learning experience and executive training programs. Integrated leadership strategies that bring various leaders from different disciplines together for training are a powerful instructional approach. This case study textbook will allow leaders to utilize transformational leadership qualities and strategies to improve organizational effectiveness, and I believe this collection is an excellent instructional tool.

Eugene T. W. Sanders, Ph.D.
Chief Executive Officer and Superintendent
Sandusky City Schools

Dr. Eugene T. W. Sanders is a former tenured professor, Chair of the Department of Educational Administration and Supervision, and Director of the Doctoral Program in Leadership Studies at Bowling Green State University. He has the unique leadership experience of being both a university faculty member and Chief Executive Officer and Superintendent of three urban public school districts in Ohio: Toledo, Cleveland, and Sandusky. He authored *Urban school leadership: Issues and strategies* (1999) and is the Chief Executive Officer of the Sanders Transformation Group, LLC, a consulting agency that works with schools and corporations on effective leadership strategies.

xiv *Foreword*

References

Gouthro, P. A. (2019). Taking time to learn: The importance of theory for adult education, *Adult Education Quarterly*, 69(1), 60–76.

Knowles, M. S. (1980). *The modern day practice of adult education: From pedagogy to andragogy* (2nd ed.). Cambridge Books.

Reviewers

The editors extend our deepest thanks to these colleagues who agreed to serve as reviewers. The fact that everyone was so responsive and helpful during such a stressful year makes the support for this work even more special. Each of these reviewers completed multiple blind reviews and provided feedback on both technical and conceptual components.

Ms. Jodi Anderson
Mr. Nathan Blust
Dr. Teresa Braun
Dr. Pamela Bruno
Dr. Gloria Gajewicz
Dr. Jennifer Groman
Dr. Sherri L. Horner
Dr. Joyce Litten
Dr. Kevin Miller
Dr. Amanda Ricketts
Dr. Abhijeet Shirsat

Contributors

Kristina N. LaVenia (0000-0001-8284-5864) is an assistant professor in the School of Educational Foundations, Leadership, and Policy at Bowling Green State University where she teaches courses on leadership for adult development, research methods, and applied statistics. Kristina's research aims to understand how leaders support improved outcomes for marginalized and/or vulnerable groups. Her current projects include: a study of the emotional demands of teaching and leading in schools; a study of interventions and programming to support educators' well-being; and an evaluation of teacher professional development designed to support culturally responsive practice. Kristina received her Ph.D. in educational leadership and policy as well as a graduate certificate in measurement and statistics from Florida State University. She also completed her doctoral studies as an Institute of Education Sciences (IES) predoctoral fellow and has served as a certified reviewer for the IES What Works Clearinghouse since 2009.

Judy Jackson May (0000-0002-4145-7475) is an associate professor of Educational Administration and Leadership Studies at Bowling Green State University. She currently serves as coordinator for the Leadership Studies Doctoral Program and is the professor of record for the Leadership Theories course. Dr. May also teaches in the Master of Educational Leadership Program and serves as coordinator for an undergraduate teacher preparation course for which she authored a textbook, *Teacher talk: A 21st century guide for beginning educators*. Before moving to higher education, she served as a speech pathologist/audiologist, a multiple handicap teacher, a school principal in urban and rural districts, and a curriculum coordinator. Dr. May has delivered over 60 presentations and workshops at the regional, national, and international levels, including Honk Kong, Tokyo, Cambodia, and South Africa. She has authored or co-authored 20 journal articles and book chapters. In her position as the Northwest Region Manager for the Ohio School Boards Association, her research interests focus on strategies to transform urban school leadership to ensure the success of 21st century students.

Anika Ball Anthony (0000-0002-1436-0635) is an associate professor of Educational Administration and Associate Dean of Academic Affairs in the Graduate School at The Ohio State University. Her research focuses on educational leadership, the systemic nature of school organizations, and the use of technology to support teaching and learning in P–12 and post-secondary settings.

Jill Fox Bernaciak (0000-0002-0088-6097) is a doctoral candidate in the Leadership Studies program at Bowling Green State University. Her research focuses on the culture for innovation in business. Jill has 20 years of experience as a corporate intrapreneur, launching over $800 million in new products. She teaches sales, entrepreneurship, and marketing, and is a Moderator for Harvard Corporate Learning. Jill is a Partner with Cleveland Social Venture Partners, that works to improve the performance of nonprofits through donations of money, time, and expertise.

Corinne Brion (0000-0001-6151-525X) is an assistant professor at the University of Dayton. She earned her Ph.D. in Leadership at the University of San Diego. Corinne's research interests include investigating the process of learning transfer among adult learners so as to understand what enhances and hinders the transfer of knowledge in different contexts.

Katherine Brodeur (0000-0002-4691-8859) is an assistant professor in the School of Teaching and Learning at Bowling Green State University, where she teaches graduate literacy courses. Previously, she worked as a high school special education teacher, a middle school reading specialist, and a literacy coach. Her research focuses on professional learning that emphasizes reflection and empowers educators to put students at the center of their instruction.

Tyrone Bynoe (0000-0002-9652-6917) is a faculty member at the University of Michigan–Flint. He teaches in the Doctor of Education and Educational Specialist programs. His primary research interests and expertise are in school finance, school business management, school leadership preparation, and comparative education. Tyrone has been a professor for 17 years.

Jasmine D. Collins (0000-0002-4181-2502) is an assistant professor of Organizational and Community Leadership in the Agricultural Leadership, Education & Communications program at the University of Illinois at Urbana-Champaign. Her research examines the experiences, environments, and resources that support college students in their development as leaders and engaged citizens, focusing specifically on developmental outcomes for marginalized student populations in an effort to inform educators and educational leaders on best practices for engaging with and supporting these students.

Denise M. Cumberland (0000-0003-4508-4386) is an associate professor in the Masters of Science in Human Resources and Organization xviii *List of contributors*

Development program at the University of Louisville. Her research interests include governance, entrepreneurship, leadership, and training within global organizations, franchise firms, and the nonprofit sector. She has authored eight book chapters and has over 30 journal articles.

Brigette S. Gibson (0000-0002-1939-1211) is a higher education professional at Bowling Green State University. She is also a third-year doctoral student in BGSU's Leadership Studies program. Brigette has experience in institutional effectiveness, student accounts, and student financial services. Her research interests include historically underrepresented minority students achievement gaps with a special focus on retention, persistence, and degree attainment; group differences in college students' sense of belonging; and student financial literacy.

Max H. Glickman (0000-0003-0339-3586) is a business consultant in the Consumer Markets practice at PricewaterhouseCoopers, where he advises clients on diversity and inclusion, and designs workforce training curriculum. Max began his career as a classroom teacher in Chicago with Teach For America and continued building his pedagogical and curriculum development skills as a student-centered curriculum specialist on assignment in Southeast Asia for the Peace Corp. He holds a BA from the University of Southern California.

Ronald S. Glickman (0000-0003-4033-952X) is an experienced executive with a proven track record for developing high potential talent and motivating culturally diverse teams to deliver breakthrough results on a global scale. Ronald holds a BBA from National University, an MBA from the University of Southern California, and an EdD from the Charter College of Education at California State University Los Angeles, where he teaches managerial leadership in the College of Business and Economics.

Alexis N. Hartley (0000-0002-2170-2314) has worked in higher education for over ten years. She is currently an academic advisor and doctoral student at the University of Tennessee–Knoxville. Her research interests include first generation college students, academic misconduct, and college student transition through luminal phases. Currently, she is examining college student experiences as they prepare for graduating college and transitioning into adulthood.

Sonya D. Hayes (0000-0002-6826-2117) is an assistant professor in the Department of Educational Leadership and Policy Studies at the University of Tennessee. Her research interests include leadership development and support for both pre- and post-service school principals, principal preparation, and leadership for learning. Specifically, she is interested in how principals are prepared and supported for the complex and demanding role of improving teaching and learning.

List of contributors xix

Jennifer A. Jones (0000-0003-4061-953X) is an assistant professor of nonprofit leadership and management at the University of Florida. She has worked in and volunteered for nonprofits for almost 20 years. Jennifer earned her Ph.D. at the University of San Diego, where she studied the intersection of adult development and nonprofit philanthropic leadership. She has published more than 28 peer-reviewed articles and regularly translates her research for practitioner audiences.

Clay Lasater (0000-0002-7702-177X) is Superintendent of Lockwood Public Schools. He has experience as a middle and high school teacher, high school principal, and superintendent.

Kara Lasater (0000-0003-2479-2615) is an assistant professor of educational leadership at the University of Arkansas. Her research interests include family–school partnerships, data use, and leadership preparation.

Deidre M. Le Fevre (0000-0002-7422-0431) is associate professor and head of graduate programs in educational leadership at the University of Auckland, New Zealand. She leads large-scale research projects investigating effective leadership, organizational, and professional learning practices for change and improvement. Deidre brings knowledge and skills in understanding organizational change, the development of professional capability, and effective leadership to her work teaching, researching, and consulting with leaders across a range of sectors and organizations.

Joanna Line (0000-0001-5529-3160) is a PhD candidate in American Culture Studies at Bowling Green State University. She has been a collegiate cross country and track and field coach for over seven years. She also works in the field of community and civic engagement. Her professional interests include social justice through sport, inclusive leadership education, and community-based research.

Jennifer L. Martin (0000-0001-6515-9395) is an assistant professor in the Department of Teacher Education at the University of Illinois at Springfield. She is the editor of *Racial battle fatigue: Insights from the front lines of social justice advocacy* (recipient of the 2016 AERA Division B's Outstanding Book Recognition Award), and co-author of *Teaching for educational equity: Case studies for professional development and principal preparation*, Volumes 1 and 2 (Roman & Littlefield). She is the 2019 recipient of the Paula Silver Case Award for Volume Year 2018, *UCEA Journal of Cases in Educational Leadership* (Volume 21): for "The Bathroom Case: Creating a Supportive School Environment for Transgender and Gender Non-conforming Students" (with Dr. Jane Beese). Follow her podcast at https://anchor.fm/doctorjenmartin/

Susan L. Massey (0000-0002-8585-0607) is an assistant professor at Upper Iowa University, where she teaches graduate courses in literacy and teacher leadership. Her research interests include literacy coaching and university-

xx *List of contributors*

based literacy clinics. She is an active presenter at local, state, and national conferences and is involved in a number of professional organizations.

Dustin W. Miller (0000-0002-8267-6498) is a clinical assistant professor and director of the EdD in Educational Administration at The Ohio State University. His research interests focus on principal professional learning, leading in times of crises, and creating supportive work environments for LGBTQ+ school leaders. Dustin teaches courses on leadership, professional learning, human resource management, and ethics. He also served for 20 years in K–12 as a high school principal, middle school principal, director of secondary education, and English teacher.

Gregory Nielsen (0000-0002-5292-6273) is committed to helping leaders translate vision into reality. He is an accomplished nonprofit CEO, having previously led the Center for Nonprofit Excellence in Louisville, KY. He is a military veteran, holds a Bachelor of Arts Degree in Government and International Relations from the University of Notre Dame, and a Juris Doctorate from Notre Dame Law School.

Lisa L. Ortmann (0000-0002-3895-0162) is an assistant professor in the department of education at Gustavus Adolphus College in Minnesota. She is a former high school English teacher and K–12 literacy and instructional coach. Her research focuses on the preparation and development of literacy educators at various stages of their career, particularly when transitioning to new professional roles or expanding beyond traditional approaches in support of student literacies and learning.

Guy L. Parmigian (0000-0002-3052-7917) is superintendent at the Benton-Carroll-Salem School District in Ottawa County, Ohio. He has also served as curriculum director, career-technical education director, high school assistant principal, and English teacher. His research interests include school finance, school leadership, and the history of education.

Rachel Roegman (0000-0002-4181-2502) is an assistant professor of educational leadership in the Department of Education Policy, Organization and Leadership at the University of Illinois, Urbana-Champaign. Her research examines the development and support of equity-focused leaders. Her work has been influenced by her experiences as a public middle school teacher and her commitment to anti-racist, equity-focused practice.

Geraldine Torrisi-Steele (0000-0002-6045-4114) is a senior lecturer in Information and Communications Technologies at Griffith University where she teaches in user experience and information systems. Her key interests are learning theory, human computer interaction, and leadership. Cutting across her interests is a belief in design with "the human at the center."

Patricia M. Virella (0000-0002-5736-3422) is a graduate professor in the Art of Teaching Program at Sarah Lawrence College and an Andrew

Carnegie Mellon Fellow. She is currently a PhD student at the University of Connecticut. Her scholarship focuses on education reform policy and implementation in oppressed communities. She also studies crisis leadership in education and principal preparation within the urban setting.

Jeremy D. Visone (0000-0003-2549-4839) is an assistant professor of Educational Leadership, Policy & Instructional Technology at Central Connecticut State University. He has served as an elementary and secondary school administrator. His primary research interests include teacher leadership, collaboration, and evaluation.

Viktor Wang (0000-0001-9557-0054) is a full-time faculty in the Department of Educational Leadership & Technology at California State University, San Bernardino. He has brought leadership to the study of education and has solidified understanding of how to conduct research into the complexities of the learning process. He has produced 240+ refereed publications, provided multiple opportunities for peers and students to develop their scholarly capabilities, and stimulated the research agendas of numerous colleagues.

Introduction

Judy Jackson May and Kristina N. LaVenia

The motivation for this edited volume stems from the editors' experiences teaching and researching leadership development. The thesis driving this book is that leadership preparation often includes an implicit focus on leadership for adult development, but that faculty, students, and practitioners can benefit from this link being made explicit. A review of several graduate programs with a focus on leadership reveals that it is common for students to have choices of courses with foci such as *Organizational Change, Leading Innovation,* or *Adult Learning,* which illustrates the importance of these areas for leadership preparation. Importantly, when faculty wish to guide students through learning activities aimed at linking leadership with adult learning and development, curricular supports are missing. This book works to meet that curricular need by not only providing real-world cases focused on leadership for adult development, but also offering cases that draw from a range of organizational and work contexts.

Case studies in leadership and adult development: Applying theoretical perspectives to real world challenges consists of 19 chapters organized into three parts. A thematic perspective anchors each part. Part I has four chapters drawn from business and industry leaders' experiences encompassing cases from nonprofit, for-profit, and non-governmental agencies. Part II has three chapters that focus on the challenges of leading through crisis. These cases explore how the Covid-19 pandemic shapes decision making and impacts leadership in both K–12 and higher education environments. Part III offers a comprehensive view of education through 12 chapters, four of which are drawn from higher education settings. Part III's balance includes cases from elementary, middle, and secondary schools and district-level leadership.

Each of the three parts includes an editors' summary that guides the reader through an overview of the chapters. Each chapter includes an illustrative teaching case accompanied by theoretical and literature perspectives, instructional activities, and extended learning suggestions. In contrast to other teaching case approaches, the editors seek to embrace each contributing author's personality by retaining as much individual style, format, technique, and creative approach as possible. The book is organized to reflect critical adult development theories that allow instructors to adapt cases to targeted learning objectives and learners to self-pace their progress. As Malcolm Knowles uncovered nearly 60 years ago, adult learning patterns are distinctly different from those of children. Knowles appropriately distinguishes between pedagogy, the art and science of helping students learn, and andragogy, the art and science of helping adults learn. This book is grounded in adult developmental perspectives of how individuals learn in adulthood. Merriam and Caffarella (1999, p. 272) capture Knowles' theory in the follow points:

- As adults mature, their self-perception moves from dependence to independence with a desire for more self-directed activity.
- Adults amass increasing depth of experiences that serve as significant sources of learning and growth.
- Adult preparedness, interest, and engagement in activities depends on the task's relevance to their current roles.
- As adults mature, they seek to apply new skills immediately as opposed to filing for later use.
- Adults are more stimulated by factors that are internal as opposed to external.

Andragogy centers on the current life circumstance of the learner. Using cases that involve diverse professionals sharing personal experiences, the editors seek to provide relatable, timely, and realistic opportunities for reader leadership growth. While the contributing authors provide research support to their cases, readers are encouraged to engage in their own "meaning-making." Meaning-making is the central theme of Mezirow's (1996) adult transformation theory, where "learning is understood as the process of using a prior interpretation to construct a new or revised interpretation of the meaning of one's experience in order to guide future action" (p. 162). This transformative learning process is "firmly anchored in the life experience. All human beings need to understand their experiences, to make sense of what is happening in their lives" (Merriam & Caffarella, 1999, p. 320). The editors of the cases in this collection provide life experiences informed by theory and moved to practice. Patricia Gouthro (2019) submits that "ensuring that adult education is a practice informed by theory enables educators to understand the complexity of the teaching and learning process" (p. 60).

Readers will note that transformational leadership theory is a consistent theme throughout this collection. The concept, first introduced by Bernard Bass nearly 40 years ago, is used extensively in the literature on leadership and remains relevant when discussing successful organizational growth. Bass and Avolio (1993) reflect on Bass' 1985 definition, which describes transformational leaders as those who "change their culture by first understanding it and then realigning the organization's culture with a new vision and revision of its shared assumptions, values, and norms" (p. 112). While this may appear somewhat cliché, the editors of this book challenge readers to contemplate why transformational leadership withstands the test of time. Regardless of the

xxiv *Introduction*

discipline, dissecting effective transformation appears to rely on three key elements: understanding the nature of the organization's members, understanding the organization's culture, and understanding how to coalesce these forces to engage the group in work that transforms the internal structure to achieve short- and long-term goals.

Although the transformation elements remain static, the strategies needed to fulfill each element will vary from organization to organization and from leader to leader. In the application of transformational leadership, consider the following analogy. All vehicles may require the same basic elements to run, such as a frame, motor, tires, and oil. However, the actual body type and model style/trim will vary from user to user and between one purpose and another (e.g., rough terrain vs. city driving). We see *leadership for adult development* as part of the necessary elements for organizational growth. This book is designed to provide critical analysis perspectives and reflection on leadership to support adult development. That so many of the contributors to this work chose transformational leadership as a focal point leads us to suggest to our readers that this is a leadership focus that is particularly relevant for those leaders working to understand and leverage adult followers' developmental processes.

References

Bass, B. M. & Avolio, B. J. (1993, Spring). Transformational leadership and organizational culture. *Public Administration Quarterly*, 17(1), 112–121.

Gouthro, P. A. (2019). Taking time to learn: The importance of theory for adult education. *Adult Education Quarterly*, 69(1), 60–76.

Merriam, S. B., & Caffarella, R. S. (1999). *Learning in adulthood: A comprehensive guide* (2nd ed.). Jossey-Bass.

Mezirow, J. (1996). Contemporary paradigms of learning. *Adult Education Quarterly*, 46(3), 158–172.

Part I

Introduction to Part I

Kristina N. LaVenia and Judy Jackson May

Organizational leaders recognize that context matters, so the editorial team worked to collect teaching cases that allow instructors, readers, and practitioners to explore leadership for adult development in a variety of contexts. This section of *Case studies in leadership and adult development: Applying theoretical perspectives to real world challenges* offers scenarios, supporting literature, and learning activities focused on business and nonprofit settings. Jones invites us to consider nonprofit leadership in the chapter "Adult Development and Nonprofit Board Leadership: The Clash of Self-Authoring Minds" using Kegan's work on development stages. The editors encourage readers to thoughtfully work through the discussion questions offered at the close of the chapter. Also, we see this case as a space to think carefully about followership and the social and relational dynamics at play between leaders and followers. For example, consider the question: *If you were a member of the board, how might readers engage in such a way that would allow Chris's perspective to unfold? What is the potential for other board members to influence Joseph's power on the board meetings? How can Chris better leverage the board as a unit?* As you answer these questions, think about how Kegan's stages of development might matter not just for dyads, such as Chris and Joseph, but also for teams.

Cumberland and Nielsen explore how philanthropic ventures might maintain their mission's integrity while securing funding to keep the effort viable. In "Helping a Nonprofit CEO Pivot Her Leadership Style," the authors seek to help readers consider multiple perspectives when resolving complex organizational issues. The authors invite readers to apply the frames of Bolman and Deal's reframing model and situational leadership to understand how to build relationships with stakeholders, understand the utility of aligning leader style with follower readiness, and increase strength by sharing power. This case appropriately asks how leaders can effectively reflect on their leadership to understand the choices that might be engaged to move the organization forward. Goffee and Jones (2000) open an engaging article published by *Harvard Business Review* by noting, "If you want to silence a room full of executives…ask them 'Why would anyone want to be led by you?'" This is a pivotal question that any leader should be willing to ask and one we think would make an excellent reflection after careful study of the Cumberland and Nielsen case.

DOI: 10.4324/9780429331503-1

2 Introduction to Part I

Similar to other businesses, non-governmental agencies are complex systems requiring effective leadership. In "Exploring the Role of Emotion and Perceptions of Risk When Leading from the Middle," Deirdre LeFevre charges the reader to consider a paradigm where leadership emerges from the middle instead of the top of the hierarchy. The author asserts that leaders who emerge from the middle are unprotected by positional titles and are vulnerable to challenges unique to undefined leadership roles. Consider that leaders who occupy roles with a title enjoy a "positional power shield." However, leaders who emerge from the middle are often subject to the emotional stress of informally occupying leadership levels without exercising formal control. In this case, LeFevre examines the unique challenges of leading from the middle and how the role of emotion can influence the way people feel, think, and act. From a distributive leadership perspective, LeFevre contends that emotion and risk are inherent. This case helps readers understand the strength emergent leaders bring to the organizational structure and acknowledge the inherent dilemmas. The chapter offers several avenues of reflection for readers. As a positional figurehead in a complex social organization, how might readers encourage, advocate, and reduce emergent leaders' emotional risk? What organizational practices might assist in reducing uncertainty in the outcomes of risk-taking?

The utility of transformational leadership theory is likely its effective transferability across organizational disciplines. This scenario offered by Jill Fox Bernaciak shares a multinational corporation experiencing an "external disruption" due to international competition. The organization is also facing a reduction in staff, paternalistic leadership practices impacting gaining and retaining new and talented employees, and a lack of sales growth. This chapter "It's Time for Transformation! Using Transformational Leadership to Support Learning and Attract Emerging Leaders" pushes readers to consider the complexity and unpredictability of change in business. The continuing challenges to transforming the organizational structure include team conflict, internal resistance, lack of organizational motivation, cultural competence, power, and politics. Jill Fox Bernaciak shares that transformational leadership characteristics can manage resistance, create connections, raise motivation and morality, and assist in goal setting and group alignment. Reflecting on this case, what behaviors might leaders display to demonstrate the preceding transformational leadership characteristics? In addition to transformational leadership, Bernaciak engages Mezirow's leadership theory in understanding how a disorienting dilemma could lead to the creation of new problem-solving practices. However, if adults are dogmatic in what Mezirow describes as "habits of mind," their entrenched assumptions become barriers to positive practice changes. The editors invite readers to consider the generational differences highlighted in this case as one area where the adult development literature may be especially helpful to leaders. We wonder how the variation in followers' developmental stages/phases and readiness might map onto generational differences and/or life stages. We suggest reading the work of Kegan and Lahey (2009) on adult developmental processes as an excellent supplement to careful study of the Bernaciak case.

Introduction to Part I 3

Taken together the cases in this section give readers some insight to the types of challenges business and nonprofit leaders face. Although leadership and followership are part of every organizational setting and industry, and remain somewhat agnostic to field, stakeholder dynamics and organizational goals vary quite a bit. Also important for the discussion here is the consideration that employee professional identity and development needs may differ dramatically between business and industry, nonprofit, and educational settings. We encourage readers to explore the supporting literature, discussion questions, and learning activities in these chapters with the overarching question of *how might this dynamic play out in my workplace?*

1 Adult Development and Nonprofit Board Leadership

The Clash of Self-Authoring Minds

Jennifer A. Jones

Introduction

This case study uses Constructive Developmental Theory to explore the nexus of adult development and nonprofit board leadership. Nonprofit organizations address some of the world's most complex problems, including poverty and climate change. There are currently more than 1.5 million nonprofit organizations in the United States (Urban Institute, 2019), which employ about 10 percent of the nation's population (U.S. Bureau of Labor Statistics, 2018). These organizations are governed by a board of directors typically comprised of volunteers with professional expertise in a variety of fields (e.g., human resources, public relations, legal). There is a direct connection between the complexity of the board members' thinking, as measured by their developmental level (Kegan, 1982; Lahey et al., 2011) and the effectiveness of their leadership (see also, Jones, 2018; Jones & Daniel, 2018).

Case: The Clash of Self-Authoring Minds

Joseph[1], age 75, is a retired businessperson and long-time philanthropist (donor and board member). This philanthropic work is a significant part of his identity – he loves giving back and talks enthusiastically about it with anyone who asks.

Joseph's Pattern

Joseph is committed to outcomes and financial sustainability. When nonprofit leaders do not pursue outcomes with fervor, he tries to correct them. His efforts often result in bitter stalemates, with Joseph resigning his role as board member, mentor, and/or founder, and moving on to a different organization. He is beginning to become disillusioned with the nonprofit sector.

DOI: 10.4324/9780429331503-2

6   *Adult Development*

Joseph founded two nonprofit organizations himself (in his spare time) to fulfill a need he identified. One organization provides resources to parents whose children are struggling with addiction and another organization works to prevent adolescent substance abuse. He walked away from both organizations because the board members and staff did not want to take the organization in the "right" direction. As a business person, he could not in good conscience lead an organization that relied on donations or failed to produce outcomes. He felt he had no choice but to leave what he saw as a sinking ship.

The Invitation

Chris is the Chief Executive Officer of Second Chances Community Center (SCCC), a community-based nonprofit providing a variety of social services to low-income, high-risk populations. He is 45 years old and has more than 10 years of experience leading successful nonprofits. Chris recruited Joseph to the board last year. Joseph had a strong reputation for helping nonprofits operate more efficiently, even if he was known for being stubborn and dogmatic. Joseph was also known for making large financial donations.

The Conflict

Joseph joined the SCCC board with high hopes he could make a difference. SCCC had been operating in the community for 20 years – how ridiculous! A good nonprofit, Joseph believed, should a) strive to put themselves out of business, and b) should be self-sustaining in the meantime. The SCCC was still operating on a shoe-string budget that, in his opinion, was overly reliant on donations. He was determined to help SCCC become financially sustainable and become more effective; and he made his intentions clear at the first board meeting.

After Joseph's first board meeting, Chris left with a headache. He was accustomed to amicable and high-energy board meetings where board members worked together. Joseph's presence had altered the tenor of the meeting. All board members had reviewed the financial statements, but Joseph questioned every line item. He demanded to see the profit and loss statements for past fundraising events. He also asked about social enterprise activities to generate earned income, such as selling promotional items, renting out the organization's unused space, or starting a small business. Whew! The questions just kept coming, and Chris was overwhelmed.

It was clear to Chris that some of Joseph's ideas would not work at the SCCC. First of all, starting a business would potentially bring in extra money; however, it was also a huge risk. The organization would have to hire someone with the expertise to get it started and, even then, there was no guarantee. Businesses failed all the time. Second, there would likely always be a need for the SCCC. A small, community-based organization cannot eradicate poverty or its devastating effects – that was a goal best addressed through federal policy. While the SCCC could become more engaged in advocacy, the organization was really designed for grassroots social services. Third, the mission of the SCCC was far greater than just providing services. It served as the heart of the community, and it allowed neighbors to engage each other in a variety of healthy and enriching ways. For example, the SCCC Dad's Club taught young men how to become fathers; the SCCC Nutrition Education Group provided ongoing social support to people struggling with diabetes; and the SCCC Teen Club provided a safe space for high-risk youth. The organization also provided volunteers and donors an opportunity to contribute to their community in meaningful ways, ways that gave them personal satisfaction and improved their health (Swinson, 2006). Ultimately, the mission of SCCC was far bigger than Joseph perceived it to be.

During his first year as a board member, Joseph continued to pepper Chris with questions and demands, and Chris continued to respond as best he could. He provided Joseph with all the information requested, and he tried to educate Joseph about the comprehensive nature of the mission of the SCCC. But Chris' efforts were not enough. Joseph's energy transformed board meetings from an engaged and enthusiastic atmosphere to one characterized by skepticism and conflict. This tension affected other board members, and Chris was sure it would erupt soon with long-term, damaging effects. Neither Chris nor Joseph knew how to resolve the conflict.

Some (Hidden) Background

Developmentally, Joseph was assessed at the Self-Authoring stage: He mediates between different sources to develop his own opinion and goals. He pursues these goals with fervor. However, he does not regularly question the assumptions behind his own opinions and goals.

Additionally, when Joseph was in his mid-20s, he struggled professionally. His father noticed Joseph floundering and said, "I guess I'll hire you because nobody else will." This comment was devastating and haunted Joseph all his life. In fact, Joseph said, "I spent my entire career proving my father wrong."

Developmentally, Chris is also operating at the Self-Authoring stage. Like Joseph, he also mediates between different sources to develop his own opinion and goals. One of his sources of information is his many years' experience working in nonprofits. He believes he has learned to balance mission and money, and he has come to believe philanthropy provides donors with an opportunity to give, an opportunity that has rich rewards for the giver (Andreoni, 1989).

Additionally, Chris' father died when he was in elementary school. He has fond memories of his father doing charitable work in the community, such as helping repair a neighbor's roof after a bad rainstorm and giving food to homeless individuals they met on the streets. Chris feels his career is a living legacy to his father's generous spirit. Most of the time, this connection is positive. However, it pains Chris greatly when he is not able to meet the needs of the many people who come to the SCCC for help, and he feels a sense of loss and shame.

8 *Adult Development*

Discussion of Supporting Literature

This section describes the adult development and board governance literature and provides a brief analysis connecting the literature to this case.

Adult Development

Constructive Developmental Theory. Constructive Developmental Theory is a branch of developmental psychology. It purports that, over the course of a lifetime, adults develop an increasingly complex mental map (Erikson, 1959; Cook-Greuter, 1999; Kegan 1982; Loevinger & Wessler, 1970; Rooke & Torbert, 2005; Torbert, 2004). This mental map is not connected to age norms, and it influences all thoughts, behavior, and action. At early and mid-stages of development, adults are not consciously aware of this mental map. These stages can be empirically assessed through various processes, including the Subject-Object Interview (Lahey et al., 2011).

Kegan outlines four stages relevant to adult development. The Self-Sovereign Mind emerges in adolescence and is the first time a person regularly manipulates the world to get what they want. For example, a teenager who ditches school for a joy ride would likely not be thinking about how their teachers and family might feel upon realizing the teenager is missing, but rather, the teenager is wondering whether they would get in trouble. The benefit of this stage is the ability to identify and strive for what one wants; and the challenge is that the inherent thoughtlessness of this process can hurt others. The Socialized Mind emerges typically in late adolescence or in the early 20s. People with the Socialized Mind regularly consider the perspectives of others (e.g., they would recognize their mom might be scared if she realized her child had gone missing, even for a joy ride), and they use their internalized ideas of others' perspectives to decide how to behave. For example, someone in a Socialized Mind stage would determine what constituted "success at work" by considering their bosses' expectations or their parents' values. This stage promotes social harmony, but people can become cognitively trapped in dogmatic ways of thinking.

In the next stage, the Self-Authoring Mind, individuals learn to mediate between different perspectives to come to their own unique (self-authored) perspective. They might, for example, reflect upon their religious heritage and compare that heritage to what they learned in school and/or their life experience. Here, individuals can question and reflect upon a variety of influencing sources and come to a decision – a skill valuable for leaders; however, the individual cannot reflect upon the assumptions of their own perspective and can appear dogmatic or arrogant about their ideas. Most adults do not reach the fully self-authoring stage but, instead, fall somewhere in the transition between Socialized Mind and Self-Authoring Mind.

The Self-Transforming stage, Kegan's last stage, is the rarest (less than 10 percent of adults). In this stage, adults regularly and spontaneously question the assumptions behind their ideas. Adults in this stage have the ability to

Jennifer A. Jones 9

create paradigm-shattering breakthroughs; however, individuals become so engaged or enamored in questioning they may forget or neglect to act. Additionally, their ideas may seem unintelligible to their peers. Unfortunately, advanced development can but does not always lead to wise action.

As adults develop through each of these aforementioned stages, they encounter familiar circumstances from a new perspective or, in Kegan's (1982) terms, from a new "construction of self" (p. 131). This evolution involves a loss of old relationships (to people and institutions) that are replaced by new relationships (to the same people and institutions). For example, an adult in the Socialized Mind stage might perceive their supervisor's perspective as the best or most appropriate. To the onlooker, there may even seem to be a sense of adulation of the superior that comes from the embedded nature of the adult's Socialized Mind. Alternatively, the adult may have rejected the supervisor's perspective if it clashed with other perspectives in which he had been socialized. However, when that same adult begins to develop a Self-Authoring Mind, he begins to see the supervisor differently. The adult can reflect upon this supervisor and consider, for example, the personal and professional experiences that shaped the supervisor's perspective. With this reflection comes the ability to assess for the quality of the supervisor's perspective and separate himself from the supervisor's perspective. The shift from Socialized to Self-Authoring Mind happens over years or even decades and, as it happens, the adult loses his experience of the "old supervisor" and gains a new supervisor. The actual supervisor has not changed, of course, but the adult's perception of and relationship to the supervisor has changed. Kegan calls this a process of "recoverable loss" and writes "what we separate from we find anew" (p. 129).

Adult development in this case. Joseph and Chris were both assessed during a series of interviews as being in Kegan's (1984, 1992) Self-Authoring Stage. The Self-Authoring stage has strong potential for leadership capacity because it can mediate between different perspectives and identify a new, self-authored perspective. This capacity can help leaders to identify a vision, make tough decisions, and facilitate board meetings. However, this case also highlights one of its vexing challenges – people in the Self-Authoring stage do not question the assumptions behind their own goals (namely, Joseph's perspective that outcomes are paramount and Chris's ideas about the role of charity in a community).

Additionally, the comment by Joseph's dad affected his board performance. Specifically, his desire to be right about nonprofit management "best practices" was likely linked to his desire to prove his dad wrong. The concept of recoverable loss is helpful here. Joseph's dad's comment came when he was in his early 20s, and it is likely that Joseph was in or entering a Socialized Mind stage. As such, he likely revered his father's perspective, and to know his father did not think much of him would have been devastating. When Joseph transitioned from the Socialized Mind to the Self-Authoring Mind, he had the opportunity to return to his relationship with his father and meet his father anew. For example, at the Self-Authoring stage, Joseph might have asked his

10　*Adult Development*

father why he made that comment (rather than make assumptions, as one would in a Socialized Mind) or he might have considered how his father's perspectives and life experiences might have influenced that comment. However, there was no evidence Joseph was relating to his father from a Self-Authoring perspective. The wound is still fresh, and the loss is still recoverable.

Board Governance Leadership

Governance as leadership. Chait et al. (2005) developed a framework for board leadership with three levels of responsibility: fiduciary, strategic, and generative. Fiduciary responsibilities emphasize fiscal accountability and the establishment of proper procedures to protect the organization. Examples of fiduciary duties include approving the budget, reviewing the new human resource policies, and ensuring the organization has the proper level of insurance. These activities can be time-consuming. Strategic responsibilities include the development of goals and strategic planning to accomplish the mission. Examples of strategic governance includes developing a strategic plan and coordinating work plans that match the strategic plan.

Generative responsibility is the process of questioning the assumptions behind the mission and the organization. The purpose of generative leadership is to develop paradigm-breaking approaches to solve complex social problems, and it is related to system leadership (Senge et al., 2015). Generative leadership is, in part, what moves nonprofits from focusing on symptoms to focusing on root causes. It involves the messy work of generating new ways of thinking about the organization. It requires board members to stop and question their assumptions. It requires them to set aside their desires to achieve specific strategic goals and, instead, question whether they are working with the right set of goals. This is hard work, especially when compared to the relatively straight forward work of fiduciary and strategic governance.

A well-functioning board operates through all three lenses; however, Chait et al. (2005) argue that board members in general tend to focus on fiduciary and strategic governance and neglect generative governance. Given that many nonprofits, like the SCCC, operate with limited resources (including the limited resource of board members' time), the work of generative governance often gets set aside. Board members and nonprofit leaders can feel justified in focusing on fiduciary or strategic activities that appear to produce tangible results (e.g., a budget or strategic plan). This is ironic because, while seemingly unproductive in the short-term, generative work leads in the long-term to the sort of change typically embodied in the organizational mission. The focus on fiduciary and/or strategic lenses therefore minimizes the long-term effectiveness of the organization.

Joseph's leadership focus. Like many nonprofit board members, Joseph did not fully understand the mission and contexts in which he was working. He was fulfilling his fiduciary and, in particular, strategic responsibilities but not engaging in generative leadership (i.e., the type of leadership that questions assumptions about the work). Joseph's emphasis on strategic leadership is likely related to his business background and meaning-making processes – he had developed a way of thinking that works for him and was not interested in exploring new ways of thinking. He wanted results and he wanted them now.

Discussion Questions

This section contains questions that can be used for class discussion, role-plays, and/or written assignments. The questions are categorized in three main areas: adult development, old wounds and recoverable loss, and leadership.

Adult Development

- Joseph focused on outcomes and financial sustainability. These are important goals; however, he took it to an extreme.

    a   If you were Joseph, how might you have worked with Chris and the board members to advance programmatic outcomes and financial sustainability without damaging your relationships?

    b   If you were in Chris' position, how might you respond to Joseph's concerns and, at the same time, ensure his energy does not cause undue tension on the board?

- Joseph and Chris were both assessed at the Self-Authoring level according to Robert Kegan's stages of development.

    a   How does their developmental level manifest in their behavior?

    b   What are the strengths and challenges of their developmental level?

    c   How might their behavior each be different if they were operating out of a different stage of development?

Old Wounds and Recoverable Loss

- One comment from Joseph's father haunted him throughout his life and shaped his work and philanthropy. Similarly, Chris's father's death has had a long-term impact on his charity work.

    a   What are some signs that a board member might be dealing with a personal issue rather than the issue at hand?

    b   What kind of interventions might prompt greater awareness of the impact of personal experiences on board work?

- By dogmatically focusing on outcomes and financial sustainability, Joseph was able to ensure his work would be demonstratively successful thus proving his father wrong. But when Joseph's goals clashed with the real world, conflict ensued. This was a pattern in his work with nonprofit leaders.

12 *Adult Development*

    a   Why has Joseph not recognized and corrected this pattern?
    b   What should/could Joseph do when he recognizes this pattern?
    c   What is the opportunity for "recoverable loss" in this case?

- Thinking back on your life, is there a single event or memory you can point to that has shaped how you engage with the world much like Joseph's dad's words shaped him? If so, how does that event/memory affect how you exercise leadership?

Leadership

- Joseph and Chris seem to have very different understandings of the goal of the SCCC.

    a   What are the differences in their perspectives and what does each perspective lack?

- Do Joseph and Chris see governance from a fiduciary, strategic, or generative lens?

    a   How does their lens promote or hinder their effectiveness?
    b   Ideally, through what lens or lenses should they be looking at their governance responsibilities?

- Is there a relationship between their preferred governance lens and their developmental stage?

Conclusion

This case demonstrates that leadership and adult development are inextricable. How we lead is a product (in part) of how we think. And how we think is shaped by our developmental level. How we lead and think are both also shaped by the old wounds that fester just below the surface of awareness. In this case, Joseph and Chris operated out of similar developmental levels, but their perspectives were very different. Additionally, each had an old wound that influenced what they perceived to be "success" in their respective roles. Their developmental levels and their old wounds propelled them toward their versions of success and, at the same time, limited their thinking, and therefore limited the organization's capacity. The result was a conflicted board. If, instead, they had each been interested in growth, they could have learned from each other and led the organization into a future that was comprehensive, programmatically effective, and financially tenable. In this way, individual adult development can lead to organizational development.

Note

1 This case is based on a true story. Names and identifying details have been changed. The actual series of events have been fictionalized. All data were collected with approval from an Institutional Review Board.

References

Andreoni, J. (1989). Giving with impure altruism: Applications to charity and Ricardian equivalence. *Journal of Political Economy*, 97(6), 1447–1458.

Chait, R. P., Ryan, W. P., & Taylor, B. E. (2005). *Governance as leadership*. John Wiley & Sons.

Cook-Greuter, S. (1999). *Postautonomous ego development: A study of its nature and measurement*. (Doctoral dissertation). Harvard University Graduate School of Education: Cambridge, MA.

Erikson, E. (1959). *Identity and the life cycle*. International Universities Press.

Jones, J. A. (2018). The unseen lens: The relationship between philanthropists' developmental meaning making and philanthropic activity. *Nonprofit Management and Leadership*, 28(4), 491–509.

Jones, J. A., & Daniel, D. (2018). Funder's meaning making regarding complex, adaptive projects: Findings from a developmentally-oriented feasibility study. *International Journal of Nonprofit and Voluntary Sector Marketing*, 24(2), 1–7.

Kegan, R. (1982). *The evolving self: Problem and process in human development*. Harvard University Press.

Lahey, L., Souvaine, E., Kegan, R., Goodman, R., & Felix, S. (2011). *A guide to the Subject-Object Interview: Its administration and interpretation*. Minds at Work.

Loevinger, J., & Wessler, R. (1970). *Measuring ego development, Volumes 1 and 2*. Jossey-Bass.

Rooke, D., & Torbert, W. (2005). Seven transformations of leadership. *Harvard Business Review*.

Senge, P., Hamilton, H., & Kania, J. (2015). The dawn of system leadership. *Stanford Social Innovation Review*.

Swinson, J. L. (2006). Focusing on the health benefits of volunteering as a recruitment strategy. *The International Journal of Volunteer Administration*, 24(2), 25–30.

Urban Institute. (2019). *Nonprofit sector in brief*. https://nccs.urban.org/publication/nonprofit-sector-brief-2019#the-nonprofit-sector-in-brief-2019

U.S. Bureau of Labor Statistics (2018). *TED: The economics daily*. https://www.bls.gov/opub/ted/2018/nonprofits-account-for-12-3-million-jobs-10-2-percent-of-private-sector-employment-in-2016.htm

2 Helping a Nonprofit CEO Pivot Her Leadership Style

Denise M. Cumberland and Gregory Nielsen

Introduction

Leaders must continually adapt their styles to effectively navigate changing environments. This case study focuses on the experience of an organizational development consultant who was tasked with building a relationship with a reluctant client. Employing Hersey and Blanchard's Situational Leadership Model provided a lens to assess the client's approach to leadership. Bolman and Deal's reframing model offered the consultant a technique to help the client reframe how she viewed and led her board of directors.

Case: Building a Relationship with a Reluctant Client

In this case, one of the authors, Greg Nielsen, an organizational development consultant, shares the story of helping Carole Turner, the CEO of Mission Forward.

Case Context

Mission Forward is a nonprofit 501(c)(3) organization operating since 2005 focused on spotlighting and empowering military veterans in their local communities. The founder and CEO, Carole Turner, nurtured the organization, launched in Nashville, Tennessee, to an annual budget of $100,000 per year. This organization's success can be attributed to Turner's vision, will, and determination to succeed. The nonprofit operates with no staff but has a board of directors comprised of eight well-respected members of the local community.

Mission Forward provides programming that educates individuals on the many contributions military veterans bring to their community outside of their military achievements. The organization produces short films and hosts in-person events where individuals can meet military veterans and learn more about their background, experiences, and efforts in the community. Annually, more than 5,000 individuals attend these programs.

As the organization has grown, the need has arisen to generate funding for the sustainability of the mission from diverse sources in addition to event revenue. One strategy involved requests for grant funding from local philanthropic

DOI: 10.4324/9780429331503-3

foundations. In 2019, the CEO pursued three specific grants from philanthropic foundations, only to be denied each time. Never one to back down from a challenge, Turner met with each of the foundation leaders, only to hear a similar refrain – concern over the organization's lack of a formal strategic plan and lack of a succession plan beyond her leadership. In frustration, Turner reached out to one of her trusted advisors, Linda Dawson, to vent over being turned down for these grants. Dawson recommended an external consultant be brought in to lead a strategic planning process with the board. Turner balked, but two days later called and asked her friend if she would recommend a consultant who was not "full of it."

The Dilemma

This is where one of the authors joins the story. Dawson reached out to me, Greg Nielsen, to gauge my interest in the project. Dawson was familiar with my background, leadership style, and approach to consulting. I am a military veteran myself, an attorney by background, and served for over a decade as a nonprofit CEO. I asked Dawson what she thought success would look like. She responded with a twofold answer:

- Gain buy-in and support from the CEO of Mission Forward to develop a strategic plan with the involvement of the board, and
- Help the CEO identify a succession plan for Mission Forward.

Meeting the Client and Diagnosing Her Leadership Style

Those who had previously described Turner as a "force of nature" proved highly accurate. Turner is a woman with significant life experience. She leads by instinct and gut rather than theory and philosophy. She holds disdain for lengthy processes and sees little utility for any process at all.

As we spoke over lunch during our initial meeting, Turner's highly directive leadership style was evident. One of the first phrases she uttered to me, which she would frequently repeat throughout the project, was, *"All I care about is who will do what by when."* When the discussion turned to the role of the board members, Turner would quickly point out that she knew the organization far better than they did. She would have little tolerance for any efforts by the board to lead the organization down a path she viewed as out of step with her vision. As one might imagine, she reacted quite negatively when I shared the fundamentals of a strategic planning process – steps that included interviews with relevant stakeholders. I emerged from that initial meeting convinced that if Carole Turner had her way, she would just as soon sit down that afternoon and write the strategic plan herself and simply ignore the issue of succession planning. With the knowledge that Turner operates from a mindset of certainty and control, I was able to identify step one in this consulting assignment: help Turner learn how to pivot from handling each situation in the same manner. But, before I could get to step one, I had to earn her trust.

How to Build a Trusting Client Relationship to Enable Learning to Occur

After several meetings with Turner, I came to see her as quite a visionary, provided the vision was hers or aligned with hers. I also observed that while her initial reaction to suggestions was often fiercely and viscerally negative, she would often circle back days later, having digested and reflected on the thoughts I presented to her. These experiences convinced me that the key to success would be in helping her to reframe how she viewed both the board and me. I also realized the process of developing a strategic planning session would only occur if we developed trust in our relationship. This led to Turner and I agreeing to a series of tenets in our working relationship:

- She could be blunt and direct in conversations with me always, and she acknowledged that I would be blunt and direct with her in return.
- If she had a question or concern, she would contact me directly, rather than sharing it with someone else.
- I would involve her in the development of the process, and she would take no steps to sabotage the process.
- She would allow me to interview not just the board but several people who knew her well.
- I would communicate with her often.

What I Learned from the Board

As a former nonprofit CEO and now consultant, I was intrigued about what I would learn in the stakeholder interview process. My underlying curiosity stemmed from a lingering question, "How can a group of highly decorated community leaders be so courageous in their daily arena and yet so timid in the board room of Mission Forward?" As you can see below, the team Turner assembled for her board lacked neither in gravitas nor professional accomplishments.

Mission Forward's Board of Directors

David, Board Chair, is a young professional with deep family roots that tie him to the organization's mission. He is an accomplished financial planner with an impressive reputation and stable roster of clients. David has served on the board for four years.

Tracy, Vice-Chair, is a close, decades-long friend of Carole Turner. She is also a person others respect and tread lightly with, perhaps stemming mainly from her relationship with Turner. A perception exists that she is Turner's eyes and ears when it comes to the pulse of the board, having served in some capacity since the founding of the organization in 2005.

Patty, Treasurer, is straight out of central casting as an experienced tax professional and auditor who has served on the board for three years. She knows the numbers backward and forward but remains reticent to draw inferences from or tell a story of the numbers that are not first scripted by Turner.

Simon, Secretary, is a community activist, a name others recognize instantly for his entrepreneurial achievements and frequent presence at all public events where one would want to be seen. Still relatively new to the board, Simon has served for 12 months.

Rachel has served as a human resources leader for a Fortune 500 company for over a decade, garnering awards and recognition along the way. Mission Forward represents one of many nonprofit boards in which her presence (and connections) are sought. She has been on the board for five years.

Blake is a successful local bank CEO whose company has provided the primary sponsorship support for Mission Forward events for the past five years since he started serving.

Amy is new to the board, a millennial, and one who gives the impression she is bursting with ideas, although she rarely voices them. For example, she takes a lot of notes during meetings, and her facial expressions indicate she has plenty to say, but she rarely voices any opinions.

Jackson is also new to the board and a former Marine. As his military career progressed, he went from the one most often taking orders to the one most frequently giving the orders. Confident and capable, yet stoic in approach.

Board member after board member painted a picture with slightly different brush strokes that nevertheless resulted in a remarkably consistent portrait. Carole Turner saw neither experience nor individuality when she pictured the board. To her, they were all the same – foot soldiers who were capable of executing orders. Certainly, their knowledge of real estate or finance or connections to community leaders could be valuable in certain circumstances, provided their actions and approaches were scripted according to her plans and vision. Board members consistently reported that they didn't question strategy or approach, or suggest alternate visions because the culture of the team indicated those actions were neither welcome nor tolerated.

Reflecting on the comments that the board members shared, I attributed Turner's leadership style of command and control to being influenced by natural born traits and likely shaped by her success in leading soldiers while serving in Desert Storm and later Afghanistan. To help Turner see the situation differently, I had to guide her toward reframing her view of the board of directors. My goal was to help her view each board member as a unique individual with different needs based on their experiences.

The Bolman and Deal Reframing Model

Leaders with certain traits, values, and attitudes often find it easier to perform some tasks over others, and they become locked into certain behaviors and wedded to a certain style. Then, true to the old saying, *if your only tool is a hammer, every problem looks like a nail*, the leader fails to change tactics when

18 *Helping a Nonprofit CEO Pivot*

confronted with organizational issues. In this section, we offer details on a tool that effective leaders must master – the art of reframing. Bolman and Deal (2017) define a frame as a

> set of ideas and assumptions that you carry in your head to help you understand and negotiate a particular territory. A good frame makes it easier to know what you are up against and, ultimately, what you can do about it.
>
> (p. 12)

Leaders use frames to quickly assess a situation and provide a solution. Our frames not only influence how we interpret a situation, but also influence the actions we take.

Bolman and Deal's (2017) model depicts four frames: structural, human resources, political, and symbolic. Each is outlined below with a description of how leaders who view the world from a particular frame operate:

Structural Frame: Leaders assume it is their responsibility to determine what needs to be done and emphasize goals and efficiency. They focus on tasks, facts, and logic while establishing clear directions and making sure people understand they are accountable for delivering results.

Human Resource Frame: Leaders consider people as the critical domain of any organization and value relationships. They focus their attention on providing support and empowering people.

Political Frame: The leader believes they must attend to the ever-present political realities of organizational life and prepare for the inevitable conflict that is just around the corner. Because of limited resources, they see their job as that of a power broker who must negotiate and manage competing interests.

Symbolic Frame: The leader considers their most important role as providing people with something they can believe in. They focus on using their charisma to build enthusiasm and commitment so that people will feel that what they do is important.

When we prioritize solving problems and resolving issues, it is tempting to work from the premise that our views and assumptions are correct. Leaders who prefer reason and logic will naturally choose rational and structural solutions. Organizations are, however, comprised of human beings who are not always rational or logical. Hence, this technical approach to problem-solving can hit a brick wall in practice. Studies in management and leadership have found the ability to use multiple frames is correlated with effectiveness. This suggests that to be effective, leaders need to practice using all four of the frames to increase their understanding of each situation and thereby visualize more options for solving. Further, reframing (using multiple frames) requires leaders to avoid the natural tendency to respond to a situation based on their own personal worldview. It requires leaders to examine a situation from other perspectives and use context to help them determine which approach will be most salient.

The Situational Leadership Model

Successful leaders are those who can pivot their leadership behaviors based on the composition of the team they are leading and the environment in which they are operating (Gates et al., 1976). One practical way to categorize leadership behavior is by adopting the Situational Leadership Model (Hersey & Blanchard, 1969). While updated with new terminology in 1993 (Blanchard et al., 1993, p. 22), both models are based on the argument that effective leaders adapt their style of management based on subordinates' competence and commitment.

In each of the four styles described by the model, the leader approaches the situation based on whether the follower needs *more or less direction* and whether they need a *high level or low level of support*. Outlined below are the behaviors exhibited by leaders in each style:

- Style 1 (S1): Leaders use a high level of *directing* and a low level of supporting.
- Style 2 (S2): Leaders *coach* using both a high level of directing and a high level of supporting.
- Style 3 (S3): Leaders use a high level of *supporting*, and a low level of directing.
- Style 4 (S4): Leaders *delegate*, using a low level of directing and a low level of supporting.

To decide on which amount of directing and supporting to supply their followers, leaders must assess each follower's development level based on each follower's competence and motivation. The model suggests followers are in one of four developmental phases, and the style adopted should correlate to where the follower is in their development. The four Development Levels that associated subordinates are classified by are:

- Development Level 1 (D1): Enthusiastic beginner, low on competence and high on commitment.
- Development Level 2 (D2): Disillusioned learner with increasing competence and low commitment.
- Development Level 3 (D3): Capable but cautious contributor, with moderate to high competence and variable commitment.
- Development Level 4 (D4): Self-reliant achiever who is high on both competence and commitment.

In the first development level (D1) are those who have not attempted a task before. In this case, S1 (the directing approach) is very appropriate for this follower because the person has little to no experience and needs explicit direction. A person in the second development level (D2) is discouraged about

20 *Helping a Nonprofit CEO Pivot*

their ability to accomplish a task despite their attempts. The leader would be wise to adopt the S2 (the coaching approach) that combines being directive with supportive tones, enabling the follower to provide input on how to accomplish the task. When someone is further along in their development (D3), they can become less committed or even apathetic. In these instances, the leader does not need to direct but needs to listen and offer support, reassurance, and encouragement using S3 (the supporting approach). Finally, followers who are fully developed (D4) have the ability to perform the task and are also committed and confident about their abilities, thereby needing little direction and little support so that the leader would use S4 (the delegating approach).

How to Communicate Findings of the Board Interviews to the Client

If I am to be completely honest, a part of me dreaded the conversation with Turner to recap what I learned from the board and what I perceived was needed. Turner relied heavily upon, if not exclusively, the S1 approach of "telling." Directive leaders can be volatile in their initial reactions. How much detail should I share with her? It was also abundantly clear that leadership transition would, by necessity, be a focal point not only of the strategic plan document but of the upcoming board strategy retreat where succession planning had to begin.

I recognized this conversation would be a central moment in the success or failure of this project. If Carole Turner reacted negatively, this project would fail. As a consultant, I rested my reputation and the success of the project on my conviction that we had built enough *trust* to navigate the next steps together. I also had to come to grips with the realization that if Turner stopped supporting the process and refused to adjust her style, I would have no choice but to walk away.

I sat down with Turner to share the results of the board interviews in a meeting that lasted several hours. Using a series of questions, my goal was to have Turner shift from a single frame view of her role to seeing her role as one encompassing different frames. I also discussed the need for succession planning and how this had to begin with an assessment of each board member. Based only on their performance in their roles as board members, I asked her to plot each board member using a grid with high and low competence on one axis, and high and low motivation on the other axis. We then discussed how different assignments board members undertook might mean they moved from one part of the grid to another.

With the ever-present goal of gaining alignment with her on the remaining steps in the strategic planning process in mind, I gave her time to consider the information, vent at times, and yes, disagree at times. By the end of that meeting, she saw what I saw – that there was value in a thoughtful approach to how we prepared for the strategic planning session for Mission Forward. That process had to begin with the board and how her approach to leading the board needed to pivot.

What's Next for Carole Turner and Mission Forward?

A leadership journey is rarely a linear process of increasing skills and achievements. Rather, it is frequently a bumpy road of growth, disappointments, achievements, and setbacks. My journey with Carole Turner was no different. However, the significant evolution and progress she demonstrated as a leader during this project is a credit to her and the relationship of trust we built together. She successfully transformed her thinking about Mission Forward from an image of a ship that she commanded to a boat in which both she and the board must row together to arrive at the destination. The next step for Turner and Mission Forward is to extend the trust Carole and I built to include the board as a vital partner and contributor to the strategy retreat and resulting plan.

A strategy retreat can be an unsettling experience for any CEO. Ideas fly like jets, possibilities are scribbled on whiteboards and flip charts, and impending change can seem like the only sure thing. Carole Turner will be tested in this environment, as will her board of directors. They will each need to demonstrate the ability to share power – Turner by giving some up and the board by accepting some. They will bump up against uncomfortable conversations, including the inevitable need for a succession plan that will require them to embrace the uncertainty and the need to collaboratively arrive at an approach that respects the roles of CEO and board in that vital process.

Throughout the next stages, neither Turner nor the board can be expected to abandon their default leadership and communication styles. Rather, if the process has been facilitated effectively and genuine trust built, the expectation will be they have each learned enough about themselves and the other members of the team that they feel empowered and equipped to flex their styles to meet the moment.

Learning Activities

- Based on the situation the consultant has uncovered about Turner's leadership approach of "telling" the board what to do, what frame do you think Turner is operating from? Why do you think she gravitates toward this frame? What frame(s) would you suggest might help Turner in working with her board?
- Choose three board members that you believe would benefit most from your feedback or coaching. First, identify where these board members are on their competence and commitment, using the D1–D4 scale. Then, determine which style you will use to lead them from where they are at this moment on the scale (which leadership style: S1–S4). For both the D1–D4 decision and the S1–S4 decision, you need to supply the rationale for why you made that determination. Now, outline a specific coaching strategy for each of the three board members based on that board member's competence and commitment.

22 *Helping a Nonprofit CEO Pivot*

- Create a list of five to ten questions that you would have used to help Turner reframe her view of the board, how leaders operate, and what steps were needed next to prepare for the board's strategic planning session.

Discussion Questions for Case

- What are some possible reasons Carole Turner relies on the "telling/directing" leadership style?
- In what circumstances does the "telling/directing" leadership style work?
- What are the disadvantages of the "telling/directing" style for a nonprofit leader working with a board of directors?
- How can we practice reframing when challenged by organizational issues?

References

Blanchard, K. H., Nigari, D., & Nelson, R. B. (1993). Situational Leadership® after 25 years: A retrospective. *Journal of Leadership Studies*, 1(1), 21–36.

Bolman, L. G., & Deal, T. E. (2017). *Artistry, choice, and leadership: Reframing organizations* (6th ed.). Jossey-Bass.

Gates, P., Blanchard, K. H., & Hersey, P. (1976). Diagnosing educational leadership problems. *Educational Leadership*, 34, 348–354.

Hersey, P., & Blanchard, K. H. (1969). Life-cycle theory of leadership. *Training & Development Journal*, 23(5), 26–34.

3 Exploring the Role of Emotion and Perceptions of Risk When "Leading From the Middle"

Deidre M. Le Fevre

Introduction

Leadership development has tended to focus on leadership enacted at the most senior leadership level in organizations; however, including distributed notions of leadership (Spillane, 2006) where people are leading from the middle (Hargreaves & Shirley, 2020) provides a more accurate portrayal of how leadership is exercised in effective organizations. Organizations are complex systems, and it can be challenging for middle leaders to work in changing and uncertain environments with multiple and sometimes conflicting demands placed on them. Leadership is emotional work (Wang, 2020). Those who lead from the middle can feel vulnerable in their role as they work between mandates and control from the head of the organization and those on the ground (Hargreaves & Shirley, 2020). Helping middle leaders to understand and navigate this vulnerability and the role of emotion in leadership work is an important aspect of leadership development (Timperley et al., 2020). By engaging with this case, participants will be able to examine the unique challenges of leading from the middle and how the role of emotion can influence the way people feel, think, and act.

Case: Leading from the Middle

This case is set in an NGO that has a long history of providing effective, within-country social services. The staff are diverse, most have been with the NGO for 10 years or more, and the majority are highly committed to the NGO's overarching mission.

The senior positional leadership consists of a board of directors and an executive director who is employed by the board and reports to the board. The NGO is structured into three divisions and each division has a manager. The board, executive director, and three division managers make up the senior leadership team. Approximately 300 people are employed across the three divisions, and there are five project leaders. Each project leader is responsible for leading a team that includes administrative and policy staff, and field and operational managers. These project leaders are "middle

DOI: 10.4324/9780429331503-4

24 Leading from the Middle

leaders" and, in the past, have typically moved into the role after having been in the organization for a number of years having developed organizational culture knowledge of "how things are done around here." They are usually shoulder-tapped by a member of the senior leadership team, and there has not been any particular leadership prerequisite or leadership development support for being a project leader.

The appointment of a new executive director just over a year ago has shaken up the organization somewhat, with several younger employees having been encouraged to apply for project leader roles. In addition, the new executive director has worked with the board to create a change in the outreach of the NGO. Since being established three decades ago, the NGO has focused on in-country community support, but now the new executive director has worked with the board to establish a significant, additional, international outreach program. There is currently disagreement amongst the staff as to what the agenda of the NGO should be, with many of the longer-established staff resisting this change in scope toward international outreach.

This case focuses on Kari who came to work at the NGO five years ago. This is her first job after graduating with a Master's degree. She is a policy analyst and younger than most of her colleagues. When she began five years ago, she worked regular office hours in a large, shared office space, and everyone observed common work hours. Her project leader had an adjacent office and she saw her on an almost daily basis and met with her in person at least once per week. Now, five years later, flexible work hours are commonplace and meetings are often held digitally since many people work remotely. Kari goes into the NGO buildings one or two days a week, and it is rare to have more than about 20 percent of her team there on any one day.

Last year Kari was promoted to a project leader. As one of the youngest employees and after just four years working in the NGO, this was unexpected. The organizational culture up to this time had been one of "waiting in line for your turn," and some of her colleagues felt that they were better placed to be in the role. Kari was somewhat apprehensive at the time of her appointment to the middle leadership role, but also excited about the challenges this would bring. She was aware that the new director wanted to increase the leadership capacity throughout the NGO and increase internal accountability within project teams. What Kari had not realized was the emotional toll this promotion would take on her, and the emotional impact these changes would have on her team.

Tia, one of the staff in the project team Kari now leads, has been with the NGO for many years. Tia was one of the people who welcomed Kari and looked after her when she first joined the NGO, and they regard each other as colleagues and friends. Recently, Kari has received a series of complaints from the senior leadership team about the quality of Tia's work, which Kari needs to discuss with Tia. Kari feels vulnerable and is reluctant to initiate a conversation because she is worried she might damage her relationship with Tia. Her move to a middle leadership role has changed the nature of the relationships she previously had with her colleagues. Constantly running through Kari's mind is the fact she is responsible for ensuring Tia meets both her project outcomes and the senior management concerns about her performance. It makes Kari feel vulnerable being in this position in the middle, being responsible both to the senior leadership team and responsible for the work of her project team. Sometimes she worries about losing the strong sense of colleagueship and friendship she has with Tia and the others as she tries to balance developing strong relationships with achieving valued outcomes for the organization.

Recently, the new executive director has widened the scope of Kari's project team's work to include a new initiative of advisory work for another country. Kari is uncertain about some aspects of this initiative, but it has been mandated by the board so she needs to implement it. Kari is concerned her team does not currently have the knowledge and resources needed to work in such a complex, international context. She is aware of a discontent amongst her project team alongside some clearly voiced dissent regarding the new agenda of the NGO focus which now extends beyond their country. Kari has heard: "This isn't what I signed up for," "How are we going to know what to do in a different place with people we don't know?" "It's too political," and "The way we know how to do things isn't going to work anymore." Kari worries that some of her team members are resistant and not engaging with the new challenges. Several now turn off their cameras during remote meetings and some are not even there when she asks a question. Others appear to be distracted with low-priority tasks and seem to be avoiding discussing the new focus of the work. Some of her team are excited about the new international focus and already under way with work, though Kari has noticed that the person who nods with the most enthusiastic agreement during team meetings seems to be the one who is, in fact, least engaged with the tasks, does not follow through, and can be overheard saying things to his colleagues such as "This will never work." This is sad to hear because, in the past, he has been extremely committed to the agenda of the NGO, he is not paid a big salary, and for the most part he works here because he really cares about what the NGO achieves.

Trying new ways of working is not new to this project team; however, taking risks and working creatively seemed easier in the face-to-face meetings they used to have than in the "virtual space" they so often inhabit now. Kari is finding it hard to get a check on how people are actually feeling. Because many of their meetings are now undertaken remotely, she cannot see how people react, she says, "I just can't read the room in this virtual space." Meanwhile, time is ticking on and her immediate manager, Tom, who is the division manager, maintains that Kari just needs to tell the team to get on with it and do it.

Kari sometimes glances up at her policy and leadership books from graduate school on her shelf and remembers why she came here in the first place and what she hopes to achieve. She is trying to develop collective responsibility in her team and share responsibility and decision-making. What worries her is that, at the end of the day, she is accountable up the line for the project results

26 *Leading from the Middle*

of her team. She feels uncertain as to what extent she should facilitate shared decision-making and planning with the team. As a middle leader, she feels vulnerable in relation to having a limited sense of control over larger decisions made in the organization. Some days it feels like it would be easier to just tell people what to do (as her immediate boss is telling her she should do); however, she has a sense this will not actually work to develop effective and sustainable leadership in the immediate team and, indeed, throughout the organization. She wants to understand why people are feeling and acting the way they are and, in particular, understand what perceptions of risk people might have and how she can support them with these. Interestingly, Kari has not yet really had an opportunity to think much about the perceptions of risk she has for herself and her own sense of vulnerability as a middle leader.

Discussion

Distributed Leadership

Concepts of distributed leadership (Spillane 2006; Spillane et al., 2001), emotion (Hargreaves, 2005; Zembylas, 2005) and risk (Le Fevre, 2014; Twyford & Le Fevre, 2019) are central to this case. Leadership that is distributed draws on knowledge and expertise throughout an organization and "leading from the middle" is central to distributed leadership. Recent research indicates those in middle leadership roles face many challenges and dilemmas (Hargreaves & Shirley, 2020). This case identifies some of these challenges

Leadership is a social process rather than an individual practice, and effective leadership is dynamic involving collective and multi-directional activity. Human interactions are key as leadership occurs within and through relationships and networks of influence (Fletcher, 2004). The complexity of relationships Kari has experienced through her leadership is evident in this case. She faces an ongoing dilemma regarding how to develop and maintain strong relationships while also moving forward with the agenda of the NGO. This causes a conflict for her as she views one as being at the cost of the other (Argyris & Schön, 1974).

Distributed leadership is evident throughout effective organizations (Spillane et al., 2008), and it is undertaken by both those with, and those without, formal leadership positions. Kari sought to promote distributed leadership within her team and communicated her desire to create a sense of internal accountability within the team, but she was reluctant to take a top-down uni-directional leadership stance and just tell people what they needed to do. The position of leading from the middle of the organization made this challenging for her as she had expectations on her as well as having expectations of others.

The Role of Emotion in Leadership

Typically, leadership development focuses on the skills and knowledge needed in leadership, and the emotional aspects of the work are given insufficient attention (Hargreaves, 2007; Twyford et al., 2017). However, leadership is emotional work, and it is important to empower leaders to understand this (Hargreaves, 2007; Wang, 2020). Emotion is inevitable in organizations, particularly during times of change (Hargreaves, 2005). Negative emotion negatively impacts well-being (Zembylas, 2005) and can inhibit learning (Frenzel, 2014). Learning is affected when attention is distracted and people tend to lose flexibility in their thinking, fixating on unimportant details and losing capability for big-picture thinking (Frenzel, 2014). In the past, cognition and emotion have been seen as separate processes but recent research reveals that cognition and emotion are actually connected and inseparable processes (Cahour, 2013).

Kari appears to be keeping a pulse on how people are feeling in her team. She is likely observing how negative emotions are impacting on some of her team members' participation. This negative emotion is likely affecting their learning and motivation and diverting attention inwards to increased feelings of vulnerability and fatigue (Taxer & Gross, 2018). What she is also becoming more aware of is the complexity of emotions (Cahour, 2013). Emotions are intricate phenomena that include psychological processes that are affective, cognitive, physiological, motivational, and expressive (Pekrun, 2011). They are also sociological responses that are affected by political or power relations (Zembylas, 2005). A person's emotional response in a situation is influenced by both their environment and factors within themselves. Career stage and time working in an organization also influence how people experience emotion during change (Hargreaves, 2005). This helps to explain why various people in Kari's team had different emotional responses to the same changes within the NGO and it also helps explain her own experiences and feelings.

Perceptions of Risk

The concept of risk is part of everyday life; however, little attention has been given to perceptions of risk in terms of adult learning and leadership work. Risk has been defined as "uncertainty about and severity of the events and consequences (or outcomes) of an activity with respect to something that humans value" (Aven & Renn, 2009, p. 6). Perceptions of risk include uncertainty about a possible outcome and a feeling of vulnerability (or a sense of possible loss) about the possible consequences of one's actions (Twyford et al., 2017). Perceptions of risk and uncertainty are an inherent part of leadership work. People make decisions in situations of uncertainty about what the outcome will be. They might perceive risk, for example, in terms of a loss of sense of self-competence when they are asked to work in an area they are not familiar with, or a sense of loss of independence and time if they need to learn and work in new and different ways. When people are aware of this, perceptions of risk can sometimes be reduced (Le Fevre et al., 2020).

Changes in the workplace (such as those experienced in this NGO) are likely to increase uncertainty and feelings of vulnerability. Indeed, perceptions of risk are an inherent part of leadership and change and are, therefore,

28 Leading from the Middle

unavoidable. Unknown and uncertain outcomes can increase perceptions of risk (Hargreaves, 2005) as can be witnessed in this case. The NGO is made up of a diverse group of people who respond in different ways to the change that is happening. For some, the change to a broader, international focus was perceived positively while for others it was a negative. Perceptions of risk are not irrational responses, rather, they develop out of histories, circumstances, and affective and cognitive processes. Understanding the power of emotion and the impact of perceptions of risk is a critical part of being an effective leader.

Resistance is thought to be one of the key reasons why change initiatives often fail to be sustained in organizations and addressing resistance is "one of the greatest challenges leaders face" (Timperley, 2011, p. 128). This case reveals an understanding of the nature of resistance that is important for leaders, particularly for those in middle leadership roles like Kari who lead the work of engaging others in initiatives and who are situated in between those who make the decisions and those who do the work on the ground. It may be that what looks like resistance and a lack of engagement from some of her colleagues is actually a perception of risk, a sense of uncertainty and a concern regarding their possible future loss. How might these emotional responses and a sense of uncertainty perhaps have been magnified due to the change in work context where people were now working remotely to a greater extent? How might emotional responses be impacted by an expectation to change the focus of their work? These inquiries constitute the sort of questions leaders need to be investigating in their own contexts.

Learning Activities

Recent research identifies the critical role of middle leadership (Fullan & Shirley, 2020). Along with the increased understanding of the importance of the role of middle leadership comes an increased need for preparation and development learning opportunities targeted towards those in middle leadership roles (Thorpe & Bennett-Powell, 2014). What are three key areas of development that you might focus on to support Kari? Begin by identifying the key dilemmas and challenges Kari faces, and then consider some possible approaches to leadership development in relation to these.

Developing Distributed Leadership

Most research and literature poses a normative view regarding distributed leadership; in other words, it promotes distributed leadership as a desirable model that is associated with effective leadership practice. However, in this case, Kari was both keen to share decision making and responsibility and somewhat reluctant to "let go of the reins" within her team. Research has also shown that "[d]istributing leadership over more people is a risky business and may result in the greater distribution of incompetence" (Timperley, 2005, p. 417). How might a leader be supported to understand the opportunities and challenges of distributed leadership in a context such as Kari's?

Leading from the Middle

Who is leading from the middle in your organization? What roles and responsibilities do those "leading from the middle" have? What perceptions of risk might they experience? How might these perceptions of risk impact on the way they go about their work and interact with others?

The Role of Emotion for Leaders

Emotion is an inherent part of the complex work of leadership. Often the focus of research is on how leaders can support those they work with; however, leaders themselves also need support and learning opportunities. What perceptions of risk do you feel for yourself in your own leadership work? Imagine you could talk about these with a mentor/coach: What would you want your mentor/coach to understand about the risks you perceive? What questions might an effective mentor/coach ask you that would help you understand your perceptions of risk? Write these questions and then consider your responses to them.

Considering Resistance as Perceptions of Risk

Create a table with two columns. On the left you will have "Being resistant" and on the right you will have "Perceiving risk." Observe a meeting or event, or recall a meeting or event you have been a part of, where people were talking about a change initiative in their organization. Consider the comments you heard and the behaviors you observed as being in one or other column and write them in the column. How does the column (lens) you use to explain behavior change the way you understand a person and thus respond to them? For example, how does the concept of having a "perception of risk" allow you to see, interpret, and respond to someone's behavior differently than if you are to see it as "resistance"? How and when might this be helpful?

References

Argyris, C., & Schön, D. A. (1974). *Theory in practice: Increasing professional effectiveness.* Jossey-Bass.

Aven, T., & Renn, O. (2009). On risk defined as an event where the outcome is uncertain. *Journal of Risk Research,* 12(1), 1–11. doi:10.1080/13669870802488883

Cahour, B. (2013). Characteristics, emergence, and circulation in interactional learning. In M. Baker, J. Andriessen, & S. Jarvela (Eds.), *Affective learning together: Social and emotional dimensions of collaborative learning* (pp. 62–80). Routledge.

30 *Leading from the Middle*

Fletcher, J. K. (2004). The paradox of postheroic leadership: An essay on gender, power, and transformational change. *The Leadership Quarterly*, 15, 647–661. doi:10.1016/j.leaqua.2004.07.004

Frenzel, A. C. (2014). Teacher emotions. In R. Pekrun, & L. Linnenbrink-Garcia (Eds.), *International handbook of emotion in education* (pp. 494–519). Routledge.

Hargreaves, A. (2005). Educational change takes ages: Life, career and generational factors in teachers' emotional responses to educational change. *Teaching and Teacher Education*, 21, 967–983. doi:10.1016/j.tate.2005.06.007

Hargreaves, A. (2007). Inclusive and exclusive educational change: Emotional responses of teachers and implications for leadership. *School Leadership & Management*, 24(3), 287–309. doi:10.1080/1363243042000266936

Hargreaves, A., & Shirley, D. (2020). Leading form the middle: Its nature, origins and importance. *Journal of Professional Capital and Community*, 5(1), 92–114. doi:10.1108/JPCC-06-2019-0013

Le Fevre, D. M. (2014). Barriers to implementing pedagogical change: The role of teachers' perceptions of risk. *Teaching and Teacher Education*, 38, 56–64. doi:10.1016/j.tate.2013.11.007

Le Fevre, D. M., Timperley, H., Twyford, K., & Ell, F. (2020). *Leading powerful professional learning: Responding to complexity with adaptive expertise*. Corwin.

Pekrun, R. (2011). Emotions as drivers of learning and cognitive development. In R. A. Calvo & S. K. D'Mello (Eds.), *New perspectives on affect and learning technologies* (pp. 23–39). Springer. doi:10.1007/978-1-4419-9625-1_3

Spillane, J. P. (2006). *Distributed leadership*. Jossey Bass.

Spillane, J. P., Halverson, R., & Diamond, J. B. (2001). Investigating school leadership practice. A distributed perspective. *Educational Researcher*, 30(3), 23–28.

Taxer, J. L., & Gross, J. J. (2018). Emotion regulation in teachers: The "why" and "how". *Teaching and Teacher Education*, 74, 180–189.

Thorpe, A., & Bennett-Powell, G. (2014). The perceptions of secondary school middle leaders regarding their needs following a middle leadership development programme. *Management in Education*, 28(2), 52–57. doi:10.1177/0892020614529808

Timperley, H. S. (2005). Distributed leadership: Developing theory from practice. *Journal of Curriculum Studies*, 37(4), 395–420.

Timperley, H. S. (2011). Leading teachers' professional learning. In J. Robertson & H. S. Timperley (Eds.), *Leadership and learning* (pp. 118–130). Sage Publications.

Timperley, H., Ell, F., Le Fevre, D. M., & Twyford, K. (2020). *Leadership of professional learning for impact*. Australian Council for Educational Research.

Twyford, K., & Le Fevre, D. (2019). Leadership, uncertainty and risk: How leaders influence teachers. *Journal of Professional Capital and Community*, 4(4), 309–324.

Twyford, K., Le Fevre, D., & Timperley, H. (2017). The influence of risk and uncertainty on teachers' responses to professional learning and development. *Journal of Professional Capital and Community*, 2(2), 86–100. doi:10.1108/JPCC-10-2016-0028

Wang, Y. (2020). What is the role of emotions in educational leaders' decision making? Proposing an organizing framework. *Educational Administration Quarterly*, 1–31. doi:10.1177/0013161X20938856

Zembylas, M. (2005). Discursive practices, genealogies, and emotional rules: A poststructuralist view on emotion and identity in teaching. *Teaching and Teacher Education*, 21(8), 935–948. doi:10.1016/j.tate.2005.06.005

4 It's Time for Transformation! Using Transformational Leadership to Support Transformational Learning and Attract Emerging Leaders

Jill Fox Bernaciak

Introduction

Organizational leaders confront resistance to cultural changes that may be necessary when facing challenges to the organization's business plan. Resistance creates "a confluence of processes that are extremely difficult to predict and almost impossible to control," say Burke and Litwin (2016, p. 523). Transformational leaders can manage resistance by creating a groundswell of like-mindedness. Northouse (2019) advises that transformational leadership "creates a connection that raises the level of motivation and morality in both the leader and the follower" (pp. 164–165). As such, transformational leadership should provide the motivation to comply with change initiatives and commit to their success (Senge, 2006).

During change, a transformational leader can reshape roles, influence team processes, modify team interactions, and improve a team's performance. This case will give students an opportunity to explore goal setting and alignment within groups, which are closely related topics in this case, in the context of a typical internal consulting opportunity for human resource professionals.

Context of the Case

Today's Consumer Company (TCC), a multi-national manufacturer of paper, pulp, and lumber, is facing an external disruption that is eroding its market position. TCC produces paperboard and has been an industry leader for two decades in coated paperboard, containerboard, and multiple packaging. Over several years, however, lower-priced Chinese producers have taken away some of TCC's best customers. There has been no growth in sales in that time, which is a real decline, because TCC is not keeping up with the rate of inflation. Its loss in sales has been accompanied by a drop in share price, and a need to suspend dividend payments, which upsets its investors. TCC has run out of options. A reduction in staff of about 25 percent is planned, to reduce production costs and maintain TCC's profit margin, so things don't get worse. This bad news has not been announced. Only high-level managers have been told. But savvy employees know cuts are inevitable. Most employees want to

DOI: 10.4324/9780429331503-5

32 *It's Time for Transformation!*

stay and are willing to hope their jobs will be safe, or that a severance package will be offered.

But TCC has another related problem. Its historically paternalistic leadership style is turning off many of its newest, most talented staff. TCC's sales staff turnover rate has increased noticeably. The company lost three national sales account executives in the last nine months; all of whom reported to Tim Reynolds, group vice president of sales. To make matters worse, the executives persuaded an additional ten support staff members to take jobs at their new companies. Exit interviews with the 13 former employees revealed frustration that TCC's sales leadership is not responding to the situation with lost customers. Several TCC customers have expressed concern about the stability of the company. The last departure was Janice Pennington, which was especially sudden and shocking. Tim had given Janice a top salary package, a relocation package, company car, and personal mentoring from him. In her first year, Janice had exceeded her sales goals by 50 percent and built trust with several key customers. Tim was grooming her to ascend into the sales leadership ranks on a fast track. All seemed well, until Janice left in ten months, right before she would have received a 10 percent bonus.

Key Individuals

Bryan McNulty, executive director of human resources, has been a trusted resource to the sales division. He has been with TCC for 25 years since it was the undisputed dominant industry leader. Bryan suspects Tim is exercising bad judgment in his hiring and talent development practices.

Tim Reynolds, group vice president of sales, has been TCC's top sales executive for the most prestigious accounts. Tim won TCC's chairman's leadership award for four years in a row, but not last year. He fears his loss of staff has hurt his reputation. He is confused by the complexity of losing staff while sales were already declining. He feels his influence is diminished and asserts himself with sarcasm and humor. The rumor mill is swirling with speculation about Tim's future.

Rachel Johnson is TCC's diversity and inclusion director. She was hired a year ago and reports to Brian. Rachel has developed a sort of fanbase inside the company, thanks to her warmth, skill, and ability to handle sensitive human resources matters. She has a Master's degree in organizational psychology and was hired because of her solid reputation with managing organizational cultural change in large organizations.

Mary Ann Riley is group vice president of sales and Tim's supervisor. Like Brian, Mary Ann is an "old school" executive; saddened by TCC's decline. She relied on Tim for big wins in sales which made up, for a time, for some sluggishness in her department's performance. She lets Tim make staff-related decisions and focuses on customer relationships. She wants to support Tim, but her status is damaged by increasing negative perceptions of him.

Pete Digney, Mary Ann's assistant, is well-trusted across the sales division. He is a great resource when Mary Ann wants to check in on the feelings and beliefs of her staff. He is working on his Master's degree in business and has been with TCC for three years.

Jim Higgenbottom, an external consultant on cultural change and a partner from a top five global consulting firm. He is an expert in human capital management and serves clients across a range of industries. Jim authored a best-selling book on organizational change management to implement new strategies and performance improvements.

Scene 1: An Attempted Intervention

Tim Reynolds sputtered, coffee teetering. "If people like Janice don't appreciate having a good job, I say 'good-bye, good luck, and God bless'!"

"I'm trying to help you," said Bryan McNulty. Lowering his voice, he confided. "Everyone knows you're the top in the sales division. But Janice is your third loss of a sales executive this year. That doesn't reflect well on you with customers. Senior leadership wants to intervene, whatever that means. This is our chance to take charge."

Tim reacted. "The candidates you send me don't have strong sales abilities. I had no choice but to recruit Janice myself from our biggest competitor. She was amazing with customers. Then she leaves right before getting her first bonus?"

Bryan nodded. "I know, but young leaders are looking for work with purpose. If they don't see it, they move on. They don't want lifetime employment or big money. We have to do a better job of making sure there is a fit between TCC values and people we hire."

"You mean, I have to do a better job?" Tim smirked. "Hiring is your job. I can only hire who you recruit. You don't understand that money incentives work best for salespeople. But if you can help, I'm listening."

Bryan promised to set up a meeting with Tim, his boss (Mary Ann), and Rachel Johnson during the following week. He suggested they all could talk more about the values of new leaders and brainstorm some ways to improve staff retention.

Scene 2: Unbelievable Answers

Two weeks later, the group gathered. Bryan asked Rachel to moderate the discussion. Rachel had emailed Tim, Mary Ann, and Bryan an article about generational differences in workers (Smith & Turner, 2015) to read before the meeting. She opened by saying, "We can be proud of our current engagement scores on the sales staff survey. We had 198 responses, an 80 percent response rate, which is good. Of course, there are complaints," she said, stealing a sideways glance at Tim. "But, overall, our engagement scores are up, since the last survey three years ago."

34 *It's Time for Transformation!*

Janice continued. "Interestingly, many people wrote comments like 'this place is my family.' People realize our industry isn't growing. But they're loyal and don't blame TCC leadership. There were a few criticisms that leadership isn't responding well. I'd like to get your theories about what that means. You read that millennials, who are a third of the workforce, want something more than a big paycheck. They want two nonfinancial benefits: flexible work arrangements and a chance to give back to society through their work. We need to redesign our compensation program. I need your ideas, and I'm counting on your honesty and confidentiality."

Mary Ann Riley, group vice president of sales, stood up. "No one should be surprised that we have people who won't leave. But the people who won't stay should be the exception. You've got to find us better people! That's your job in human resources! When I see millennial staff with their faces in cell phones, I wish they would leave, if they don't find their work to be engaging. Can we get some outside ideas about how to fix things?"

"I agree with Mary Ann," Tim said. "My trusty methods didn't work with Janice. If I think about it, the other people I lost seemed happy too. They probably left for a little more money or a more stable employer. I can't help it if prices are driven down by the Chinese!"

Rachel nodded. "Ok, I'll get an outside consultant and will get us back together this month. The layoffs are coming later this quarter. Morale will suffer. Somehow, and quickly, we've got to create an opportunity out of this problem."

Scene 3: Fact-Finding

Mary Ann called Pete Digney into her office. "Pete, I'm on a team about improving talent retention. You're new here, but I'm sure you have some insights. We've lost a few top people recently with no warning. Everyone knows our sales aren't growing, but I'm told people are incredibly happy here. Is there a problem we can't see?"

Smiling, Pete said, "I could get input from a few employees. The staff survey is okay, but no one really thinks it changes anything."

"See what feedback you can get confidentially," Mary Ann said. "I don't want people complaining or feeling compelled to speak. Get back to me in a few days."

In a few days, an article appeared on Mary Ann's desk. A signed note from Pete said, "Could this happen here?" The article was about a global company that required that 20 percent of staff time be used as event time; when people step away from tasks and deadlines, giving unstructured time to develop ideas, work on personal projects, or even to socialize.

Mary Ann intercepted Pete on the way to lunch. She laughed. "Pete, thanks for that article. Event time sounds expensive. What's the payoff?"

Pete stood tall. "Mary Ann, event time isn't a giveaway. It's job-related. People in the sales division have been passing this article around. It's just one idea. Companies that generate ideas this way have been shown to make significant profits from the new products and services it generates. Innovative companies (the article says) respect the desires of people for flexibility, personal growth, connectivity, and a chance to give back to the world. They say payroll costs can be reduced and a more market-attuned culture can be developed."

Mary Ann looked at Pete in silence. "Okay, I'll think about it," she offered.

Scene 4: Reconvening the Team

More silence resulted when the team read through the article together two weeks later. Tim blurted, "Looks like the word has gotten out that we need help!" he chortled. "What are we supposed to do when we can't afford to sponsor social hours?"

Rachel interjected. "Many things improve the climate of an organization. But they don't necessarily improve the culture. We can't be over-confident in our beliefs. For example, we discussed how millennials have their faces in their cell phones a lot. Cell phones are their preferred work tools. Maybe we need to change our perceptions about the right way to work. At our next meeting, a facilitator will guide us through an idea generation session about how to incentivize emerging leaders."

Tim reacted. "I've talked to my best people. Some of them are excited about cultural changes. Let's leverage their enthusiasm. But let's also be realistic. Some great salespeople won't want to deal with culture change. They already have more important problems, like the industry decline, which means they make less money right now, no matter what any of us do."

Side conversations started. Rachel reminded the group: "We're exploring, not committing. I agree we can't force cultural change. Still, some people said our culture was 'paternalistic' and 'cult-like' in the sales staff survey. Those aren't qualities the emerging workforce would get excited about."

The Challenge of Change

"I thought we were going to get outside ideas!" Tim exclaimed, upon joining the first "TCC Sales Culture Design Thinking" meeting. "This is the same old group!"

Jim Higgenbottom, facilitator, shook Tim's hand. "I'm Jim. I've been retained to moderate these discussions. I'll ask you to suspend disbelief for now. Is that alright?"

Tim shrugged, indicating a skeptical "yes."

Rachel introduced everyone to Jim. "Based on Rachel's description of TCC's needs," Jim began, "we decided to use today as an educational session about the qualities of innovation, which is what is needed during change. I'll share examples of the behaviors and qualities of innovative groups. I'd like your thoughts on how you might model supportive behaviors at TCC."

"I've always heard modelling is fun," Tim joked, striking a pose.

Jim smiled. "Your positive spirit is going to help! We will also ask you to identify influencers from your division who might help our cause. We will

36 *It's Time for Transformation!*

gradually build a wellspring of support and ideas we can test across the company. In other words, we'd like to create some widespread optimism."

Discussion: The Opportunity Presented by Transformational Leadership

In the case, resistance to change came from the "top down" (i.e., senior leadership) and from the "bottom up," from followers. According to Northouse (2019), "transformational leadership is the process whereby a person engages with others and creates a connection that raises the level of motivation and morality in both the leader and the follower" (pp. 164–165).

An organization can become a learning organization that constantly transforms itself, enabling it to remain competitive by doing what is in the best interest of the organization into the future (O'Keeffe, 2002). Transformational leadership, according to Bass (2018), changes individuals and groups through positive elements that develop followers by enhancing their motivation, morale, and performance. As shown in Exhibit 1, the four elements of transformational leadership connect the follower's sense of self to an organization's collective identity and mission, and the collective identity of the organization. Followers are encouraged to take ownership of their work. Leaders are viewed as inspiring role models who understand their strengths and weaknesses and provide them with tasks that optimize their performance.

Exhibit 1

Elements of Transformational Leadership

Idealized Influence (also known as Charismatic Leadership), the Leader's Role – Transformational leaders act in ways that make them role models. They are respected, admired, and trusted. Followers identify with them and describe them in terms that imply extraordinary capabilities, persistence, and determination. These leaders are willing to take risks. They can consistently be relied upon to do the right thing, displaying high moral and ethical standards.

Inspirational Motivation (Collaborative Culture) – These leaders embody the term "team spirit." They show enthusiasm and optimism, providing both meaning and challenge to the work at hand. They create an atmosphere of commitment to goals and a shared vision.

Intellectual Stimulation (Organizational Identity) – a Transformational Leader encourages creativity and fosters an atmosphere in which followers feel compelled to think about old problems in a new way. Public criticism is avoided.

Individualized Consideration (Structural Systems) – Transformational leaders act as mentors and coaches. Individual desires and needs are respected. Differences are accepted and two-way communication is common.

These leaders are considered good listeners, and along with this comes personalized interaction. Followers of these leaders move continually toward development of higher levels of potential.

Source: The Bass handbook of leadership: theory, research, and managerial applications

Transformational Learning

In his Transformational Learning Theory, Jack Mezirow (1991) advises that a disorienting dilemma is an experience that does not fit expectations or does not make sense and that cannot be solved by one's previous approaches. In the case, the concurrent dynamics (i.e., new hiring trends and an impending layoff) have created a disorienting dilemma. The work climate could be impacted quickly, and the effects can alter the organizational culture, negatively.

Tim exhibits what Mezirow calls "habits of mind" (assumptions), which are obstacles to solving disorienting dilemmas. For example, Tim was incorrect in the assumption that Janice's salary and perks would retain her. These assumptions, Mezirow (1991) explains, define and shape individual perceptions, thoughts, and feelings. They determine what people think, feel, and do. People are reluctant to abandon them.

To transform TCC into an organizational culture that attracts and retains top talent, its leaders can transform their own perspectives through learning (for example, by responding to the generational data that Rachel provided). Mezirow's theory also calls for the transformation of feelings, as well as ideas, as Exhibit 2, through his Ten Phases of Perspective Transformation. This transformation creates new behaviors that leaders can model for others.

Exhibit 2

Ten Phases of Perspective Transformation

1. Disorienting dilemma
2. Self-examination with feelings of guilt/shame
3. Critical assessment of epistemic, sociocultural, or psychological assumptions
4. Recognition that one's discontent and the process of transformation are shared and that others have negotiated a similar change
5. Exploration of options for new roles, relationships, and actions
6. Planning a course of action
7. Acquisition of knowledge and skills for implementing one's plans
8. Provisional trying on of new roles
9. Building of competence and self-confidence in new roles and relationships
10. A reintegration into one's life based on conditions dictated by one's new perspective

38 *It's Time for Transformation!*

Leader Behaviors and Team Conflict

If TCC employs transformational leadership and transformational learning theories, it must be prepared to manage cognitive and affective conflict to make changes that are, say Kotlyar and Karakowsky (2006). Group members led by transformational leaders are more likely to challenge fellow members and fight harder to defend their positions. There is also more potential for generating dysfunctional conflict. The following discussion questions will help students to use theories and facts from the case to anticipate possible outcomes.

Learning Activities

Discussion Questions:

1. What were the factors that helped or hindered Tim's ability to retain talent?
2. What are your team's behaviors and attitudes that uphold your organization's values? How can you use roles, processes, interactions, and measures to reinforce these norms?
3. What examples of transformational learning did you see in this case, which were a result of transformational leadership practices?
4. How could TCC improve in the areas of idealized influence, inspirational motivation, intellectual stimulation, or individualized consideration?

Research: Find your organization's resources for optimizing talent recruitment and retention. Evaluate the measures taken by Tim in dealing with Janice's hiring and development.

Role-play: "You are …," is an activity that examines the case from multiple perspectives. Assuming the position of a stakeholder allows the students to discuss and debate controversial issues related to the importance of diverse values and perspectives.

The opinions on the role-play cards are intentionally exaggerated to exemplify viewpoints and in no way represent the opinions of the author.

Directions:

- Place the stakeholders listed below on separate index cards (one stakeholder per card).
- Have students randomly choose an index card.
- Each student will represent the viewpoint of the stakeholder they selected, even if it opposes their own true opinion.
- Assign the student who randomly selected the role of Brian to be the moderator of the meeting where the issues are discussed.
- Allow 5 minutes for every student to prepare for their role. (Use the index card as a guide).

- Allocate 20 minutes for the role-play.
- Finally debrief and allow students to share their true point of view if they choose to.

    a Do you think issues of power and privilege were relevant in this scenario?

    b Would the scenario differ if the executives or employees involved were of different race, gender, or ethnicity?

    c Would the scenario differ if the executives or employees involved represented different levels of authority, or different functional areas of the company, such as Manufacturing, Engineering, Marketing, Human Resources, IT, Legal, or Administration?

Roles:

1. You are the CEO, Karen Grace. After attending a group meeting, you are upset that anyone is questioning the values that created decades of quality products and customer service. You are concerned about the apparent divisiveness among senior leaders. You're not going to give this team long to develop recommendations before you decide whether to dismiss at least one person on the team.

2. You are Bryan McNulty. You believe the TCC must change. You believe that employees already know that layoffs are imminent. TCC will wind up stronger than ever. You are determined to lead this discussion with authenticity.

3. You are Mary Ann Riley. Your employee, Pete, is a key influencer in the company and is your eyes and ears. You trust Pete but are worried about your peers' perceptions of his ideas.

4. You are Pete Digney. You can understand why Janice left. In your view, Tim is unimaginative and she was over-qualified. A shake-up might be healthy for the company. True leaders, in your opinion, have nothing to fear.

References

Silverman, R. E. (2014, Oct 1). At work: The clock hurts your creativity: New study shows employees are more creative, happier without a clock. *Wall Street Journal (Online)*https://search-proquest-com.ezproxy.bgsu.edu/docview/1566679938?accountid=26417

Smith, C., & Turner, S. (2015). The radical transformation of diversity and inclusion. https://www2.deloitte.com/content/dam/Deloitte/us/Documents/about-deloitte/us-inclus-millennial-influence-120215.pdf

Barakat, M., Mountford, M., Poole, D., & Pappas, D. (n.d.). *Tidal wave: A university's response to transformational learning objectives.* https://journals.sagepub.com/doi/10.1177/1555458919831335

Bass, B. M., & Bass, R. E. (2008). *The Bass handbook of leadership: Theory, research, and managerial applications* (pp. 618–648). Free Press.

Burke, W. W., & Litwin, G. H. (2016;1992). A causal model of organizational performance and change. *Journal of Management*, 18(3), 523–545. doi:10.1177/014920639201800306

40 *It's Time for Transformation!*

Kotlyar, I., & Karakowsky, L. (2006). Leading conflict? Linkages between leader behaviors and group conflict. *Small Group Research*, 37(4), 377–403. doi:10.1177/1046496406291388

Mezirow, J. (1991). *Transformative dimensions of adult learning.* Jossey-Bass.

Northouse, P. G. (2019). *Leadership: Theory and practice.* SAGE Publications.

O'Keeffe, T. (2002). *Organisational learning: A new perspective. Journal of European Industrial Training*, 26(2/3/4), 130–141. doi:10.1108/03090590210422012

Silverman, R. E. (2014, Oct. 1). At work: The clock hurts your creativity: New study shows employees are more creative, happier without a clock. *Wall Street Journal* (Online) https://search-proquest-com.ezproxy.bgsu.edu/docview/1566679938?accountid=26417

Smith, C., & Turner, S. (2015). The radical transformation of diversity and inclusion. https://www2.deloitte.com/content/dam/Deloitte/us/Documents/about-deloitte/us-inclus-millennial-influence-120215.pdf

References

Goffee, R., & Jones, G.(2000). Why should anyone be lead by you?In Harvard Business Review. *On what makes a leader*(pp.153–175). Harvard Business School Press.

Kegan, R., & Lahey, L. L. (2009). *Immunity to change: How to overcome it and unlock potential in yourself and your organization.* Harvard Business Press.

Part II

Introduction to Part II

Kristina N. LaVenia and Judy Jackson May

Perhaps more than any other time in contemporary history, recent events, both nationally and worldwide, have shaped the definition of crises. Merriam Webster defines a crisis as a turning point for better or worse, a condition or period of instability and difficulty, and the point where decisive change occurs. In light of the global pandemic caused by Covid-19, however, this definition feels incomplete. While tragic, most crises available for study in organizational change can be framed based on a beginning and an end. One of the early lessons we have from the pandemic is that some of the most challenging leadership work during this crisis stems from uncertainty around the actual timeline and/or temporal aspect. At the time of this writing, more than one year after initial acknowledgement of the pandemic in the United States, we are warned of future waves and ongoing need for social distancing. Across organizations in all sectors, leaders are faced with the *what next* and *when will this end* challenges from followers. This part includes three chapters that share the theme of dealing with leadership challenges during times of crisis.

In "Responding to School Crisis Through Compassionate Leadership: A District's Journey with Covid-19," Lasater and Lasater invite readers to consider the importance of compassion during crisis leadership. The authors ask us to think about how compassionate leadership may provide the support that helps followers experience growth and resilience following a crisis. The editors encourage readers to reflect on what this might look like for leader-follower dyads, leader-follower sets/groups in the community, as well as taking a systems perspective.

How would a compassionate educational system be described? How might a system designed intentionally to center compassion differ in policy, resource allocation, and decision-making? We assert that compassion is critical to the work of education and that educators tend to be compassionate people. How, then, do we design for compassionate systems that support, reward, and acknowledge compassionate leadership? What about compassionate followership? These are questions in need of examination by practitioners, policy makers, and researchers. The Covid-19 pandemic has provided a shared crisis experience. Although each person and organization has a unique story regarding how they are personally impacted, the pandemic's universality may

DOI: 10.4324/9780429331503-6

42 *Introduction to Part II*

provide an entry point for multiple perspectives and initiatives to center compassion in our learning organizations. As Lasater and Lasater point out, compassion demands that we extend our educational care ethos to action that alleviates suffering; we invite our readers to explore ways of achieving this in their own work settings. Finally, we ask leadership preparation faculty to consider how our programs may better meet the need for developing compassionate leaders.

Engaging non-traditional learners has become a new but significant focus for higher educational institutions. The second chapter in this section utilizes adult learning theory to understand recruitment, enrollment, and retention of "student" populations whose characteristics are distinctly different from the case setting's traditional students. Readers might consider how to address predicted demographic shifts while managing unpredicted crises. In "Higher Education Leadership in an Unprecedented and Uncertain environment: The Case of a Midwestern Private Institution," Brigette Gibson raises important questions that become even more urgent in light of the pandemic. The chapter describes the leadership considerations for cabinet members of a small private liberal arts residential institution.

Given that post-secondary institutions are historically slow to change, how do higher educational leaders manage the loss of traditional students while engaging non-traditional students in the wake of Covid-19? Gibson asserts that Schlossberg's transition theory provides a vehicle to understand how non-traditional adults adjust for success in new environments. Readers will explore how situational leadership, transition theory, and adult learning theory inform the what, how, and why of leading pre-, during, and post-pandemic. We urge readers to move beyond focusing only on challenges to consider which special opportunities might be discovered as a result of the pandemic? Thinking about the Gibson case in light of the Lasater and Lasater reading, how might leaders in higher education embrace compassionate leadership to meet the needs of non-traditional learners? Where are there opportunities to meet organizational goals – and live up to stated missions – with innovation and compassion combined?

The onset of the pandemic impacts every school system in the nation, whether public, private, community, charter, elementary or secondary. The nation's superintendents are compelled to make life and death decisions in a shorter span of time than many take to select their produce. Parmigian chronicles a public school superintendent's decision-making process making life-altering decisions within unimaginable timelines.

"Dr. Remote Instruction: Time Constraints and Critical Consciousness in Crisis Leadership" explores critical questions in play for school leaders facing Covid-19. The chapter explores the decision-making considerations in the "exurban" setting of the case study. Parmigian engages readers with critical theory of adult development and adaptive and technical leadership to make sense of the leadership dilemmas. Readers are asked to consider how to address embedded cultural norms that support deficit thinking and low expectations for low-income students. How to present the moment's

Introduction to Part II 43

immediacy to school board members, district administration, community members, media, and external stakeholders? How to ensure that students are receiving appropriate remote instruction? The editors encourage reflection on how leaders might advocate for students who have been historically left behind, as well as how to prepare for leading the district in the aftermath of such uncertainty. This case, too, illustrates the need for compassionate leadership and quick responses to changing demands. Perhaps more than any other section in this book, the three chapters here beg to be read as a "set" so readers can think carefully about *compassionate leadership for adult development* in pursuit of organizational goals.

5 Responding to School Crises through Compassionate Leadership

A District Leader's Journey with Covid-19

Kara Lasater and Clay Lasater

Introduction

The Professional Standards for Educational Leaders (PSEL) call on school leaders to promote the success and well-being of all students and adults within the school community (National Policy Board for Educational Administration [NPBEA], 2015). This is cognitively, emotionally, physically, and spiritually demanding work – particularly during school crises. School crises are events that threaten or disrupt the school's core values or foundational practices (Pepper et al., 2010), and they serve as a direct threat to individual and organizational well-being.

Leaders must respond to crises in ways that restore organizational functioning and facilitate individual healing, growth, and well-being. Attending to the well-being of others during crises requires compassionate leadership. Compassionate leadership involves the intentional, coordinated efforts of leaders to create and support organizational routines, structures, and processes that acknowledge and respond to others' vulnerability and suffering (Ali & Terry, 2017; de Zulueta, 2016). Not only does this approach to leadership facilitate compassion and care for others, but it is also responsive to the developmental changes spurred by crisis events. **Thus, this case explores the nexus between compassionate leadership and school crises.**

Smithville School District

Smithville is a small, rural community located in the Midwest. Smithville School District consists of grades Pre-K–12 with a total enrollment of approximately 350 students. There are two schools within the district: Smithville Middle and High School (grades 7–12) and Smithville Elementary School (grades Pre-K–6). The administrative team for the district consists of superintendent, Mr. Ramey; elementary principal, Mrs. Marshall; secondary principal, Mr. Wolfe; K–12 curriculum coordinator and elementary teacher, Mrs. Welch; and K–12 counselor, Mrs. Lawrence.

The 2019–2020 school year marked Mr. Ramey's fifth year as Smithville superintendent. Previously, he served six years as Smithville's secondary

DOI: 10.4324/9780429331503-7

46 *Responding to School Crises*

principal and ten years as the middle school math teacher. Mr. Ramey firmly believes compassionate leadership is the key to assisting Smithville through the pandemic and supporting the overall well-being of students, faculty, and community members.

March 27, 2020

In response to the Covid-19 pandemic, Mr. Ramey and his administrative team prepare to close school for the remainder of the 2019–2020 school year. Mr. Ramey initiates the meeting by encouraging the team to remain focused on the holistic well-being of students and adults within the school community. "I've spent considerable time reflecting on the best course of action, and I keep circling back to four questions," Mr. Ramey stated. **"First, how do we provide a meaningful learning experience for students outside the school walls?"**

"*Can* we require students to complete work?," Mr. Wolfe interjected. "If not, how can we give students credit? Some students were not passing courses when school dismissed. If we don't allow them to complete work, they'll fail."

Mr. Ramey could sense Mr. Wolfe's angst. "Those are good questions, and I fully understand why those questions are important to you as the high school principal. I've thought about them too. But I also realized those questions distracted me from the heart of the issue – providing a meaningful learning experience for students. While we cannot ignore pragmatics, let's start with what matters most." And with that, the administrative team began brainstorming.

For several minutes, the team shared ideas related to virtual classrooms, online activities, and/or the compilation of hardcopy materials. "I like many of the ideas I've heard," Mr. Ramey commented, "But as we're discussing, we should consider my second question: **How can we ensure the learning experience we provide students is equitable?"**

"That's what I keep thinking," Mrs. Marshall added. "Many students don't have internet. They either can't get it where they live, or they can't afford it. How can we expect these students to do anything that requires the internet?"

"And not all students have family support with their learning at home," Mrs. Welch offered. "I'm not saying parents don't care or aren't willing to help, but many parents are still working full-time. Elementary students struggle to work independently. Are parents supposed to work all day and do homework all night?"

"That's my concern," Mr. Ramey replied. "Part of the equity equation is recognizing that all families are in different circumstances as a result of Covid. To think that all families can support students in the same way seems unrealistic and incredibly insensitive – which leads to my third question: **How can we ensure the learning experience we provide students is value-added and not additionally burdensome to families?** Families are already under extreme stress. Whatever we provide must *assist* students and families – not further burden them."

"So do you think we should require students to do anything," Mrs. Marshall asked, "or should we just provide supplemental materials?"

"At the high school, no one would complete optional assignments," Mr. Wolfe added. "I hate to ask teachers to develop assignments no one will complete."

"You care about your teachers and respect their time," Mr. Ramey reflected. "Their lives have been disrupted too. The care and concern you demonstrated speaks to my final question. Above all, **how can we ensure Smithville students, families, faculty, and community members know they are cared about and supported?**" With all four questions under consideration, the administrative team spent the next several hours developing a plan of action.

April 15, 2020

Each morning since Smithville enacted its plan for remote learning, Mr. Ramey opened his inbox to a new set of challenges. This morning, Mr. Ramey took a deep breath and read:

Dear Mr. Ramey,

I am contacting you as a concerned parent and citizen. Covid-19 abruptly forced schools to change. These changes were unprecedented and unpredicted. Consequently, I recognize how little time the district had to prepare for non-traditional schooling, and I appreciate the district's efforts to quickly adapt. However, I sincerely hope the district is much more prepared should Covid force school closures next year. As the parent of two high school students, I believe the district's current approach lacks the rigor necessary for my children to reach their academic and career goals. My children are increasingly disinterested in schoolwork. After looking at their assignments, I understand why. The assignments are superficial and lack complexity. This is a missed opportunity for the district, as now is an ideal time to challenge students to think deeply about the world around them. I attribute the school's rudimentary approach to inadequate time for preparation. Now that ample time is available, I anticipate the district will provide students with a more rigorous, engaging curriculum in the 2020–2021 school year. My children's futures depend on it.

Sincerely,

Dr. Richard Nelson

Mr. Ramey re-read the message four times – each time with a new emotion rolling over him. He drafted a response but found the tone of the message too defensive. Instead, he picked up the phone and dialed Dr. Nelson's number.

April 20, 2020

As he pulled into the driveway, Mr. Ramey could hear his children's laughter. It brought much-needed respite from the otherwise constant stress and anxiety of Covid-19. But he was only home a few minutes when his phone rang.

48 *Responding to School Crises*

"It's my sister," Mrs. Lawrence quietly cried. "She'd been sick for a few days but thought it was a cold. She feared Covid exposure, so she refused to go to the doctor. This afternoon, she started feeling short of breath. Her husband called the ambulance, but it was too late. She's gone, and we can't even be together as a family or give her the service she deserves!" When she finished her sentence, Mrs. Lawrence's quiet cries turned to sobs.

Mr. Ramey's heart broke for his colleague and friend. He wished there was something he could say or do to alleviate the pain she felt. *But what could he say or do that would bring comfort amid such sudden, tragic loss?*

May 4, 2020

Mr. Ramey leaned back in his chair exhausted. For eight straight weeks, the school provided supplemental learning activities, prepared meals for students, planned summer and fall activities, and developed contingency plans given the continued unknown. He also checked in frequently with Mrs. Lawrence. But Mr. Ramey knew the pandemic was far from over. He was contemplating the continued challenges in front of him when his office phone rang.

"Hello, Mr. Ramey?" a voice hesitantly asked. "This is Sarah Carter. My four kids attend Smithville Elementary."

"Hello, Mrs. Carter," Mr. Ramey replied. "Thank you for calling. What can I help you with today?"

"For weeks now, my kids have received homework from their teachers. Many assignments require the internet, but we can't get internet where we live. I park outside public places to get free Wi-Fi, but it's hard to do every night after work. My husband and I are fortunate to have our jobs, but we can't keep up with schoolwork. The youngest two kids can't work independently, so we have to sit beside them and do homework all night."

"I understand your concerns," Mr. Ramey empathized. "My own family has experienced similar challenges."

"I'm already hearing rumors that schools might close again this fall. I wanted to speak up before that happens. Students need to be in school. They need to be around their friends and learning from teachers! *If* schools are forced to close, it's ridiculous to assign all this homework. It ends up falling on parents' shoulders, which isn't feasible for working parents."

Mr. Ramey understood her concern. In truth, his family *had* experienced similar challenges. He not only had three school-aged children at home, but one of his children had a disability, which required additional academic support. With two working parents, this spring had been incredibly difficult for his family. *How could parents work full-time and simultaneously provide an education for their children at home?*

But there were also families experiencing other challenges. Several parents in his community were laid off from their jobs. They were trying to juggle their children's schoolwork while simultaneously grappling with tremendous financial stress. *How could these families focus on schoolwork with looming financial concerns?*

The Dilemma

For such a small community, there was considerable diversity in families' needs and experiences as a result of Covid-19, and Mr. Ramey knew it was his responsibility to recognize and attend to families' diverse needs. *But how could he develop an educational experience for each student that was responsive to families' unique needs? How could he nurture others' well-being amid tremendous stress and uncertainty? How could he foster a culture of compassionate care within the district when everyone was experiencing the pandemic in such different ways?*

Discussion: School Crises and Compassionate Leadership

School crises create a multitude of challenges for leaders. For Mr. Ramey, the challenges created by Covid-19 were evolving and highly complex, and they required swift decision-making. In response, Mr. Ramey worked to facilitate post-traumatic growth and support individual and organizational well-being by enacting compassionate leadership.

School Crisis

School crises unfold at both the individual and organizational levels. At the individual level, crises disrupt existing schemas and subsequently create considerable emotional distress (Kegan, 1980; Tedeschi & Calhoun, 2004). At the organizational level, crises disrupt basic functions and systems in ways that threaten the viability of the organization (Pepper et al., 2010). Consequently, crises create situations in which leaders must work to restore the organization's functioning while simultaneously supporting the growth and healing of diverse stakeholders.

School crises are obvious in their manifestation, but they emerge from complex, obscure, and uncontainable circumstances (Pepper et al., 2010). Throughout Covid-19, information about the virus and its health consequences were obscure, and responses to the pandemic were complicated by the complex structure of school governance and competing demands of external and internal stakeholders (Pepper et al., 2010). Ultimately, these circumstances created the types of "frightening junctures" that threaten individual and organizational autonomy, control, dignity, and direction (de Zulueta, 2016, p. 2).

School crises also necessitate urgent decision-making from leaders – decisions that are of great consequence to individuals and organizations (Pepper et al., 2010). Unfortunately, schools often lack adequate data to guide decision-making during crises. This was evidenced during Covid-19 when leaders were forced to make decisions about school closures and alternative methods of instruction amid limited, and sometimes distorted, data. These types of public, high-stakes decisions place considerable pressure on leaders and lead to emotional exhaustion (Mahfouz, 2020).

50 *Responding to School Crises*

Compassionate Leadership during School Crises

Compassionate leadership can help leaders respond to school crises and facilitate post-traumatic growth in the aftermath of trauma. Post-traumatic growth refers to the type of transformational development that occurs in response to highly challenging life events that alter existing schemas (i.e., crises; Calhoun & Tedeschi, 2004). Growth in the context of crises requires "cognitive rebuilding that takes into account the changed reality of one's life after trauma" and leads to the development of new, more resilient schema (Tedeschi & Calhoun, 2004, p. 5). Crises in-and-of themselves do not lead to growth. In fact, they can be emotionally, psychologically, and physically debilitating (Burke Harris, 2018). But growth in the aftermath of crisis is possible (Calhoun & Tedeschi, 2004), and compassionate care could help support this process.

Compassionate care refers to an awareness of and responsiveness to an individual's vulnerability or suffering (Ali & Terry, 2017). It involves noticing, feeling, and responding to others' pain, vulnerability, and suffering (Frost et al., 2006, p. 846). Compassionate leadership, in turn, fosters and sustains compassionate care within organizations (de Zulueta, 2016). It involves the intentional and systematic promotion of compassion within organizational practices, policies, structures, and routines (Ali & Terry, 2017).

Compassionate leadership requires attention to both the interpersonal and organizational aspects of compassionate care. Interpersonal compassionate care involves "the effortful handling of interpersonal interactions" (Frost et al., 2006, p. 846). It requires highly sophisticated skills related to noticing, open listening, empathetic responding, reframing, personal reflection, appreciative inquiry, conflict management, storytelling, and feedback (de Zulueta, 2016; Dewar & Cook, 2014; Dewar et al., 2013; Frost et al., 2006). These skills subsequently provide opportunities to understand others' vulnerability and to engage in open, restorative dialogue about suffering and care (Dewar et al., 2013; Dewar & Cook, 2014). When leaders utilize these skills, it can serve as a "healing force" in times of crisis (Frost et al., 2006, p. 843).

Organizational compassion "involves a set of social processes in which noticing, feeling, and responding to pain are shared among a set of organizational members" (Kanov et al., 2004, p. 816). These social processes: legitimize compassionate feelings and behaviors through intentionally crafted practices and policies; they propagate compassionate responses through organizational systems; and, they coordinate collective responses to others' suffering (Frost et al., 2006; Kanov et al., 2004). Leaders can support organizational compassion by providing training, implementing programs of well-being, facilitating supportive interpersonal connections between stakeholders, and sharing knowledge, skills, and work associated with compassionate care (de Zulueta, 2016).

There are multiple ways compassionate leadership can facilitate growth and healing during crises. First, crises lead to intense feelings of stress, anxiety, and fear, and this "struggle with the trauma" is essential for post-traumatic growth

(Tedeschi & Calhoun, 2004, p. 4). But compassionate leaders seek to be fully present in others' suffering (de Zulueta, 2016; Murphy, 2016), and in doing so, they facilitate healing by offering a safe space for others to process their evolving understanding of the world.

Second, compassionate leaders can assist in the reconstruction of meaning-making systems by engaging in caring conversations. Caring conversations elicit information about a person's experiences, who they are, and what matters most to them (Dewar & Cook, 2014). This crafting of one's personal narrative subsequently allows for emotional expression, facilitates intimate connections, and assists in reconstructing schemas and goals following crises (Tedeschi & Calhoun, 2004). The narratives elicited through compassionate, caring conversations allow people to make sense of who they are following crisis (Frost, 2006), and these new meaning-making systems "incorporate the trauma and possible events in the future" and "are more resistant to being shattered" (Tedeschi & Calhoun, 2004, p. 5).

Finally, compassionate leadership can help sustain educators as they respond to crises. Attending to others' well-being, particularly in high-stress circumstances, can be cognitively and emotionally draining work (Shirley et al., 2020), but leadership for compassionate care "requires acknowledging and making provision for the difficulties and challenges of working in an anxiety-laden context" (de Zulueta, 2016, p. 1). Thus, leaders must intentionally attend trainings, foster connections, and craft organizational systems that support them in developing distress tolerance, self-compassion, and a supportive network for compassionate care (de Zulueta, 2016; Murphy, 2016). With adequate support and opportunities for honest reflection and open dialogue, compassionate care is energizing, rejuvenating, and deeply satisfying for practitioners (Dewar et al., 2013).

Discussion Questions and Learning Activities

The following questions and activities can facilitate critical reflection/dialogue on compassionate care during school crises and support leaders in developing the interpersonal skills necessary to demonstrate compassionate care.

- Compassionate care is a reciprocal relationship. It requires intimate, relational knowledge about who people are, what matters to them, and how they feel about their own experiences (Dewar & Cook, 2014). This knowledge is subsequently used to ensure compassionate care is enacted in ways that are meaningful to the individual experiencing suffering (Dewar et al., 2013). In the above case, people experienced suffering in different ways. What were the various ways they experienced suffering, and how could this knowledge be used to provide individualized compassionate care?
- Leaders play a critical role in developing a school culture of compassionate care by establishing organizational structures, practices, systems,

52 *Responding to School Crises*

routines, and policies that foster collective compassion (Kanov, 2004; Frost, 2006). School cultures of compassion not only influence how current crises are addressed, but they shape the organization's response to future tragedy and suffering (Frost, 2006). How did Mr. Ramey work to establish a culture of compassion within the district? What impact did Mr. Ramey's actions, or inactions, have on the district's culture of compassion? What types of routines, systems, practices, or structures could Mr. Ramey create that would help him respond to the suffering of others and craft a compassionate culture within the district?

- Compassionate care is cognitively and emotionally-demanding work; thus, the sustainability of compassionate care is predicated by care-providers' personal well-being, ability to tolerate distress, and willingness to demonstrate self-compassion (Ali & Terry, 2017; de Zulueta, 2016; Murphy, 2016). What were likely sources of distress for Mr. Ramey? Why is it important for Mr. Ramey to practice self-compassion amid personal distress? As a school leader, what are the personal and professional consequences of inadequately practicing self-care and self-compassion? How will you promote self-care and self-compassion in your current or future work as a school leader?

- Mr. Ramey aimed to demonstrate compassionate leadership in his work as superintendent. On March 27, Mr. Ramey used four questions to guide the district's response to Covid-19. What is your perspective on the four questions? Were they helpful in guiding the district's response? Did they orient the district toward compassionate care? What other questions might have been helpful in framing the district's response?

- The demonstration of compassion involves highly skilled performative elements (Frost et al., 2006). These performative elements can be nurtured through role-play. Role-play provides a valuable mechanism for enhancing adult learning by engaging learners in deliberate practice and providing them constructive feedback (Hubbard, 2014). Identify a role-play partner. Role play the conversation between Mr. Ramey and Dr. Nelson. Practice responding to Dr. Nelson's concerns in ways that demonstrate compassion. Immediately following the role-play, ask your partner for feedback. Feedback should focus on ways you effectively demonstrated compassion and areas of needed improvement. Follow the same process for role-playing the conversation between Mr. Ramey and Mrs. Lawrence.

Suggested Readings and Exercises

- Pepper et al. (2010) offer a self-audit inventory that leaders can use to assess their schools' preparedness for crises (p. 253–263). The first aspect of this inventory involves the identification of core values. This provides a meaningful opportunity for leaders to consider the extent to which compassion and care are represented within the school's core values and foundational practices. As the inventory progresses, leaders can align their crises plans to reflect the school's commitment to compassion, care, and well-being.

- In *Dancing in the Rain: Leading with Compassion, Vitality, and Mindfulness in Education*, Murphy (2016) describes the importance of approaching school leadership from a compassionate, mindful perspective. This text offers many useful exercises that can assist school leaders in developing compassionate habits of mind.

References

Ali, S., & Terry, L. (2017). Exploring senior nurses' understanding of compassionate leadership in the community. *British Journal of Community Nursing, 22*(2), 1–7. doi:10.12968/bjcn.2017.22.2.77

Burke Harris, N. (2018). *The deepest well: Healing the long-term effects of childhood adversity.* Houghton Mifflin Harcourt.

Calhoun, L. G., & Tedeschi, R. G. (2004). The foundations of posttraumatic growth: New considerations. *Psychological Inquiry, 15*(1), 93–102. doi:10.1207/s15327965pli1501_03

Dewar, B., Adamson, E., Smith, S., Surfleet, J., & King, L. (2013). Clarifying misconceptions about compassionate care. *Journal of Advanced Nursing, 70*(8), 1738–1747. doi:10.1111/jan.12322

Dewar, B., & Cook, F. (2014). Developing compassion through a relationship centered appreciative leadership programme. *Nurse Education Today, 34*, 1258–1264. doi:10.1016/j.nedt.2013.12.012

de Zulueta, P. C. (2016). Developing compassionate leadership in health care: An integrative review. *Journal of Healthcare Leadership, 8*, 1–10. doi:10.2147/JHL.S93724

Frost, P. J., Dutton, J. E., Maitlis, S., Lilius, J. M., Kanov, J. M., & Worline, M. C. (2006). Seeing organizations differently: Three lenses on compassion. In C. Hardy, S. Clegg, T. Lawrence, & W. Nord (Eds.), *Handbook of organizational studies*, 2nd ed. (pp. 843–866). Sage.

Hubbard, G. B. (2014). Customized role play: Strategy for development of psychiatric mental health nurse practitioner competencies. *Perspectives in Psychiatric Care, 50*, 132–138.

Kanov, J. M., Maitlis, S., Worline, M., Dutton, J. E., Frost, P. J., Lilius, J. M. (2004). Compassion in organizational life. *American Behavioral Scientist, 47*(6), 808–827. doi:10.1177/0002764203260211

Kegan, R. (1980). Making meaning: The constructive-developmental approach to persons and practice. *Journal of Counseling & Development, 58*(5), 373–380. doi:10.1002/j.2164-4918.1980.tb00416.x

Mahfouz, J. (2020). Principals and stress: Few coping strategies for abundant stressors. *Educational Management Administration & Leadership, 48*(3), 440–458. doi:10.1177/1741143218817562

Murphy, J. T. (2016). *Dancing in the rain: Leading with compassion, vitality, and mindfulness in education.* Harvard Education Press.

National Policy Board for Educational Administration. (2015). Professional Standards for Educational Leaders 2015. http://www.npbea.org/wp-content/uploads/2017/06/Professional-Standards-for-Educational-Leaders_2015.pdf

Pepper, M. J., London, T. D., Dishman, M. L., & Lewis, J. L. (2010). *Leading schools during. crisis: What school administrators must know.* Rowman & Littlefield.

Rogers, J. (2019). For school leaders, a time for vigilance and caring. *Educational Leadership*, 77(2), 22–28.

Shirley, D., Hargreaves, A., & Washington-Wangia, S. (2020). The sustainability and unsustainability of teachers' and leaders' well-being. *Teaching and Teacher Education*, 92, 1–12. doi:10.1016/j.tate.2019.102987

Tedeschi, R. G., & Calhoun, L. G. (2004). Posttraumatic growth: Conceptual foundations and empirical evidence. *Psychological Inquiry*, 15(1), 1–18.

6 Higher Education Leadership in an Unprecedented and Uncertain Environment

The Case of a Midwestern Private Institution

Brigette S. Gibson

Introduction

Higher education as an industry has always been slow to change as it is largely based on traditions and values. Increasingly, however, internal factors and external environmental pressures to solve many economic, retention, and social issues have caused the industry to adapt faster than it typically would to meet stakeholders' needs (Buller, 2015; Burke, 2018; Hersey et al., 2001). It is not a matter of if things will change, but when they will change. In an unprecedented environment, such as the Covid-19 global pandemic and economic downturn, and as stakeholders' needs and expectations rapidly change, many colleges and universities are challenged to remain sustainable. The pandemic is caused by the novel coronavirus (Centers for Disease Control and Prevention [CDC], n.d.). It is currently the most unpredictable, disruptive, and uncertain global public health crisis of our lifetime (Fernandez & Shaw, 2020; Tesar, 2020). Covid-19 has impacted every aspect of life, and many higher education institutions swiftly shifted policies, practices, instructional modes, and protocols to ensure the health and safety of stakeholders while working to maintain operational effectiveness.

The recruitment, enrollment, and retention of non-traditional adult learners (NALs) is an uncharted area for many private liberal arts higher education institutions. The National Center for Education Statistics (NCES; 2017) reports that by 2025 approximately 10 million NALs will be enrolled in colleges and universities. The report also states that NALs are projected to constitute over 41 percent of postsecondary students, and this number is expected to continue to grow.

Voorhees and Lingenfelter (2003) define NALs as someone 25 years of age or older involved in postsecondary learning activities. Additionally, Horn (1996, as cited in Chen, 2017) states the following:

> Non-traditional adult learners, usually defined as aged 25 and over, also include those under 25 but who have characteristics indicative of adult responsibilities, such as working full-time, being financially independent, has non-spousal dependents, is a single parent, as well as having a

DOI: 10.4324/9780429331503-8

nontraditional educational trajectory, such as delayed enrollment into higher education or did not complete high school.

(p. 1)

While colleges and universities experience a decline in enrollment of first-time, full-time undergraduate students due to Covid-19, another phenomenon that will soon impact enrollment is the demographic shift. The pending demographic shift, also referred to as the higher education enrollment cliff, is a result of fewer traditional direct-from-high-school graduates that will be college-bound in certain areas of the United States like the Midwest and Northeast. This enrollment decrease is precipitated by the 2008 economic recession, birth rate decline patterns, and migration (Bransberger & Michelau, 2016; Bransberger et al., 2020; Grawe, 2018). These demographic shifts mean that in the Midwest and other parts of the United States, college and university enrollments are projected to increase for the Hispanic and Black student population and decrease for the White student population (Bransberger & Michelau, 2016; Bransberger et al., 2020; Grawe, 2018). This shift will directly impact the core student population of Midwest College, the case study institution.

While Midwest College primarily enrolls traditional college-age students, the institution must pivot to accommodate enrollment decreases because of Covid-19 as well as the impending demographic changes. Traditional college-age students are typically between 18 and 24 years old, enrolled full-time, reside on campus, and financially dependent on parents (NCES, n.d.; Pelletier, 2010; McGregor et al., 1991; Hurtado et al., 1996). Midwest College leaders must strategically pursue opportunities to increase their market share of the population of students of color, specifically Hispanic and Black students, as well as the NALs populations.

Due to Covid-19, many colleges and universities have reimagined their strategic plans and shifted from the standard of in-person instructional delivery; students and their families have had to adjust to virtual pedagogical learning environments, virtual work, health and safety, and economic challenges. Additionally, NALs are more likely to experience disruptions in their employment status, as compared to traditional college students. NALs are increasingly enrolling or re-enrolling in college in a virtual environment to strengthen their skills or obtain a first or secondary degree. As it relates to adult transitions, Schlossberg et al. (1995) broadly define Schlossberg's transition theory as one that focuses on the transitions that adults experience throughout life and how they cope and adjust to those transitions.

In this environment of uncertainty, it is critical that Midwest College's leaders understand and engage situational leadership. It is understood that the pandemic has created a crisis situation that demands that leaders: effectively communicate to all stakeholders and employ adult learning theory for the development and design of curriculum and programs for NALs in transition. Through the exploration of this case, readers will be able to identify and explain situational leadership, consider how both Schlossberg's transition theory and adult learning theory can be applied to situational leadership, and predict their personal leadership behavior and approach to the situation.

Case Scenario

Midwest College is a private, four-year, selective, liberal arts, residential institution in Ohio with an approximate undergraduate enrollment of 2,500 students as of fall 2020. The College offers undergraduate degree programs in a variety of majors in the liberal arts, sciences, and humanities. Midwest College's tuition and fees for the academic year 2020–21 is $30,000, and room and board are an additional $10,000 per year for a total of $40,000. The College has an $80 million endowment as well as a $50 million operating budget derived mostly from tuition, fees, and auxiliary revenue. With 85 percent of students residing on campus, Midwest College enjoys a vibrant student life with more than 120 student organizations. Students have many ways to engage inside and outside of the classroom. The College enjoys a 90 percent first- to second-year retention rate, and 70 percent four-year graduation rate. Midwest College is a predominantly White institution (PWI) with student demographic breakdown as follows: 90 percent White, and 10 percent students of color, which includes, Blacks, Hispanics, American Indians, Asians, and students of two or more races. Furthermore, gender breakdown is as follows: 60 percent female, 39 percent male, and 1 percent of students at Midwest identify as non-binary.

In academic years 2018–19 and 2019–20, Midwest College enrollment remained steady but flat at 2,500 students. However, because of Covid-19, there was a slight 1 percent enrollment decline in fall 2020, which accounted for an approximate loss of 25 enrolled students and approximately $1 million loss in tuition and fees revenue. For a small institution, this is a huge loss in revenue. Therefore, the college instituted a hiring freeze, furloughs, and a pause on annual staff raises and travel. Due to Covid-19 disruptions in spring 2020, such as the College's transition to virtual teaching, learning, and work environments, Midwest College projected the fall 2020 enrollment decrease. Covid-19 has caused significant public health, safety, and financial concerns for Midwest College. Any additional enrollment decreases will cause a crippling blow to the sustainability of the institution.

The College leaders have contemplated multiple perspectives and considerations for incorporating NALs in their educational community. They conducted initial exploratory and fact-finding research on how to expand their academic and student support services. This included work to understand how to develop pedagogical and andragogical models of teaching and learning with the goal to better prepare for NALs. The senior leadership team is aware that the programs and curriculum they currently utilize for traditional-aged college students will need to gear toward the specific needs of NALs based on their workplace and personal

58   *Higher Education Leadership*

life demands. Furthermore, with anticipated institutional changes (cultural, fiscal, personnel, services, and programmatic), the College must develop a recruitment strategy that includes preparation for NALs in the same classroom and online environments as traditional-aged college students. Several stakeholders will be involved in the strategic leading and guiding of Midwest College through this challenging time. Given this scenario, the case will feature multiple actors such as Midwest College President, Cabinet, and other college leaders, including a select group of academic Deans, faculty members, public health officials, and student leaders to demonstrate the importance of institutional collaboration among different stakeholders.

The Dilemma

How can Midwest College scale up and strategically plan to focus on efficiently and effectively utilizing their human, capital, technological, physical, and intellectual resources during and post-Covid-19? How does Midwest College pivot to include NALs in their educational community? Is it an effective strategy?

Learning Activities/Discussion Questions

An instructor can initiate small group discussions framed within the approach to situational leadership to address the following specific questions:

1. What should Midwest College do to prepare for the pending demographic shift and Covid-related challenges? How important is leadership during an institutional transition or change?
2. How should Midwest College leverage its strengths and opportunities, address weaknesses, and mitigate threats in such an unprecedented and challenging external environment?
3. How might the pending demographic shift, institutional changes, and transitions as a result of Covid-19 change the College's mission, vision, and priorities? What might an envisioned future look like?
4. What leadership behaviors and styles most align with these institutional changes as Midwest College implements new strategies that change the direction of the College?
5. How do Midwest College leaders keep faculty, staff, and the College community motivated and engaged throughout these challenging institutional changes?

Midwest College's President also has important questions and considerations for the Cabinet and the taskforce assigned to assist with planning for the pending demographic shift and institutional changes because of Covid-19. The instructor will assign a student to act as the College President. The actor portraying the College President will then select classmates as Cabinet members, and academic leaders on their taskforce. The instructor will also organize a mock town hall meeting and invite faculty and students to encourage stakeholder participation and provide feedback to the President and the taskforce. The town hall should be structured as an open forum discussion where attendees will ask questions of the academic leaders in attendance. The President will raise the following questions to these specific academic leaders relative to the pending demographic shift and Covid-19:

Questions for the Provost

1. How do we develop the right mix of undergraduate and graduate degree and certificate programs to meet NALs workforce needs and support student success during Covid-19 and beyond?
2. Are our faculty culturally, linguistically, and technically responsive to teach students of color and the NALs demographic online and in person? How will we know the answer to this question?

    a   What can we do to improve our readiness in these domains?
    b   What are the primary challenges to developing our ability to be culturally responsive?

3. Is the College well situated to offer distance education degree programs?

Questions for the Vice President for Student Affairs

1. How will we support this new student demographic?

    a   What are the resource implications?

2. Does staff have the appropriate competency level to support this new population?
3. How will the out-of-classroom experience need to change?
4. How will we ensure the health and safety of all students?

Questions for the Chief Financial Officer

1. What are the financial implications for such an institutional change during Covid-19 and beyond?

    a   Can Midwest College afford this change?
    b   What is the strategy for meeting this need?

2. Do we have the right financial aid model? Is it appropriate?
3. Should we be increasing or freezing tuition?
4. What are some opportunities for cost savings and greater efficiencies?

60　*Higher Education Leadership*

Questions for the Vice President for Enrollment Management

1. What specific enrollment management strategies are best utilized for attracting and recruiting students of color and NALs during and post-Covid-19?
2. Which degree and certificate programs present the best growth opportunities?

Supporting Literature

This case presents three relevant theoretical frames: situational leadership, Schlossberg's transition theory, and adult learning theory in order to explore the challenges of a private college facing an unprecedented event and transition that threatens its sustainability.

Situational Leadership

Leadership is most effective and successful when the appropriate behavioral style is used based on the situation in the environment (Hersey et al., 2001). This case demonstrates the importance of diagnosing the environment, adapting behaviors based on the situation, and effective and efficient communication—all critical leadership competencies. Although there are several situational approaches to leadership, to assist with analyzing this case, we will utilize the Vroom-Yetton Contingency Model, a situational model that suggests that leadership is contingent or depends on the current situation. In addition, the Hersey-Blanchard Tridimensional Leader Effectiveness Model, a leadership model which focuses on task behavior and relationship behavior (Hersey et al., 2001), will be applied. The learning activities outlined for readers in this case have Midwest College leaders utilize a consultative, collaborative, or democratic leadership style in situations where other colleagues' feedback and considerations are included in decision-making. This leadership style also aligns with Hersey-Blanchard relationship behavior where decisions are made by a group. Note that there are situations where the College President provided a directive and was autocratic in style, which is indicative of task behavior.

As Midwest College reimagines their future demographic profile and the long-term impact of Covid-19 on their operations, they also must contend with a worsening economy and its impact on college affordability for students and their families. As a result of rapid changes in the internal and external environment, it will be important for College leaders to diagnose the environment, analyze and conduct environmental scanning and awareness, and be adaptable in their leadership style to fit situational changes (Hersey et al., 2001).

Planning for a demographic shift of this magnitude in a current and post-Covid-19 environment requires innovation, and "thinking outside the box" is likely critical for sustainability. Midwest Colleges' leaders may envision changes in their academic programs and student services, faculty modes and methods of instruction, pedagogical to more andragogical teaching and learning or an integration of both, personnel job functions, and visibility of the College to external constituents. Each of these necessary shifts may require different decision styles based on the situation.

Schlossberg's Transition Theory

Goodman et al. (2012) identify three types of transitions: anticipated or predictable, unanticipated or nonscheduled, and nonevent. There may be some overlap with individual experiences, as NALs may be in the midst of one transition and concurrently have other transition experiences. For example, starting in spring 2020, Covid-19 became an unanticipated global event or transition that impacted not only higher education but also the workforce/job sector(s). As a result of this event, NALs are forced to manage and cope with many unanticipated, unique, professional, and personal transition challenges and adjustments concurrently.

Additionally, Goodman et al. (2012) further specify the 4S model: four factors that influence coping mechanisms during transitions: (a) situation, (b) self, (c) support, and (d) strategies. The 4S model describes "the factors that make a difference in how one copes with change" (p. 61). These factors are important especially in an unprecedented, unanticipated transition such as Covid-19, as well as the downstream implications (e.g., lack of childcare, schools closing/moving to fully online, loss of nonessential employment options). *Situation* describes what is happening; in this case scenario, Covid-19 is the unanticipated event; *self* describes whom the transition is happening to, that is, NALs; *support* describes available assistance, which are academic and student support services; and *strategies* describes strategies utilized to navigate the transition.

There have been many unfortunate transitions since Covid-19 began in the United States. The percentage of minorities experiencing joblessness and furloughs. Employee lay-offs have been higher for minorities than for their White counterparts (Harper, 2020; Jan & Clement, 2020). Research shows that Covid-19 is negatively impacting students and families of color disproportionately based on historical and systemic health, social, and educational disparities. It has brought to the forefront long-standing structural and societal inequities that have impacted racial and ethnic minorities (CDC, n.d.; Harper, 2020; Jan & Clement, 2020; Tai et al., 2020). In 2020, many Midwest College students and families lost their jobs because of economic and financial strains, which reduced both new and returning student enrollment due to student and families' financial hardships. Research shows that lost income from financial aid and student employment may impact students' decisions about returning to college even flexible instructional options (e.g., virtual) are offered. These factors, along with declining state budgets, and institutional enrollment, may result in accelerated financial instability as a

62   *Higher Education Leadership*

result of Covid-19 (Brown, 2020; Center on Budget and Policy Priorities, 2020; Polikoff et al., 2020). It can be argued that the leadership demands of Covid-19 are extreme and not predictable.

Adult Learning Theory

Knowles et al. (2015) describe adult learning theory as a combination of andragogy, which is "an intentional and professionally guided activity that aims at the change in adult persons," and andragogics, or the "methodological and ideological systems that govern andragogy" (p. 39–40). Andragogy is based on six principles that are critical to NALs: (a) their need to know, (b) self-concept, (c) prior experiences, (d) readiness to learn, (e) orientation to learning, and (f) motivation to learn (Knowles et al., 2015; Merriam, 2004). Additionally, Frey and Alman (2003) posit that, "adult learning theory helps faculty to understand their students and to design more meaningful learning experiences for them. There is not one adult learning theory that successfully applies to all adult learning environments" (p. 8). It is important for Midwest College to understand the different perspectives of NALs and make the necessary considerations for NALs to be successful; adult learning theory can help meet this need.

NALs have busy lives; these students are more likely juggling work, family, and other responsibilities. Online programs may provide their only chance for continuing education. However, quality online programming has its own challenges. Cercone (2008) stated that "adults have many challenges today, such as multiple careers, fewer stable social structures to rely on, living longer, and dealing with aging parents" (p. 139). It is important for colleges and universities to prepare for learners who have such complex lives combined with a zeal to learn. Chao et al. (2007) stated that, "online education has shown significant growth, particularly with NALs, and appears to have great potential for helping more institutions serve NALs more effectively" (p. 12). Midwest College leadership have discussed the prospects of having an online instruction option for NALs.

Implication of Theories for Midwest College

NALs are a unique population of students, and integrating the necessary pedagogical and andragogical learning models to support NALs may be challenging for Midwest College. One important consideration that situational leadership helps us focus on is the fact that leaders' approach and behaviors are contingent on the situation at hand, as well as the leader's assessment of the situation. It is important to note that when facing a volatile and fluid external environment, higher education must increase its adaptive capacity to better handle the transitions internal stakeholders experience as a result of Covid-19. While implementing transformational organization changes, it is critical for Midwest College to consider the six principles of andragogy that might facilitate a successful transition for NALs.

Suggestions for Further Reading

In preparation for discussions on the case, an instructor can ask students to read the following article to better understand the pending demographic shifts: WICHE's 10th edition of *Knocking at the college door: Projections of high school graduates.* The instructor can also ask students to read *Strategic diversity leadership* (Williams, 2013) to understand the type of leadership it takes to successfully lead transformational institutional change with a diversity mindset. Additionally, the instructor may find value in utilizing the following sources on leadership, organizational change, demographic shifts, and NALs in higher education:

- Adult development, and the adult learner and online education: Knowles et al. (2015) and Cercone (2008).
- Organizational change, strategic, operational, and tactical level planning in higher education: Burke (2018), Fullan (2011), Rost (1991), Hinton (2012).
- Enrollment management: The Conference for Adult Learner Enrollment Management (CALEM), Strategic Enrollment Management Quarterly (2018), American Association of Collegiate Registrars and Admissions Officers (AACRAO.org).
- Leadership styles and behavior: Hersey et al. (2001).

References

Bransberger, P., Falkenstern, C., & Lane, P. (2020). *Knocking at the college door: Projections of high school graduates* (10th ed., pp. 1–71). Western Interstate Commission for Higher Education.

Bransberger, P., & Michelau, D. K. (2016). *Knocking at the college door: Projections of high school graduates* (9th ed., pp. 1–160). Western Interstate Commission for Higher Education.

Brown, S. (2020). When covid-19 closed colleges, many students lost jobs they needed. Now campuses scramble to support them. *The Chronicle of Higher Education.*

Buller, J. (2015). *Change leadership in higher education: A practical guide to academic transformation.* Jossey-Bass.

Burke, W. W. (2018). *Organization change: Theory and practice* (5th ed.). Sage Publications.

Center on Budget and Policy Priorities. (2020). States grappling with hit to tax collections. https://www.cbpp.org/

Centers for Disease Control and Prevention. (n.d.). Coronavirus (COVID-19). https://www.cdc.gov/coronavirus/

Cercone, K. (2008). Characteristics of NALs with implications for online learning design. *Association for the Advancement of Computing in Education Journal, 16*(2), 137–159.

Chao, E. L., DeRocco, E. S., & Flynn, M. K. (2007). NALs in higher education: Barriers to success and strategies to improve learners. Employment and Training Administration Occasional Paper2007–03, 1–61.

Chen, J. C. (2017). Nontraditional NALs: The neglected diversity in postsecondary education. *Sage Open Journal, 7*(1), 1–12.

Fernandez, A. A., & Shaw, G. P. (2020). Academic leadership in a time of crisis: The coronavirus and COVID-19.. *Journal of Leadership Studies, 14*(1), 39–45.

64 *Higher Education Leadership*

Frey, B. A., & Alman, S. W. (2003). Applying adult learning theory to the online classroom. *New Horizons in Adult Education*, 17(1), 4–12.

Goodman, J., Schlossberg, N. K., & Anderson, M. L. (2006). *Counseling adults in transition: Linking practice with theory* (3rd ed.). Springer.

Grawe, N. D. (2018). *Demographics and the demand for higher education.* John Hopkins University Press.

Harper, S. (2020). COVID-19 and the racial equity implications of reopening college and university campuses. *American Journal of Education*, 127(1), 153–162.

Hersey, P., Blanchard, K. H., & Johnson, D.E. (2001). *Management of organizational behavior: Leading human resources.* Prentice-Hall.

Jan, T., & Clement, S. (2020). Hispanics are almost twice as likely as whites to have lost their jobs amid pandemic. https://www.washingtonpost.com/

Knowles, M. S., Holton, E. F., & Swanson, R. A. (2015). *The adult learner: The definitive classic in adult education and human resource development* (8th ed.). Routledge.

McGregor, L., Miller, H. R., Mayleben, M. A., Buzzanga, V. L., Davis, S. F., & Becker, A. H. (1991). Similarities and differences between "traditional" and "non-traditional" college students in selected personality characteristics. *Bulletin of the Psychonomic Society*, 29, 128–130.

Merriam, S. (2004). *The changing landscape of adult learning theory.* In J. Comings, B. Garner, & C. Smith (Eds.), *Review of adult leaning and literacy. Connecting research, policy, and practice: A project of the national center for the study of adult learning and literacy* (pp. 199–220). Routledge.

National Center for Education Statistics. (2017). *Projections of educational statistics to 2025.* https://nces.ed.gov/pubs2017/2017019.pdf

Pelletier, S. G. (2010). Success for adult students. *Public purpose*, 2–6.

Polikoff, M., Silver, D., & Korn, S. (2020). What's the likely impact of COVID-19 on higher education? https://www.insidehighered.com/

Schlossberg, N. K., Waters, E. B., & Goodman, J. (1995). *Counseling adults in transition: Linking practice with theory* (2nd ed.). Springer.

Tai, D., Shah, A., Doubeni, C. A., Sia, I.G., & Wieland, M. L. (2020). The disproportionate impact of COVID-19 on racial and ethnic minorities in the United States. *Clinical Infectious Diseases*, 1–4.

Tesar, M. (2020). Towards a post-covid-19 'new normality?': Physical and social distancing, the move to online and higher education. *Sage Journals*, 18(5), 556–559. https://doi-org.ezproxy.bgsu.edu/10.1177/1478210320935671

Voorhees, R. A., & Lingenfelter, P. E. (2003). NALs and state policy. http://www.sheeo.org

Williams, D. A. (2013). *Strategic diversity leadership: Activating change and transformation in higher education.* Stylus Publishing, LLC.

7 Dr. Remote Instruction

Time Constraints and Critical Consciousness in Crisis Leadership

Guy L. Parmigian

Dr. Remote Instruction: Time Constraints and Critical Consciousness in Crisis Leadership

Dr. Eloise Scricca, age 51, was in her second year as superintendent at River Run Public School District. An exurban school district in the Midwestern United States comprises 1,800 students and about 250 staff members housed in four elementary schools, one middle school, and one high school. An "exurb" is much like a suburb but is considered more rural. While just 40 minutes away from the nearest city, River Run, like most districts, carried its own cultural footprint. In terms of electoral politics, the community had traditionally been a majority of reliably Democratic voters from pro-union households. Over the last 20 years, however, the school district and Ottabula County have trended Republican mainly based on socio-cultural considerations. Feeling uneasy with reports of the nation's coloring and perceptions of losing financial standing and power, the community voted overwhelmingly Republican in recent state and national elections.

A Weekend Getaway from River Run....or Not?

Thursday, March 12, 2020, the day that began the coronavirus crisis for Dr. Scricca, had a familiar start with a 7:00 AM meeting of her administrative cabinet, including six building principals, assistant superintendent, and the director of curriculum. Her primary agenda item was to direct subordinates to prepare their schools and departments for the possibility that the county health department would close schools due to the coronavirus in a few weeks. Based on her reading of facial expressions and overheard whispering during the meeting, some of her administrators seemed to pooh-pooh her directive as overly alarming. Dr. Scricca ignored high school principal Jim Scranton when he mocked at the end of the meeting that "We will just get lots of hand sanitizer and show these kids what it means to persevere and have grit in a crisis!"

With the administrative cabinet meeting over, Dr. Scricca began to mentally count down the workday hours. She planned to play hooky and get a jump start on a short, impromptu vacation with her spouse, Dale. She

DOI: 10.4324/9780429331503-9

66 Dr. Remote Instruction

completed some small tasks in her office, straightened up her desk, and excitedly slipped out of the building. An hour into the trip, she and Dale listened in stunned silence in the car as the local NPR station flashed news of the State Health Commissioner's order. The Commissioner ordered all K–12 school buildings in the state would be closed to students effective Monday, March 16, due to what was now being called a pandemic. The order declared that education would continue remotely at the sole discretion of each local school district. Within moments Dr. Scricca's cell phone exploded with text messages and phone calls.

Dale recognizing the look of panic on his wife's face and broke the silence with a whisper saying, "They can handle it. You have a great team in place, baby. Let's just keep going." With a tone back to normal, he said, "You need this little break! We will be back soon enough." After a short chat, Dr. Scricca said emphatically, "I can't, I can't, I just can't; I'm sorry, I've got to go back!" Dale turned the car around without another word and sped back toward River Run. Dr. Scricca's first call from the car was to her assistant, where she called for a 5:30 PM "crisis planning meeting" with the administrative cabinet. "Order some pizza, too," she told him. They arrived at home. Dale got out, and Dr. Scricca jumped in the driver's seat, waved goodbye, and hit the gas.

Her mind was swimming with the details of the meeting: Who should be there? How should it be organized? How much time do I have? What decisions need to be made? Dr. Scricca ran a red light and came within inches of smashing into a large truck. She could feel the anxiety building and took a deep breath to calm herself. As she pulled into the district headquarters parking lot, she thought that she better invite the Board, too, and proceeded to text them. Dr. Scricca again became anxious thinking about having her boss (the five members of the Board of Education) and her subordinates, the administrative cabinet, in the same room sitting in judgment of her crisis leadership skills. Envisioning the personalities in the room, Dr. Scricca thought deeply about what each would expect of her leadership and felt a twinge of paranoia and self-doubt. "But now is not the time for that," Dr. Scricca reasoned out loud and continued to conceptualize the crisis planning meeting. Nearly every detail of every department, every employee and student expectation, and almost every norm of operation of her school district was to be adapted to the remote instruction order.

Walking into HQ, Dr. Scricca surveyed the stunned and anxious employees' faces, which ironically brought her a sense of calm. Dr. Scricca saw the district's savvy and well-respected teacher union president Cindy Baxter talking with the assistant treasurer and proceeded to invite her to the crisis planning meeting.

Preparing for the meeting, Dr. Scricca feared the questions that needed to be answered about re-tooling and adapting the school district to move to remote instruction. She knew the questions would not lend themselves to easy answers because they are related to values and beliefs. For example, what student assignment deadlines in the plan for remote instruction would be relaxed due to the chaos, economic uncertainty, and mass layoffs in the wake of coronavirus uncertainty?

Dr. Scricca was surprised and comforted that her thoughts suddenly wandered back to her graduate school coursework and Ronald Heifetz's theory of adaptive leadership. For Heifetz, adaptive leadership means engaging with "adaptive challenges," or value-laden questions that do not lend themselves to easy answers. She was amazed to recall some keys to adaptive leadership challenges. Leaders do not fulfill the expectation for ready solutions; instead, leaders facilitate the questions that lead people to feel the impending threat to stimulate adaptation.

Momentarily, Dr. Scricca's thoughts wandered back to when she had implemented adaptive leadership quite successfully over the years. She recalled last year when she successfully navigated the long-festering issue of the student dress code. The dress code was not a technical matter that lent itself to a clear solution but rather an adaptive challenge that involved gender, race, class, and especially values. She navigated the dress code issue with a series of parent and student meetings over several weeks, which involved asking probing questions about the dress code's purpose until consensus began to emerge.

Leading adaptive challenges fit with Dr. Scricca's personality as facilitator and collaborator who sought consensus. Reality set in, and she again thought aloud, "I just don't have time to embrace that process." In this crisis, she had roughly three hours to figure out what value and judgment questions would be raised. She anticipated questions like who would be allowed to work from home, who would be required to report to buildings, and the expectations of student learning during remote instruction. Dr. Scricca felt the greatest pressure from the time constraints. It *had* to be her values and expertise that would drive decisions, and this felt uncomfortable to her. How would she navigate moving from Dr. Scricca to Dr. Remote Instruction....Extraordinaire?

Dr. Remote Instruction

As she sat in her office, Dr. Scricca's mind was racing, thinking about how to move effectively through this crisis. Certainly, it could not last for too long. She decided that she would need to use a balance of charisma, decisiveness, and whatever else she could muster to become Dr. Remote Instruction: The one with all the answers. From past experiences, Dr. Scricca knew that her followers would not be looking for a consensus builder at this time but would want guidance and reassurance to feel as stable as possible.

As her new role of *Dr. Remote Instruction*, Dr. Scricca had approximately an hour before the crisis planning meeting to collect her thoughts. She first established the meeting's end goal, which was to provide the remote instruction plan for River Run School District. This would hopefully provide everyone at the meeting the ever-important initial perception that she and the district were prepared for success. She walked slowly to her office window and peered outside. She wondered how everything had changed in such a short time. With an eye toward this end goal, Dr. Scricca decided that she would meet with the Board and administrators, and then provide a press release to

68   *Dr. Remote Instruction*

the rest of the community by 9:00 PM that night. Dr. Scricca shut her door (a rare occurrence), searched for a yellow legal pad, sat down behind her desk, and began to scribble down all of the questions that she felt would need to be addressed.

The Meeting

Dr. Scricca began the crisis planning meeting with 18 members: six building principals, the assistant superintendent, four directors and one manager (curriculum, special education, HR, operations, and food service), the treasurer, the school board, and the union president, Cindy Baxter. Everyone gathered tightly in the conference room, seated around a rectangular table that had to be extended with a card table. Her tactic for the meeting was to methodically read each question that she had contemplated, provide her solution to each question, ask for input, and record the information on chart paper for all to read. She would also work to terminate any extensive and repetitive conversation on any one topic. She was somewhat heartened that the 18 attendees offered largely supportive input on her initial recommendations. The final action plans were recorded on chart paper and stuck to the walls around the room.

Plan of action decisions came relatively swiftly, one after another, on critical value-laden issues, even though she knew there was plenty of room for error and ego in this administration. Recalling some of the seemingly endless discussions about the most trivial topics in administrative cabinet meetings over the last two years—discussions that were important despite the tedium. During the previous sessions of seemingly endless minutia, Dr. Scricca had surprised herself with her calm decisiveness, where she easily "handled" the few instances of dissent to her decisions. Somewhat intoxicated by the aura of the crisis, Dr. Scricca was suddenly conscious of how proud she felt of her history dealing with such calamities. The March 12 crisis planning meeting concluded with a clear remote instruction plan communicated to the news media at 9:10 PM. Exhaustion met and got the better of an inflated ego, and Dr. Scricca drove home.

The Aftermath: Embers, Smoke, and Flame

On the drive home, she replayed the meeting in her head and reflected on the pockets of impending discord that she knew would move from embers to flame. And history taught her that the show of harmony last night had a very brief shelf life. For example, she and union president, Cindy Baxter, joined forces on handling student grading. Both of them had insisted on a high degree of flexibility on student grades during the period of remote instruction. With little commentary from the group, Dr. Scricca directed that teachers would be highly accommodating with students during the fourth quarter of this school year to allow flexibility. She added that the teachers needed to consider the uneven resources students have available to complete work at home. While no one commented to the group, Dr. Scricca noticed an immediate sidebar conversation between Herman Smalls and River Run High School principal Jim Scranton. This worried her due to the biographies of the two men.

Board of education member Herman Smalls had once been a mathematics teacher at River Run High School. Following a "grade-fixing" scandal in which he accused the principal, the principal was fired, and Mr. Smalls assumed the role. A few years later, Herman was forced to resign because of his own grade-fixing scandal involving a football player's academic eligibility. Despite this, Herman remained a respected figure in the community. Herman had always been active in Ottabula County politics, having served as the county Republican Party Chairman for 17 years. At the age of 79 and still grieving the loss of this wife after 56 years of marriage, Herman was elected to the River Run Board of Education several years ago.

As Principal of River Run High School for the last decade, Jim Scranton was a strong ally of Herman Smalls. It was rumored that Jim, who married Herman's second cousin, was the one who recruited him to run for an open seat on the school board. By all accounts, Jim Scranton was a traditional high school principal who had good relations with most veteran high school staff and "ran a tight ship."

The Case

Three weeks following the crisis planning meeting, Dr. Scricca had a tense meeting with Jim Scranton in her office to discuss final exams, graduation, and other issues. Dr. Scricca and Jim's relationship had been strained from the start, and she always detected that he had trouble taking orders from a woman. She began by sharing her thoughts for high school graduation, which she felt should be held in the parking lot while students and families remained in their cars. Then she moved to engaging Jim on upcoming high school final exams. Dr. Scricca told Jim that she felt that they should be eliminated considering the pandemic and the uncertainty of delivering consistent or effective instructional delivery.

Jim did not respond and fumbled through his papers. Perturbed, Dr. Scricca moved to her "teacher tone" to ask Jim what he had done to ensure teachers would demonstrate grading flexibility. During the meeting, she said that each principal would need to provide the professional development required to implement her expectations to engage flexible grading.

Jim looked at her blankly, and Dr. Scricca added, "It is essential that teachers acknowledge and understand the importance of flexibility with grading in this crisis context. And it sounds like some just aren't getting it."

Clearly angry, Jim broke his silence and roared back, "So, I guess student accountability and grading is out the window; I guess that's how we roll from now on?"

There was a pause, and Dr. Scricca was surprised at Jim's insubordinate tone. Her face growing redder by the second, she shot back, "No, Jim! We

70   *Dr. Remote Instruction*

need student accountability, but we have to be rational. There has to be a balance that considers our student households' context where anxiety about how mom is going to buy next week's groceries is more important than education. You have seen our poverty numbers skyrocketing over the last decade—right? I mean, we have students living in dysfunctional homes too. Do you think that just stops all of a sudden, and those adults forget their lives and become tutors only focusing on education? How many of our parents have three or four kids at home and are just overwhelmed? Come on, Jim, don't you get it?"

Jim's blank stare continued, but his tightening facial expression suggested he was working up to something. "Can I be honest?" Jim stated in more of a statement than a question. He stood up, folded his papers, and stuck them half-way into his pants like a football coach on a sideline. He stared out the window for a few seconds.

Dr. Scricca waited and then impatiently said, "What?"

Jim lowered his voice and said, "Are you trying to lead a revolution here with this pandemic being your opportunity? You seem to take joy in blowing up the norms of our graduation traditions of being on the football field for some white trash drive-through graduation in the name of safe social distancing."

Dr. Scricca tried to interrupt: "Now, Jim, you know as well as—"

But Jim cut her off and continued ranting. "On top of that, you are blowing up the norms of grading and accountability in the name of some poverty baloney. Grading is a natural fact of life, and everyone gets it, even our kids, except you! Ya' know those 'poverty people' you wanna coddle always find the money for their cigarettes, cell phones, and beer. Now you want to make everyone just like them by saying no exams? You seem to want to use this crisis to turn things upside down."

"So, this is how you talk about our kids? Really?" Dr. Scricca shouted.

Jim walked out of her office and passed the outer desk, and Dr. Scricca followed. Jim turned to her and said, "I just know our kids need consistency and structure now more than ever. Grades are part of that. You are not gonna use this pandemic as your opportunity to shove this agenda of coddling all and overturning tradition down our throats." Jim walked out to the hallway, and Dr. Scricca was furious.

The following day, Dr. Scricca received an email from school board member Herman Smalls demanding that she set up a special school board meeting. The purpose of the meeting was to discuss several concerns he and other board members had, including "Watered-down student expectations and grading" and "failure to uphold River Run High School traditions." Dr. Scricca's heartbeat accelerated as she felt very isolated.

Discussion

The crisis at River Run offers a myriad of views for analysis including, but not limited to adult development, leadership, followership, societal and cultural norms, and the ethics of education. Theoretical perspectives that will be examined in this discussion include critical theory of adult learning, adaptive and technical modes of crisis leadership, and leadership ethics.

Critical Theory of Adult Learning

Education is a political enterprise reflecting the tenants of a bureaucratic system, and school leaders must be willing to critique the system. Critical theory "questions the framework of the way we organize our lives or the way our lives are organized for us" (Foster, 1986, p. 72). Critical pedagogy addresses challenges of power, oppression, conflict, and control (Merriam & Cafferella, 1999). Critical theory of adult learning focuses on how adults learn to recognize and challenge ideological domination and manipulation. Brookfield asserts that a critical theory of adult development and learning is a theory of "social and political learning" and should illuminate "how adults learn to challenge the ideology that serves the interests of the few against the well-being of the many" (p. 20–21). The case story illustrates attempts to advocate for practices from the stance of a positional leader and draws attention to the significance of other bases of power (French & Raven, 1959) and ethical student considerations.

As a result of the pandemic, deeply rooted cultural issues bubbled to the surface, unmasking the discrepancy between what is ethically ideal and what realistically exists. In critical consciousness, Dr. Scricca faced "the discrepancy between the real and the possible, between the apparent and the authentic truth" (Marcuse, 1964, p. 229). In this case, the orthodox, yet arbitrary, system of grading in the traditional American high school has the appearance of being "natural" thanks to what Marcuse (1964) calls a "preconditioning which shapes the instinctual drives and aspirations of the individuals and obscures the difference between false and true consciousness" (p. 32). For Jim Scranton's preconditioned false consciousness, an effort to overthrow the "natural fact of life" of their high school grading during a global pandemic is a threat that angers him. Bourdieu (1998) explains that the "mildest attempt" to modify school programs encounters great resistance due to teacher interests tied to the established academic order.

> Matters of culture, and in particular social divisions and hierarchies associated with them, are established as such by the actions of the state which, by instituting them both in things and in minds, confers upon the cultural arbitrary all the appearances of the natural.
>
> (p. 38)

Jim Scranton's resistance to Dr. Scricca is a defense of an established order whose novel feature is "the overwhelming rationality in this irrational enterprise" (Marcuse, 1964, p. 32). Thus, traditional grading systems and the social reproduction they help to perpetuate are falsely seen as natural. One of the psychically jarring results of a crisis like the coronavirus pandemic is a new and/or heightened consciousness of what was previously taken as a natural order.

72   *Dr. Remote Instruction*

Adaptive vs. Technical Modes of Leadership in a Crisis

This case study engages Heifetz's theory of adaptive leadership challenges, or "systemic problems with no ready answers" (Heifetz & Laurie, 1997, p. 124), toward understanding Dr. Scricca's strategy and goals during the crisis planning meeting. Heifetz (1994) explains that adaptive leadership challenges involve diagnosing the situation in light of the values at stake and then unbundling the issues that come with them. As such, the leader poses questions about the definition of the problem solutions (p. 127). Adaptive leadership challenges require sustained learning about both the problem and the solution (p. 76). In adaptive situations, the leader disorients current roles, gives work to all the organization's stakeholders, and encourages all to raise hard questions and generate distress around defining the problem and determining the solution (p. 127–128).

In contrast with adaptive leadership situations, Heifetz's theory explains "technical situations" where leaders define both the problem and the solution with clear authority lines in a chain of command. Technical situations may also be very complex and critically important. Still, they have known solutions that "can be resolved through the application of authoritative expertise and through the organization's current values and ways of doing things" (Linsky & Lawrence, 2011, p. 7). An example of a technical situation is the decision to close school due to poor weather conditions. Information is gathered from subordinates, and a decision is made by the leader.

Given the distinction between adaptive and technical situations, Heifetz's theory acknowledges that problems do not come neatly packaged as adaptive or technical (Linsky & Lawrence, 2011, p. 7). Heifetz (1994) acknowledges that "life is fluid" and that even in adaptive situations, the authority figure will have to make "tactical decisions to move between technical and adaptive modes" depending on factors including the severity of the problem and time (p. 126). This suggests a balance between the two modes of leadership that Dr. Scricca may have worked, a balance Heifetz refers to as "walking a razor's edge" (1994, p. 126–127). The coronavirus presented both technical and adaptive situations, both requiring strong leadership. In the end, Dr. Scricca's approach to crisis planning provided much-needed "direction and security" to many district followers. But the emergence of deep-seated issues relative to culture, values, and biases exacerbated existing conflicts and highlighted new challenges. These challenges will require effective leadership to meet both short- and long-term district transformation.

Questions for Discussion

1. Lynn Wooten (2005, 2015), a crisis leadership scholar and President of Simmons University, has articulated that leaders looking at a crisis through a political framework must know their organization's political terrain well, and further understand key power brokers and networks of

relationships. What networks of relationships and power brokers seem critical to this case? What other networks of relationships or power brokers would you want to learn more about if you were advising Dr. Scricca?

2. What other stakeholders might have been missing from the crisis planning meeting?

3. Dr. Scricca felt isolated when she received the email from Herman Smalls requesting a special board meeting. Could this feeling of isolation be prevented? How should Dr. Scricca prepare for the special meeting?

4. Did Dr. Scricca go too far with her advocacy approach to grading during the global pandemic? Should she modify her position to align with Jim Scranton?

5. Did Dr. Scricca find the right balance between technical and adaptive leadership modes during the crisis planning meeting? Could there have been more of a balance "on the razor's edge?" Is there a different strategy or tactic you would have taken at the crisis planning meeting?

6. Dr. Scricca's shortened timeline for scheduling the crisis planning meeting was driven by her desire to establish a positive first perception of her remote instruction plan to prove district preparedness. Were the time constraints in the best interest of the district? Were the self-imposed timelines warranted?

References

Brookfield, S. (2001). Repositioning ideology critique in a critical theory of adult learning. *Adult Education Quarterly*, 52(1), 7–22.

Bourdieu, P. (1998). *Practical reason*. Stanford University Press.

Burns, J. M. (2006). *Roosevelt: The soldier of freedom*. History Book Club.

Caro, R. A. (2012). *The years of Lyndon Johnson: The passage of power*. Alfred A. Knopf.

Foster, W. (1986). *Paradigms and promises: New approaches to educational administration*. Prometheus Books.

French, J. R. P., & Raven, B. (1959). The bases of social power. In D. Cartwright & A. Zander. *Group dynamics*. Harper & Row.

Gilligan, C. (1982). *In a different voice*. Harvard University Press.

Halverson, S. K. et al. (2004). Charismatic leadership in crisis situations. *Small-Group Research*, 35(5), 495–514.

Heifetz, R. A. (1994). *Leadership without easy answers*. The Belknap Press of Harvard University Press.

Heifetz, R. A., & Laurie, D. L. (1997). The work of leadership. *Harvard Business Review*, 124–134.

Linsky, M., & Lawrence, J. (2011). Adaptive challenges for school leaders. In H. O'Sullivan, & J. West-Burnham, (Eds.), *Leading and managing schools* (pp. 3–15). Sage.

Marcuse, H. (1964). *One-dimensional man*. Beacon Press.

Wooten, L. (2015, September 15). *How to lead in a crisis: Michigan Ross School of Business* [Video file]. https://www.bing.com/videos/search?q=lynn+wooten+leading+in+a+crisis+you+tube&docid=608036320832914631&mid=1CAFFDCAD5FC95268DF51CAFFDCAD5FC95268DF5&view=detail&FORM=VIRE

Wooten, L. P. (2007). Leadership in a crisis situation: An opportunity for framing to learn. *Human Factor*, (2)1, 76–80.

Part III

Introduction to Part III

Judy Jackson May and Kristina N. LaVenia

The educational system in America is experiencing unprecedented change. That said, leadership challenges in the 21st century are far too similar to those from the 20th century. Research continues to show that we have yet to adequately and equitably educate significant numbers of our school-aged population, primarily students of color and those living in poverty. The advent of the Covid-19 pandemic further exacerbates the significant issues facing public education. In a Harvard EdCast episode, Jill Anderson (2020) interviewed Dr. Jewell-Sherman, a former superintendent and Harvard Professor of Practice in Educational Leadership, who noted, "a crisis of this magnitude has been unimaginable." Laid bare through the pandemic are the persistent and historical social, racial, and economic inequities that have plagued our society and school systems for more than a century. The perseverance of such familiar issues illustrates that there has never been a more critical period to explore educational leadership's efficacy. Whether debating elementary, secondary, or post-secondary settings, current challenges illustrate the need to create avenues to ensure we are working today to develop adult leadership for tomorrow.

Historically, leaders in K–12 settings readily identified school challenges as distinctly urban, suburban, or rural. However, the 21st century's educational difficulties, more urgently the years leading up to and including the Covid-19 pandemic, serve to reduce these distinctions along the lines of urbanicity. The disparity in achievement based on race has long been a focal point of school failure in urban school centers. However, the widening gaps between poor and affluent students have now taken center stage (Reardon, 2011), given that rural students are 50 percent more likely to be poverty-stricken (WestEd, 2019). Long-term trends also show that students from high poverty environments score 26 points below their more affluent peers on standardized assessments (NCES, 2020). While poverty still disproportionately affects students of color, lower incomes brought on by the pandemic impact are pushing more families into poverty. The World Bank (2020) observes that the crisis is the most devastating trauma levied on public schools, and "the pandemic now threatens to make education outcomes even worse" (p. 1). More and more often, districts with student populations from 1,000 to 40,000 share similar concerns relative to student achievement.

DOI: 10.4324/9780429331503-10

76 Introduction to Part III

The shifting racial demographics in public schools further fuel existing concerns relative to school leadership. According to the NCES (2020), of the 50 million students in the nation's schools, more than 50 percent are students of color. These statistics, juxtaposed to reports noting that 78 percent of the nation's school leaders are White (National Teacher and Principal Survey, 2018) as are 83 percent of the nation's classroom teachers, remain troubling trends. The lack of educators of color has endured for decades. The social, cultural, behavioral, and academic dilemmas and conflicts occurring based on demographic incongruencies and cultural mismatches present significant leadership barriers that are important for student outcomes.

The 12 chapters in this part of the book discuss perspectives focusing on the persistent leadership challenges in educational settings. While uniquely different in scope, the cases each draw attention to the need to understand the interconnectedness of school leadership competencies. The case contributors discuss transformational leadership, professional development, social justice, the role of trust in collegiality, cultural mismatch, implicit bias, and building the mission and vision in school settings.

Developing a critical consciousness in addressing persistent and embedded social justice inequities undergird the chapters authored by Roegman and Collins, and Jennifer Martin. These two chapters invite readers to consider how stable versus flexible organizational structures offer unique challenges and opportunities for leaders' communication skills. Or how might unquestioned practices based on implicit biases impact the ability to recognize power structures that disproportionately disadvantage certain students? "Activating and Sustaining Motivation for Social Justice Leadership in Secondary Education" by Roegman and Collins offers an opportunity to consider how leadership challenges may vary based on whether the leader works within an organization that is designed more for stability (e.g., public schools) or an organization designed more for flexibility (e.g., for-profit or start-up).

The analysis of Martin's chapter, "The Sharpie Incident: Coloring in the Lines and School Policing of Black Hair," offers readers an opportunity to consider if public schools can promote social change. Or are public schools stuck in maintaining the status quo? Martin identifies belief systems that enable policies and practices that contribute to cultural mismatches and inequitable practices. This "ripped from the headlines" case challenges readers to think critically about the school leader's role in addressing inequities at the building level. Given that societal norms support the school practices perpetuating inequalities, the leader's moral compass and commitment to equality are exceedingly significant. Further, Roegman and Collins encourage readers to think carefully about what linking developmental readiness and social justice leadership might look like in practice. These theories – taken together – require thought about school success as a form of ecological and communal consciousness. The editors challenge our readers to consider: How can leaders develop a critical consciousness around each of Furman's dimensions that Roegman and Collins highlight?

Introduction to Part III   77

The cases presented by Jeremy Visone, Tyrone Bynoe, and Patricia Virella focus on implementing comprehensive transformational leadership strategies at the elementary and middle school levels. Two of the cases highlight how new building leaders approach sweeping change. In his case "We Can Do This! Transformational Leadership for School Improvement" Visone tackles the issue of underachieving students and educator apathy. This problematic dynamic is what many educators note as one of the most challenging issues facing the school learning environment. Visone's case study focuses on an economically depressed district bordering one that is considered affluent. This reading draws attention to student achievement disparities, insufficient financial and human resources, and the leadership challenge of overcoming deficit thinking among faculty. Additionally, Visone delves deeply into the issues of a newly named principal who takes over a building on the heels of a "respected and well-liked" leader. Given the school variables, the case asks readers to explore the strategies most likely to transform the culture through an adult learning and development framework lens.

The case "Visionary and Mission Minded School Leadership Grounded in Adult Learning Theory" asks readers to diagnose the pitfalls in a junior high school retreat geared toward refining the district's vision and mission statements. Bynoe identifies notable literature for review to understand the tools required for laying the foundation for adopting the core values of a vision. The case offers three areas of research to explore when developing a schoolwide plan. In addition to the literature on building a mission and vision, Bynoe's essential competencies include developmental models of supervision and key principles for transforming adult learning. In a junior high school setting, Bynoe asks the reader to identify appropriate strategies to foster teacher collegiality and co-authorship in vision development. The core of the case deals with promoting collaborative work with diverse personalities and perspectives while focusing on student achievement.

Using a large city charter school backdrop, Patricia Virella's chapter, "I Can't Hear You: Incorporating Developmentally Appropriate Feedback for Adults in Balkor Elementary Charter School," illustrates the strength of adult development research. The story describes a principal assuming leadership in a school that has, up until recently, enjoyed strong student enrollment and high achievement. Populated primarily with students of color, they have experienced high leadership turnover and declining student achievement over the last couple of years. In approaching schoolwide transformation, the new principal is focusing on building trust and developmentally appropriate feedback. Virella utilizes Drago-Severson and Blum-DeStefano's adult development theory to inform her plan of action. This case strategically engages the reader in understanding how leaders provide supportive frameworks to promote effective feedback for instructional growth.

Engaging a variety of theoretical perspectives on transforming educator practices, three cases include compelling views on the critical role of the "through-line" for high yield instructional practices. The through-line refers to

78 *Introduction to Part III*

understanding the relationship between district and practices, and measurable student improvement. In the chapter "Leading for Transformation? Decisions of New Coaches Matter," the authors Ortmann, Brodeur, and Massey highlight the importance of collegial relationships between leaders and followers. In particular, supporting the learner's ability to engage in premise reflection, and interrogating the assumptions one is making about a particular problem or challenge. This process calls for a focus on the importance of trust in collegial relationships. We invite readers to consider research on collegial trust with a particular eye toward reflecting on our attitudes, beliefs, and behaviors in the workplace and how they may support or undermine our ability to extend and receive collegial trust. Further, we ask readers who are higher in the organizational flowcharts to ask themselves how they might support trust-building with their personnel. Which policies, for example, might hinder the opportunity for trust-building? Knowing that instructional coaching requires repeated interactions to build the strength of the communications and relationships between coach and teacher, how might an administrator work to facilitate ongoing coaching opportunities? Are there building or district level policies for how coaches are utilized that work against shoring up necessary relational components to achieve strong communication and trust?

Corinne Brion's chapter on "Learning Transfer: The Missing Link to Leading the Successful Implementation of Professional Development in Schools" critically examines the pervasive failure of schools to ensure professional development is anchored in the school culture for measurable instructional improvement. The setting of the case is a middle school where teachers actively question why they are not included as active decision-makers in creating professional development opportunities. One of the many noteworthy points of the chapter is that transferring new knowledge to measurable classroom practices requires collaborative adult development and efficacious leadership. While some educators seek to transform classroom practice willingly, others may seek a less rigorous path resistant to change. Brion's Multi-dimensional Model of Learning Transfer (MMLT) supposes that "Culture" impacts all aspects of the learning transfer cycle. The MMLT combined with John Kotter's Eight Steps to Transformation provides a clear and descriptive path to building a learning transfer culture. This chapter leads the reader to critically analyze why teachers are not encouraged to take more ownership in professional growth opportunities.

Dustin Miller and Anika Ball Anthony's chapter also speaks to teachers' need to assume ownership of their professional development. "Preparing Educators to Lead Professional Learning in P–12 Schools: Applying Research on Leadership Development and Adult Learning" advocates professional learning plans to promote growth in educator thinking. While this chapter setting is a large high school in the Midwest, the professional learning plan elements, including problems of practice, goals, timeline, and evaluation, are research-based practices applicable across professional disciplines. Like other contributors in this part, Miller and Anthony draw attention to the lack of

Introduction to Part III 79

connection between professional development training and instruction. Additionally, this case appropriately addresses educator philosophy that is too seldom addressed: Why do organizations focus mainly on changing student practices before critiquing adult behavior? This chapter is extremely enlightening for school leaders seeking to focus energy on a singular issue or problem of practice, which in this case is collaboration. Relying on Knowles' perspective of adult development, Miller and Anthony engage the instructional round approach to improve student growth. The use of peer observation and feedback is offered as a best practice for instructional growth. Readers are charged with critically examining their organization to identify the problem of practice for the strongest path to success.

A college degree remains a significant path to what many call the "American dream," and four-year degree earners can expect to earn nearly 60 percent more than non-degree holders. The economic development of the nation is dependent, in part, on the success of the nation's higher education institutions, with statistics showing that 65 percent of all jobs require post-secondary training (Georgetown Public Policy Institute, 2013). However, between 2010 and 2016, only 52 percent of the students entering four-year institutions graduated with a degree (Hess, 2016). Like the P–12 sector, higher education institutions also face leadership challenges with students and leaders.

Four chapters in this part discuss the higher education experience, including how leaders foster personal, emotional, and leadership growth of students and how theoretical perspectives are valued as necessary leadership tools for administrators. Contributors Ronald and Max Glickman note that post-secondary institutions are accountable for preparing the students they serve whether or not the leadership has adapted to multigenerational student populations. This chapter shares the challenges of a recently appointed president in a four-year public institution who is charged with positioning the university to prepare the next generation of leaders to meet the state's workforce pipeline. However, in the initial phase of the president's plan, she is met with a "full stop" when a dispute develops between the two faculty members selected to create a "world class" leadership development program. One full-time faculty member believes leadership is best taught by reading tried and true theories of the 20th century. The second member, a successful executive who teaches part-time, believes in a combination of presentation mediums and action learning exercises. In "Curriculum and Pedagogy Considerations for Connecting Personal Growth and Leadership Development," Glickman and Glickman dive into the divergent views between authentic leadership and self-authorship. The dilemma focuses on the president's ability to maneuver authentic leadership, self-regulation, relational transparency, and self-authoring leadership.

Viktor Wang and Geraldine Torrisi-Steele also discuss a case illustrating the misalignment of theory and practice in higher education. "The Gap Between Theory and Practice: A Scenario from Higher Education" depicts the lack of standardized ascension patterns of higher education leaders. Unlike other

80 *Introduction to Part III*

professions where criteria, such as a license denoting a level of training, may be necessary for promotion to leadership roles, post-secondary ascension is often based on seniority, academic acumen, and political savvy. Research by co-author Torrisi-Steele asserts that members assume roles with significant positional power typically without formalized leadership training or evidence of ethical decision-making skills. This particular case chronicles a "leader" who is repeatedly rewarded with promotions in the wake of leadership failure. Readers are encouraged to consider the long-term organizational impact of such practices on financial and program growth, faculty morale, trust, commitment, and student growth. Does an organization remain viable with individuals holding leadership posts who lack knowledge of systems thinking? What framework for change is suitable and viable for building a learning organization?

A learning organization continually evolves to meet current demands while creating the capacity for future growth. Success in higher education, like other educational settings, depends on fostering student growth. However, organizations often demonstrate inverted human capital value systems, where those at the top of the hierarchy are perceived as more significant than those who provide essential services. Alexis Hartley and Sonya Hayes illustrate this dynamic in their chapter "Because They Are Worth It: Utilizing Servant Leadership to Increase First Generation College Persistence." The chapter shares how higher education institutions are increasingly dependent on academic advisors to improve student retention and persistence rates, most notably of first-generation college students. Academic advisors are significant in providing direct support to students including, but not limited to financial, emotional, and academic concerns. Trends show that while increasing academic advisors' expectations and responsibilities, universities are adopting models that reduce funding and support for service delivery. The case draws on social capital theory and servant leadership to diagnose the complex functioning of an overworked academic advisor working to assist a first-generation college student. What type of leadership is needed for advisors to increase first-generation students' social capacity through servant leadership?

How might a feminist pedagogical approach to leadership challenge traditional hegemonic leadership paradigms? Joanna Line addresses this question in "Using a Feminist Approach to Leadership Education to Promote Coalition Among Women Collegiate Student-Athletes." This chapter examines how traditional leadership perceptions influence how female collegiate athletes perceive their opportunities for leadership roles. Utilizing Batliwala's feminist leadership theory diamond, which asserts that everyone possesses leadership capacity, Line draws on her collegiate coach experiences. The case reflects Line's desire to empower athletes to self-identify with leadership roles that have historically aligned with hegemonic structures. The case argues that the leaders' ability to aid in removing systemic barriers hinges on understanding student experiences. Guided by a feminist theoretical approach, the term leadership is replaced with the term coaction. Coaction frames leadership as a

Introduction to Part III 81

process that includes resisting oppressive systems rather than the possession of specific characteristics. The chapter provides a compelling lens to engage readers in challenging hegemonic structures that may inhibit the potential of minoritized identities. While Line focuses her case on women collegiate athletes, readers will recognize the value of feminist pedagogy in empowering emergent student leaders in any environment.

Each of the cases in this part of the text offers opportunities for instructors, readers, and practitioners to engage with real-world leadership scenarios and supporting literature. The contributors have worked to make the application of leadership for adult development central to their cases, and each of the discussion questions and activities for learning are designed with these pillars of adult development and leadership in mind. We encourage interested readers to explore Oliver Robinson's (2020) *Development through adulthood* as a supplemental text for extending the ideas presented in this part of the text.

8 Activating and Sustaining Motivation for Social Justice Leadership in Secondary Education

Rachel Roegman and Jasmine D. Collins

Introduction

Students of color, students with disabilities, and low-income students continue to experience inequitable policies, opportunities, and outcomes in K–12 settings (e.g., Milner, 2012; Morris, 2016). Social justice leadership, the practice of leadership that "focuses on the experiences of marginalized groups and inequities in educational opportunities and outcomes" (Furman, 2012, p. 194), is needed to address these inequities. However, K–12 administrators face pressure from teachers, parents, community members, and superiors to maintain policies and practices that privilege white, middle class students (Theoharis, 2007). Even leaders who know that change is needed often engage in silence and inaction (Gooden & Dantley, 2012; McMahon, 2007).

Given the need for social justice leadership, and the challenges that social justice-oriented leaders encounter, it is necessary to support leaders in sustaining this type of practice. The theory of developmental readiness offers a foundation in considering how leaders assess their ability to develop and prepare themselves for growth as leaders in complex organizational contexts. Developmental readiness is a leadership theory that considers both the *motivation* and *ability* of leaders and stakeholders to develop and change (Avolio, 2016).

Through the exploration of this case, participants will be able to identify and explain social justice leadership, consider how developmental readiness theory can be applied to sustain social justice leadership, and reflect on their own leadership practices.

Case: Tackling Disproportionality in Discipline Data

In this case, we share the story of Principal Ruth Wells, who, after receiving a phone call from a parent, identified alarming patterns of racial disproportionality in discipline data. Students of color were significantly more likely to receive referrals for subjective misbehavior, and more likely to be suspended, than white students. We follow Principal Wells as she shares these data with her staff.

DOI: 10.4324/9780429331503-11

84 *Leadership in Secondary Education*

Case Context

Lincoln High School (LHS) is a comprehensive high school that serves 2,100 students in a small city. The city and school are both racially and socio-economically diverse: the student body is about 40 percent white, 35 percent Black, 10 percent Latinx, and 10 percent multiracial, and about two-thirds are classified as economically disadvantaged. LHS faculty includes 100 teachers. The majority, 80 percent, are white, 10 percent are Black, and 10 percent are Latinx. They are diverse in terms of years teaching, but homogenous in other aspects – over two-thirds graduated from LHS, they are middle class, and most profess generally progressive beliefs. At the same time, several maintain a color-neutral attitude ("I don't see race") and believe that schooling is a benevolent institution that rewards students who work hard.

Key Individuals

Ruth Wells has been the principal for five years. She is well-liked. As a white woman, she has made intentional efforts to get to know families of color. Teachers see Principal Wells as someone who is dedicated to students and open to new ideas.

James Jamison is in his third year as Dean of Discipline. Although he is new to LHS, he has experience working in other schools. Dean Jamison believes that if students misbehave, they need consequences. Dean Jamison is a white man who professes that he does not see race; he just sees behavior.

Larry Smith, an experienced teacher in his 20th year, is seen by many colleagues as their representative voice with administration. He enjoys this role, working with teachers and administration to address concerns. Mr. Smith is a white man who thinks the school is doing a pretty good job in terms of race.

Adrianna Pell, an experienced teacher leader in her 15th year, is an active participant in many school-level committees, including the leadership team. Her peers see her as an advocate for social justice. As a Black woman, Ms. Pell is seen by many students and families of color as their main voice in the school, and she sees herself as responsible for holding students of color to high standards.

Scene 1: The Phone Call

Principal Wells was in shock. She had just gotten off the phone with a parent, whose son received a one-day suspension for "disrespect." Among other accusations, the parent told her that it was unfair for her child to be suspended for standing up for himself. *All he did was tell the teacher that he didn't understand the question. He just needed the teacher to explain it again. Maybe he got loud, but he was frustrated. Instead of helping,* the parent said, *the teacher kicked him out. How is this fair? Why do Black boys get kicked out of class just for asking for help? This is just like what's happening in the news.*

Principals Wells realized the parent was referencing the recent attention to a series of police killings of unarmed Black men. Principal Wells wanted to look at her school's data to see if the parent's claims of disproportionality were true. She asked Dean Jamison to create a spreadsheet of the previous year's referrals and suspensions, disaggregated by race. His response was "Why?" After she explained, Dean Jamison told her that the whole system was color-neutral, but he would prepare the file as directed. He also suggested this was a good time to review the referral form, since he was frustrated that teachers would sometimes send a student out of class without completing it.

Scene 2: Analyzing the Disciplinary Data

Principal Wells could see that LHS disciplinary procedures were unequivocally resulting in patterns of racial disproportionality. Students of color received harsher punishments for the same offense as white students and were significantly more likely to receive referrals for subjective misbehavior, such as "disrespect." In a subjective incident, the teacher relies on personal judgment – different teachers likely have different definitions of disrespect, for example. In contrast, objective behavior refers to incidents in which all, or almost all, adults would agree that a rule has been broken, such as a physical altercation.

Table 8.1 Teacher Referrals, Disaggregated by Race and Offense

	Total	White	Black	Latinx	Multiracial
Defiance	352	15	244	15	78
Dress Code Violation	412	38	276	3	95
Disrespect	333	33	228	33	39
Physical Altercation	112	29	26	22	35
Disrupting the Class	298	16	220	10	52
Tardy	132	43	40	27	22
Inappropriate Use of Technology	355	62	179	85	29
Destruction of Property	42	10	11	11	10
Inappropriate Language	265	5	201	17	42

Table 8.2 Discipline Consequences, Disaggregated by Race

	Total	White	Black	Latinx	Multiracial
In-School Suspensions	262	65	131	37	29
Out-of-School Suspensions	118	19	71	9	19
Expulsions	4	0	3	1	0

86   *Leadership in Secondary Education*

Principal Wells was confident that when faculty saw the data, they, too, would agree that they needed to rethink how they approached discipline. She created a presentation to share at the next faculty meeting.

Scene 3: Sharing the Data with the Faculty

Mr. Smith spoke first. "Those kids have more referrals because they misbehave more," he argued. "I never have a white student talk under their breath. I only give referrals to students who misbehave. I don't see kids' race."

Ms. Pell started to talk, pointing out that teachers and students might have different understandings of respect, but Mr. Smith cut her off. "You have to give respect to get respect," he said, "and if you talk under your breath, that is a ticket to Dean Jamison's office."

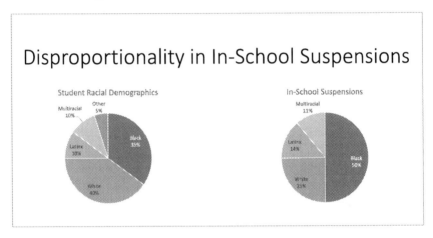

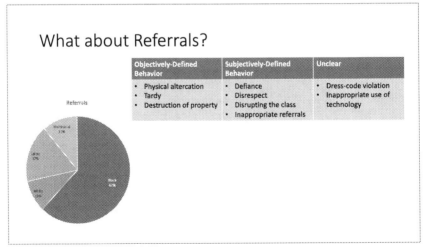

Figure 8.1   Sample Slides from Principal Wells's Presentation

As Mr. Smith talked, other teachers nodded their heads. They were adamant that students of color received more referrals because they misbehaved more. Principal Wells pushed through with her presentation, but each slide was met with similar remarks. She looked pleadingly at Ms. Pell, who she knew agreed with her, but Ms. Pell looked away.

The Dilemma

Principal Wells's initial motivation to address an issue that seemed so obvious was beginning to wane. She knew that the discipline process was not equitable, but few faculty seemed to care. What could she do? How could she help teachers see their "color-neutral" practices were harming students of color? How could she develop her own skills to be a better leader for students of color?

Discussion: Social Justice Leadership and Developmental Readiness

This case brings together two important theories – social justice leadership and developmental readiness – within the context of a school facing persistent racial inequities that most faculty were unwilling to name or address.

Social Justice Leadership

To help analyze the case presented here, we look to Furman's (2012) praxis-dimensions-capacities framework of social justice leadership. This framework offers a conceptual way to analyze social justice leadership that includes both theoretical and practice-oriented components.

Praxis, drawing on Freire's (1998) work, is the combination of reflection and action. As leaders reflect on their beliefs and understandings of inequities, "[t]his discovery cannot be purely intellectual but must involve action" (p. 65); at the same time, action should not "be limited to mere activism, but must include serious reflection" (p. 65). Neither reflection nor action on its own is sufficient; instead, social justice-oriented leaders engage in a constant cycle of both (Furman, 2012).

The *dimensions of praxis* refer to the multiple, varied, and overlapping contexts that influence leaders' work (Furman, 2012). Educational leadership is not an isolated practice; rather, it is situated within multiple contexts that create possibilities and constraints (Roegman, 2017). Furman (2012) identifies five critical dimensions of leadership: personal, interpersonal, communal, systemic, and ecological. Each dimension guides leaders to reflect on specific aspects of themselves and their leadership context, and each carries its own set of actions. For example, the communal dimension refers to ways that leaders build community across diverse stakeholder groups through inclusive and democratic practices. Reflection requires leaders to be aware of how they approach different groups and to be aware of community history. Through

88   *Leadership in Secondary Education*

reflecting, action requires the leader to implement specific strategies to engage all stakeholder groups.

Finally, *leader capacities* are an individuals' skills, knowledge, and dispositions to engage in social justice work. Furman (2012) identifies specific capacities aligned to each praxis dimension. For example, successful praxis around the communal dimension requires knowledge of different cultural groups, as well as the skill to develop inclusive and democratic engagement strategies. In contrast, the ecological dimension, which acknowledges broader sociopolitical contexts, requires that leaders reflect on their school's role in advancing or challenging systemic issues, such as racism and poverty. Furman (2012) suggests that action, in concert with reflection, involves "designing pedagogical experiences for both teachers and students related to these broader issues" (p. 212). Capacities related to this dimension include knowledge of broader issues and how they impact schooling, as well as the skill to engage others in conversations about these issues.

Developmental Readiness

Developmental readiness (DR) is a multilevel leadership theory focusing on the *motivation* and *ability* of leaders, followers, stakeholders, and the context to develop and change (Avolio, 2016). A central purpose of DR is to shift the conversation from "How can we better develop leaders?" to "How can we get leaders and their organizations to be better ready to develop?" (Hannah & Avolio, 2010, p. 1182). Development refers to ways that individuals and organizations incorporate new knowledge, skills, abilities, and attributes into existing structures of knowledge and identity (Hannah & Avolio, 2010; Lord & Hall, 2005).

Motivation to Develop

Motivation to develop oneself or others stems from intrinsic interests and goals, goal orientation, and developmental efficacy (Hannah & Avolio, 2010). Motivation – the internal process that drives direction, intensity, and persistence of behavior – affects a leader's decisions to take on specific leadership responsibilities (Chan & Drasgow, 2001). Leaders may be motivated by passion, duty, or desire to make a difference (Bronk & McLean, 2016; Chan & Drasgow, 2011; Collins, 2019). The level of motivation determines the intensity of effort and persistence (Chan & Drasgow, 2011).

Goal orientation is the next facet of motivation to develop. It refers to ways that individuals approach challenges – namely, whether they will enter the situation with the intention to learn (learning orientation) or to demonstrate competence (performance orientation) (Culbertson & Jackson, 2016; Hannah & Avolio, 2010). Setting learning goals improves performance over time as individuals seek feedback and seek to challenge themselves (Culbertson & Jackson, 2016). Conversely, performance goals tend to result in less transformative effects (Locke & Latham, 2002).

Developmental efficacy refers to leaders' confidence in their ability to develop and employ the knowledge, skills, and attributes necessary to lead effectively (Hannah & Avolio, 2010). Higher levels of efficacy are associated with the drive to take on developmental challenges (Hannah et al., 2008).

Ability to Develop

Ability to develop is promoted through self-concept clarity (SCC), cognitive complexity, and meta-cognitive ability (Hannah & Avolio, 2010). SCC is defined as "the extent to which self-beliefs are clearly and confidently defined, internally consistent, and stable" (Hannah & Avolio, 2010, p. 1183). Leaders' propensity to develop may be heightened or dissuaded given the relationship of new knowledge, skills, and attitudes to their pre-existing beliefs and biases (Hannah & Avolio, 2010; Lord & Hall, 2005).

Cognitive complexity describes how well a leader is able to differentiate and integrate various sources of information (Hannah & Avolio, 2010). This is central to leader developmental readiness, because cognitive complexity allows leaders to utilize more multidimensional approaches (Keegan & Lahey, 2010). Leaders consider individual, institutional, and cultural factors that promote readiness to develop employees' cognitive complexity (Avolio, 2016; Keegan & Lahey, 2010).

Meta-cognitive ability refers to the ability to "think about thinking" (Hannah & Avolio, 2010, p. 1183). Self-reflective leaders uncover how emotions influence their interpretation of feedback, how new experiences provide insights germane to development, and how implicit biases influence their ability to develop (Hannah & Avolio, 2010). Implementing regular opportunities for self-reflection and formative assessment is useful for promoting meta-cognitive development among members and leaders (Levi, 2015).

Bringing the Theories Together

One critique of DR is the tendency to focus exclusively on leaders (Avolio, 2016). It is important to note that followers, supervisors, other stakeholders, and contextual elements all play a role in accelerating or stifling developmental readiness (Avolio, 2016). One's *motivation* to learn, reflect, and act in social justice-oriented ways can be affected by the readiness of followers, stakeholders, and the organizational environment. If teachers possess low learning orientations and are more concerned with appearing competent, for example, it is possible that the principal's developmental efficacy may be diminished due to the formidable barriers that this situation presents (Hannah & Avolio, 2010).

When it comes to identifying and addressing persistent inequities, leaders must anticipate resistance as they challenge norms and disrupt order (Heifetz & Linsky, 2017). Organizations are incredibly stubborn and notoriously immune to cultural change (Heifetz et al., 2009; Keegan & Lahey, 2009) and many institutions ignore issues of equity (Bonilla-Silva, 2013; Roegman et al., 2018).

90   *Leadership in Secondary Education*

Changing cultures requires individuals to assess their currently held beliefs and look deeply into themselves and their institutions. However, fear of being accused of racism (DiAngelo, 2018) and fear of what may be lost in the change process (Heifetz et al., 2009), among other fears, prevent change. Thus, increasingly complex conditions, combined with deeply held beliefs and willful ignorance, contribute to climates wherein individuals will outright refuse to acknowledge inequity, even in the face of hard evidence (Dugan, 2017).

For leaders such as Principal Wells, developmental readiness provides a lens into the difficulties in sustaining social justice leadership, in terms of the leader's own motivation to develop and the leader's ability to develop school personnel's skills, knowledge, and dispositions needed to eliminate existing inequities in schools.

Learning Activities

Data Analysis: Review discipline and demographic data presented in the case.

1. Calculate the risk index, composition index, and/or relative risk ratio for referrals, in-school suspensions, and out-of-school suspensions (see Fergus, 2016 for formulas).
2. What patterns stand out?
3. What other information would you want to investigate this issue in greater depth?
4. What questions do these data make you ask?

Role-Plays: With a partner, act out the scenarios, considering both social justice leadership and developmental readiness.

1. One week after the faculty meeting, Principal Wells evaluated Mr. Smith's teaching as part of his annual review. She gave him the second-highest rating, not the highest, because of his large number of out-of-class referrals. This was Mr. Smith's first time to receive this rating, and he is angry. Role-play the conversation in which Mr. Smith and Principal Wells discuss the evaluation.
2. Principal Wells and Dean Jamison are modifying the referral form. Principal Wells is interested in addressing subjectively-defined behavior, while Dean Jamison is focused on streamlining the form. Role-play their conversation as they create a workable document.
3. Some parents have formed a working group aimed at holding LHS accountable for disproportionate patterns in discipline. The superintendent does not want this issue making the news. Role-play conversations that might take place between Principal Wells and the working group, and between Principal Wells and the superintendent.

Discussion Questions

1. In what ways did Principal Wells show a lack of understanding of her faculty's readiness to talk about race?
2. In what ways did Principal Wells show a lack of understanding of her own readiness to talk about race?
3. How might Furman's (2012) praxis-dimensions-capacities framework support Principal Wells in moving forward? How might focusing on different dimensions of praxis support Principal Wells in identifying her next steps?
4. Think about your own practice. In what ways do you engage in social justice leadership? Are there times when you avoid raising issues, and what are your reasons for doing so? In what ways do you support the social justice practice of others?
5. How do you maintain motivation when you face resistance? What supports you and keeps you focused?

References

Fergus, E. (2016). *Solving disproportionality and achieving equity: A leader's guide to using data to change hearts and minds*. Corwin Press.

Hannah, S. T., & Avolio, B. J. (2010). Ready or not: How do we accelerate the developmental readiness of leaders? *Journal of Organizational Behavior*, 31, 1181–1187.

Keegan, R. & Lahey, L. (2009). *Immunity to change: How to overcome it and unlock the potential in yourself and your organization*. Harvard Business Review Press.

Khalifa, M. (2018). *Culturally responsive school leadership*. Harvard Education Press.

Theoharis, G. (2009). *The school leaders our children deserve: Seven keys to equity, social justice, and school reform*. Teachers College Press.

Avolio, B. (2016). Introduction: The golden triangle for examining leadership developmental readiness. In B. Avolio (Ed.), *Leader developmental readiness: Pursuit of leadership excellence* (New Directions for Student Leadership, No. 149, pp. 7–14). Wiley.

Bonilla-Silva, E. (2013). "New racism," color-blind racism, and the future of Whiteness in America. In *White out* (pp. 268–281). Routledge.

Bronk, K. C., & McClean, D. C. (2016). Introduction: The role of passion and purpose in leader developmental readiness. In B. Avolio (Ed.), *Leader developmental readiness: Pursuit of leadership excellence* (New Directions for Student Leadership, No. 149, pp. 7–14). Wiley.

Chan, K. Y. & Drasgow, F. (2001). Toward a theory of individual differences and leadership: Understanding the motivation to lead. *Journal of Applied Psychology*, 86(3), 481–498.

Collins, J. D. (2019). A comparative group factor analysis of the SIAS: Implications for measuring social justice leadership capacity. *The Journal of Leadership Education*, 18(3), 20–40.

Culbertson, S. S., & Jackson, A. T. (2016). Orienting oneself for leadership: The role of goal orientation in leader developmental readiness. In B. Avolio (Ed.), *Leader developmental readiness: Pursuit of leadership excellence* (New Directions for Student Leadership, No. 149, pp. pp. 7–14. Wiley.

DiAngelo, R. (2018). *White fragility: Why it's so hard for white people to talk about racism*. Beacon Press.

Dugan, J. P. (2017). *Leadership theory: Cultivating critical perspectives*. Wiley.

92 *Leadership in Secondary Education*

Fergus, E. (2016). *Solving disproportionality and achieving equity: A leader's guide to using data to change hearts and minds.* Corwin Press.

Freire, P. (1998). *The pedagogy of hope.* The Continuum Publishing Company.

Furman, G. (2012). Social justice leadership as praxis: Developing capacities through preparation programs. *Educational Administration Quarterly, 48*(2), 191–229.

Gooden, M. A., & Dantley, M. (2012). Centering race in a framework for leadership preparation. *Journal of Research on Leadership Education, 7*(2), 237–253.

Hannah, S. T., & Avolio, B. J. (2010). Ready or not: How do we accelerate the developmental readiness of leaders? *Journal of Organizational Behavior, 31,* 1181–1187.

Hannah, S. T., Avolio, B., Luthans, F., & Harms, P. D. (2008). Leadership efficacy: Review and future directions. *The Leadership Quarterly, 19,* 669–692.

Heifetz, R., Grashow, A., & Linsky, M. (2009). *The practice of adaptive leadership: Tools and tactics for changing your organization and the world.* Harvard Business Review Press.

Heifetz, R., & Linsky, M. (2017). *Leadership on the line: Staying alive through the dangers of change.* Harvard Business Review Press.

Keegan, R. & Lahey, L. (2009). *Immunity to change: How to overcome it and unlock the potential in yourself and your organization.* Harvard Business Review Press.

Keegan, R. & Lahey, L. (2010). Adult development and organizational leadership. In N. Nohria & R. Khurana (Eds.). *Handbook of leadership theory and practice* (pp. 769–787). Harvard Business Review Press.

Levi, D. (2015). *Group Dynamics for Teams* (5th ed.). Sage.

Locke, E. A., & Latham, G. P. (2006). New directions in goal-setting theory. *Current Directions in Psychological Science, 15,* 265–268. doi:10.1111/j.1467-8721.2006.00449.x

Lord, R. G., & Hall, R. J. (2005). Identity, deep structure and the development of leadership skill. *The Leadership Quarterly, 16,* 591–615.

McMahon, B. (2007). Educational administrators' conceptions of whiteness, anti-racism and social justice. *Journal of Educational Administration, 45*(6), 684–696.

Milner, H. R. (2012). Beyond a test score: Explaining opportunity gaps in educational practice. *Journal of Black Studies, 43,* 693–718.

Morris, M. W. (2016). *Pushout: The criminalization of Black girls in schools.* The New Press.

Roegman, R. (2017). How contexts matter: A framework for understanding the role of contexts in equity-focused educational leadership. *Journal of School Leadership, 27*(1), 6–30.

Roegman, R., Samarapungavan, A., Maeda, Y., & Johns, G. (2018). Color-neutral disaggregation? Principals' practices around disaggregating data from three school districts. *Educational Administration Quarterly, 54*(4), 559–588.

Theoharis, G. (2007). Social justice educational leaders and resistance: Toward a theory of social justice leadership. *Educational Administration Quarterly, 43*(2), 221–258.

9 Learning Transfer

The Missing Link to Leading the Successful Implementation of Professional Development in Schools

Corinne Brion

Introduction

This teaching case study is relevant to practicing and prospective principals and educational administrators because it raises issues related to leading change and the effective implementation of professional development. The following operational definitions are used in this case:

Professional development: a lifelong collaborative learning process that nourishes the growth of educators both as individuals and as team members to improve their skills and abilities (Speck & Knipe, 2005, p. 4).

Learning transfer: the effective and continuing application by learners – to their performance of jobs or other individual, organizational, or community responsibilities – of knowledge and skills gained in the learning activities (Broad, 1997, p. 2).

Culture: everything you believe and everything you do that enables you to identify with people who are like you and that distinguishes you from people who differ from you (Lindsey et al., 2018, p. 29).

Professional development is an important element in improving both teachers' and school leaders' skills and abilities that may impact student academic achievement (Hattie, 2003; Koonce et al., 2019; Reeves, 2010). Currently, school budgets are often spent on professional development that does not result in the hoped-for improvements in student learning outcomes and performance (Hess, 2013). In fact, despite the millions of dollars spent on professional development nationally, learning outcomes continue to stagnate or dwindle, discipline issues often skyrocket, and teacher morale plummets (Hess, 2013). This may be due, in part, to the lack of attention being paid to learning transfer after professional development, as well as the difficulties leaders face when they attempt to lead change.

Case Narrative

The author used pseudonyms to describe the community, the school district, and the school itself. Murtle (population 60,000) is a city located in the Southwest

DOI: 10.4324/9780429331503-12

94   *Learning Transfer*

United States. Most recent census data indicate that the city's racial makeup is 63 percent White, 20 percent Black or African American, 15 percent Latino, and 2 percent Native American. In the past two years, Murtle welcomed many refugees and immigrants. The mayor is thrilled about having a more diverse community. He attributed this migration to the "affordable housing and good quality of life." The mayor works closely with the school superintendent, Mr. Moxley, to find solutions to equitably serve the refugee and immigrant students who face language and cultural difficulties when they enter the American school system.

Murtle School District serves approximately 7,000 students. The district has nine elementary schools, two middle schools, and one high school. Fifteen years ago, the district was named in the "Top 100" school districts by *Money* magazine, a recognition that has remained in the minds and hearts of locals. In recent years, however, the district's academic results have declined. The superintendent blames the decrease in performance on the overwhelming focus from the state on standardized testing. Others blame the leadership for not adapting and tackling the academic decline adequately.

Mr. Rupert has been the principal of Murtle Middle School (MMS) for eight years. MMS serves 600 students grades 6–8. The student demographics closely mirror the city's demographics with 60 percent White students, 20 percent Black or African American students, and 20 percent Latino students. Mr. Rupert oversees 20 teachers, two building operators, three administrators, one counselor, one nurse, and one athletic director. Although the school is well known for its strong athletic performances, academic results are dwindling, and discipline issues are rising. As a result, Mr. Rupert decided to allocate more money to professional development (PD). Based on his research and conversations with his colleagues in other districts, he decided to allow $5,000 per teacher for his PD budget. This amounts to a total of $100,000 allocated for PD.

Prior to assuming his administrative role, Mr. Rupert was a science teacher. As such, he understands the value of PD and is proud to offer many PD opportunities to his teachers. For the past two years, the principal has focused his PD on implementing Positive Behavior Interventions and Supports (PBIS), which is a new framework that aims to help with his school's discipline issues. PBIS is a proactive approach to establishing the behavioral supports and social culture needed for all students in a school to achieve social, emotional, and academic success. Mr. Rupert also allocated other PD funds to focus on Science, Technology, Engineering, and Mathematics (STEM) in order to support educating students in these disciplines.

Over the past months, three teachers have been increasingly dissatisfied with Mr. Rupert's PD plans. These teachers continually criticize Mr. Rupert for having too many mandatory PD events that do not pertain to their subject areas. Specifically, they have been vocal "that STEM PD is irrelevant for those of us teaching English Language Art (ELA), English as a Second Language (ESL), social studies, art, music, or physical education."

During one of the staff meetings, one of the three teachers said to Mr. Rupert, "I do not know, and nobody knows, why we do not choose the PD we need for our particular subject areas. It is done like that in other districts. Right now, you are wasting our time, and quite frankly, students are paying the price because we could serve them better than we currently are."

Another teacher from the trio added, "Not to be disrespectful, but I teach students who just moved from Mexico, Honduras, and the Republic of Congo, and they need extra help in English. I feel that we all need extra help to teach these students because we are culturally miles apart and it shows in how they learn. We are not prepared to teach them, and it makes it hard for them to adapt to our ways of learning and teaching."

Seeing that Mr. Rupert was perplexed, the same teachers decided to write him a letter that detailed their complaints regarding PD. Their hope was that if the complaints were in writing, it would force the principal to react. The letter read:

> Dear Mr. Rupert,
>
> While we know that you have the best intentions with PD, we feel that PD, as it currently stands, is a waste of our time and a waste of our tax-payers' money. PD should be linked to our professional goals and to our teaching evaluations. As such, we should not attend STEM PDs if we teach other subject matter. Also, regarding PBIS, the consultant is always lecturing, which is not an effective way to teach adults. We often wonder why we do not use the wealth of knowledge that exists in this building instead of always contracting with expensive consultants who do not know our school context and culture. We wonder why we are asked to indivi-dualize teaching but are not offered individualized PD? For example, it is ironic that consultants come in and out but never ask us about our learning styles. Also, as it stands, a few of us implement new strategies learned during our PD, but most teachers do not because they are not held accountable. We also know that, based on our student demo-graphics, all of us could benefit from training in culturally responsive teaching. We teach refugee and immigrant students as if they were born and raised in this culture, which is unfair to them!
>
> We thank you for your time and consideration.
> Sincerely,
> Mrs. Parker, Mr. Fox, and Miss Dearden

When Mr. Rupert read the letter, he did not know what to do and felt totally unappreciated. Based on the surveys he sent after each PD, teachers seemed to be pleased with their opportunities for learning. To make things worse, the three dissatisfied teachers had sent a copy of the letter to the superintendent who immediately asked Mr. Rupert to come for a meeting. The principal explained the situation. "Teachers are fine with PD. It is just those three."

The superintendent asked the principal to show him his school's data in terms of discipline and results. There were evident gaps in learning outcomes for the refugee and immigrant students. There was also a large number of

96 *Learning Transfer*

male African American students being disciplined. Mr. Moxley took the side of the three teachers and said, "Mr. Rupert, I think your three teachers have a point here. I know it does not feel good to be criticized, but why don't you reflect on this letter and your school's data, and show me your plan of action and how you are going to change your PD practices? The PD offered this year needs to be transferred to practice because too much money is spent in vain. I expect you to be prepared to demonstrate how the PD investments you're making are both relevant for teachers and leading to improved practice."

Back in his office, Mr. Rupert asked himself, "How am I supposed to lead this change and convince all teachers that we need to change our PD model? Teachers are set in their ways and it will be hard to alter their mindsets. They will feel like I betrayed them."

The situation at MMS is far from being resolved. Mr. Rupert has to convince his staff to embrace a new PD model that includes providing quality and relevant PD and ensuring that teachers transfer the new knowledge to their classrooms and are accountable for improved practices. This case study is relevant, and its solutions are applicable, to many districts in the United States because it is rare that leaders take into consideration learning transfer when planning, implementing, and evaluating PD. This case study uses Kotter's (2012) model of change and the Multidimensional Model of Learning Transfer (MMLT) (Brion, 2020) as a conceptual framework to raise critical questions relative to change and learning transfer.

Supporting Literature

Leading Change

Being a facilitator of change is one of the most important aspects of leadership. Leaders need to understand that resistance to change is inevitable but not necessarily a negative. Leaders may benefit from viewing change as an opportunity for growth. Leading change is demanding and often requires leaders to enhance their performance. For example, during periods of change, employees deserve good planning, involvement, decision making, and timely communication (Hess, 2013). Having trusting relationships with all stakeholders is also critical to the success of major organizational change. Kotter (2012) offers a model of change that leaders can use to frame their work when organizations need to change. Kotter posits that leading change involves the following elements:

- Establishing a sense of urgency
- Creating a guiding coalition (and allies) and encouraging participation
- Developing a vision and clear goals as to align programs to those goals
- Communicating regularly to develop buy-in
- Empowering action in others and removing barriers

- Generating short-term wins
- Consolidating gains and keeping the momentum going
- Incorporating changes into the culture and, if necessary, writing new norms

Kotter (2012) adds that communication is critical before, during, and after the change takes place. He reminds us to involve people and that collecting data is one way to include follower voice. Kotter warns leaders to be wary of the early excitement and urges them to take risks while also being thoughtful and careful. I extend Kotter's charge to include asking leaders to be open-minded, listen to feedback, and understand that challenges will arise when leading change.

Learning Transfer

Learning transfer is the primary objective of teaching, yet it is possibly the most challenging goal to reach (Foley & Kaiser, 2013; Furman & Sibthorp, 2013; Hung, 2013). Every year, billions of dollars are spent on training in the United States, and some estimates suggest only 10 percent results in transfer of knowledge, skills, or behaviors in the workplace or at a loss of 87–90 cents per dollar spent on professional development (Broad & Newstrom, 1992). These findings demonstrate the lack of attention placed on learning transfer and indicate that is not sufficient to simply offer PD events if organizations hope to see meaningful development of employee's skills.

Broad and Newstrom (1992) identified six key factors that can either hinder or promote learning transfer in adults: (a) program participants, their motivation and dispositions, and previous knowledge; (b) program design and execution including the strategies for learning transfer; (c) program content that is adapted to the needs of the learners; (d) changes required to apply new learning; (e) organizational context such as people, structure, and cultural milieu that can support or prevent transfer of learning values (Continuing Professional Development [CPD]); and (f) societal and community forces.

The process of learning and developing is socio-cultural in nature. Our cultures impact how we interact and learn; thus, our culture affects learning transfer. Because everyone brings their own culture to work, these diverse cultures, worldviews, and core values form the organizational culture. This organizational culture affects policies, practices, actions, and behaviors (Muhammad, 2009). Building on Broad and Newstrom's (1992) work as well as data collected in schools in five African countries over a period of six years, Brion (2020) proposed a Multidimensional Model of Learning Transfer (MMLT) in which Culture (with a capital C) influences all other dimensions of the learning transfer process.

For the MMLT, Culture includes individual, sectional, departmental, organizational, regional, and national cultures, as well as cultures related to a continent. The author asserts that Culture is the predominant enhancer and inhibitor to transfer, and that Culture affects the entire learning transfer phenomenon (Brion, 2020). Considering Culture as the main enhancer or inhibitor to transfer is innovative and useful because schools spend large amounts

98 *Learning Transfer*

of money and resources on PD, yet the money invested often does not lead to the desired outcomes.

In the MMLT, the author affirms that Culture affects all dimensions of learning transfer: pre-training, learner, facilitator, material and content, context and environment, and follow-up. Ignoring cultural issues in schools presents numerous risks including reinforcing stereotypes, increasing intolerance among stakeholders, raising misunderstandings, and yielding poor outcomes (Caffarella & Daffron, 2013). The MMLT provides an effective way to organize, deliver, implement, and assess PD and learning transfer.

As Figure 9.1 indicates, *pretraining* includes the orientation of supervisors and facilitators so that they can support the professional development event once it has begun. In the case study presented, Mr. Rupert did not orient the facilitators and consultants who were coming to provide the PD. The facilitators and consultants were also not briefed about their audience's needs. Pretraining also includes communicating expectations to trainers and trainees and explaining who will benefit from the training (Yang et al., 2009). The case presented suggests that Mr. Rupert did not think carefully about teachers' implementation of what was learned during training.

Learner refers to the learner's levels of motivation, understanding the cultural background of the facilitators and self, and comprehending how history and social events affect stakeholders (learner, facilitator, peers, and colleagues). The learner dimension also includes understanding cultural differences in learning styles (e.g., collectivistic vs. individualistic cultures), as well as language and writing differences. Learner is also comprised of the participants' beliefs and attitude toward their job (Yelon et al., 2013), whether or not they have the freedom to act, and the positive consequences of that application. Finally, this dimension involves participants' belief of their efficacy to implement the knowledge and skills learned (Yelon et al., 2013). At MMS, three teachers did not believe that the PD offered was beneficial to their growth.

Facilitator includes the understanding of the trainer's own cultural background, the background of the participants, and how history and social events affect stakeholders (facilitator, learner, peers, and colleagues). It also refers to the understanding of language and writing differences, setting goals, and the selection of PD participants (Yang et al., 2009). Once again, at MMS, facilitators came in and out without taking the time to understand the participants' cultural backgrounds and learning styles. The facilitator domain also includes the dispositions of the facilitators. A competent facilitator understands the difference between teaching and learning transfer. Teaching is the delivery of content, whereas a facilitator of learning works with participants to create knowledge that is applicable to their jobs and personal lives.

Content and materials involves using evidence-based, culturally-relevant, and contextualized materials. Adults learn by doing, sharing their own experiences, seeing how the new knowledge can be beneficial to them, and reflecting.

Corinne Brion 99

Figure 9.1 Multidimensional Model of Learning Transfer (MMLT)

100 *Learning Transfer*

Consultants hired to lead PD at MMS were often not using content and materials that align with the MMLT components.

Context and environment is comprised of the training environment and the work environment such as the school culture. It also refers to having enough time to transfer knowledge, the support for action or resources, the freedom to act, and peer support (Facteau et al., 1995). Finally, context and environment refers to the training incentives such as intrinsic incentives (provides employees with growth opportunities) and extrinsic incentives (rewards or promotion) (Facteau et al, 1995). In this case, Mr. Rupert might have done more to support the learning of his teachers if he had provided them with resources and prioritized the transfer of PD knowledge into teachers' practice.

Sustainable follow-up is important after PD in order to avoid skill decay and training relapse. This follow-up can include tutor facilitated networks via mobile technology, micro-learning using mobile technology (Brion, 2018), coaching, testimonials, professional learning communities (PLCs) or community of practice (COPs), apprenticeship, coaching, and e-coaching (Wang & Wentling, 2001). Follow-up should include frequent and detailed feedback, upkeep of networks, modeling, and reflection. At MMS, there was no follow-up, mechanism for feedback post-training, or accountability for transferring the new knowledge.

Learning Activities

Next, you will have the opportunity to reflect on the case study and apply what you have learned. Use the supporting literature provided in the reference list to help you complete the activities.

Activity on Leading Change

Using the eight elements of Kotter's (2012) model of change, in pairs or at your table, create a *matrix of ideas* for each of the elements. Put yourself in Mr. Rupert's shoes:

1. What would you do to establish a sense of urgency?
2. What would you do to create a guiding coalition (and allies) and encourage participation?
3. What would you do to develop a vision and clear goals as to align programs to those goals?
4. What would you do to communicate regularly and develop buy-in?
5. What would you do to empower action in others and remove barriers?
6. What would you do to generate short-term wins?
7. What would you do to consolidate gains and keep the momentum going?
8. What would you do to incorporate changes into the culture? Be ready to share your ideas.

Activity on Learning Transfer

1. In pairs, discuss why the three teachers are frustrated with the PD offerings. Have you experienced similar frustrations?
2. Discuss and explain your understanding of the MMLT as a group. Discuss whether or not you believe culture is important to consider for learning and learning transfer.
3. Decide what Mr. Rupert could do in each of the MMLT dimensions to enhance the transfer of learning and the implementation of new knowledge in the classrooms post PD.
4. Discuss whether you believe the MMLT might be useful at your school. Why or why not? If you believe it would be useful in your setting, then how would you use it?

Recommendations for Further Reading and Research

The MMLT provides an effective way to organize PD events, facilitate learning and its implementation, while also assessing PD and learning transfer. It could be used systematically by educational leaders who wish to lead change and improve the efficiency of their PD programs. The MMLT includes seven dimensions that can enhance or hinder the transfer of learning. These dimensions include culture, pretraining, learner, facilitator, content and materials, context and environment, and sustainable follow-up. Upon understanding which of the seven dimensions supported or prevented the transfer of training, learners and facilitators can adapt their teaching, content, conditions for learning, pre-training activities, and follow-up methods.

References

Brion, C. (2018). Keeping the learning going: Using mobile technology to enhance learning transfer. *Educational Research for Policy and Practice (ERPP)*, 18(3), 225–240. doi:10.1007/s10671-018-09243-0

Brion, C. (2020). Learning transfer: The missing linkage to effective professional development. *Journal of Cases in Educational Leadership*, 23(3), 32–47.

Broad, M. L. (1997). *Transferring learning in the workplace: Seventeen case studies from the real world of training*. American Society for Training and Development.

Broad, M. L., & Newstrom, J. W. (1992). *Transfer of training: Action-packed strategies to ensure high payoff from training investments*. Da Capo Press.

Caffarella, R. S., & Daffron, S. R. (2013). *Planning programs for adult learners: A practical guide*. John Wiley & Sons.

Facteau, J. D., Dobbins, G. H., Russell, J. E., Ladd, R. T., & Kudisch, J. D. (1995). The influence of general perceptions of the training environment on pretraining motivation and perceived training transfer. *Journal of Management*, 21(1), 1–25.

Foley, J. M., & Kaiser, L. M. R. (2013). Learning transfer and its intentionality in adult and continuing education. *New Directions for Adult and Continuing Education*, 2013(137), 5–15.

Furman, N., & Sibthorp, J. (2013). Leveraging experiential learning techniques for transfer. *New Directions for Adult and Continuing Education*, 2013(137), 17–26.

102 *Learning Transfer*

Hattie, J. (2003). *Teachers make a difference: What is the research evidence?*Australian Council for Educational Research (ACER).

Hess, F. M. (2013). *Cage-busting leadership.* Harvard Education Press.

Hung, W. (2013). Problem-based learning: A learning environment for enhancing learning transfer. *New Directions for Adult and Continuing Education*, 137, 27–38.

Koonce, M., Pijanowski, J. C., Bengtson, E., & Lasater, K. (2019). Principal engagement in the professional development process. *NASSP Bulletin*, 103(3), 229–252. doi:10.1177/0192636519871614

Kotter, J. P. (2012). *Leading change.* Harvard Business Review Press.

Lindsey, R. B., Nuri Robins, K., Terrell, R. D., & Lindsey, D. B. (2018). *Cultural proficiency: A manual for school leaders*, 4th ed. Corwin.

Muhammad, A. (2009). *Transforming school culture: How to overcome staff division.* Solution Tree Press.

Speck, M., & Knipe, C. (2005). *Why can't we get it right? Professional development in our schools.* Corwin Press.

Wang, L., & Wentling, T. L. (2001, March). The relationship between distance coaching and the transfer of training. In Proceedings from the Academy of Human Resource Development Conference. Tulsa, Oklahoma.

Yang, B., Wang, Y., & Drewry, A. W. (2009). Does it matter where to conduct training? Accounting for cultural factors. *Human Resource Management Review*, 19(4), 324–333.

Yelon, S. L., Ford, J. K., & Golden, S. (2013). Transfer over time: Stories about transfer years after training. *Performance Improvement Quarterly*, 25(4), 43–66.

10 Leading for Transformation? The Decisions of New Coaches Matter

Lisa L. Ortmann, Katherine Brodeur and Susan L. Massey

Introduction

Transformational leadership "involves inspiring followers to commit to a shared vision and goals for an organization ... developing followers' leadership capacity via coaching, mentoring, and provision of both challenge and support" (Bass & Riggio, 2006, p. 4). The success of transformational leadership models in K–12 schools hinges on the willingness of teachers, administrators, and other key personnel to engage in capacity building processes. Often these processes look like the "capacity building tools" of teacher leadership teams, small learning communities, professional development institutes, and instructional coaching (Mangin, 2016, p. 945). When schools are committed to teacher transformation, adopting an instructional coaching model focused on the cycle of learning and reflection has shown to be successful. Coaching provides a vehicle of interaction and communication around organizational goals for individual growth, learning, and change (Solansky, 2010). However, too often the coaching model is not designed to leverage the capacity building of a crucial individual: the instructional coach, particularly in the area of engaging teachers in the sometimes-difficult practice of critical reflection (Cranton, 2013).

This case explores the complexities of transformational leadership through the lens of a new coach as she engages in coaching decisions before, during, and after a coaching dialogue, thus highlighting the successes and missed opportunities for supporting a teacher's critical reflection on practice. Transformational leadership hinges on the deep, critical reflection of an individual's professional practice, which coaches are well-positioned to support; however, as middle-level leaders they often face tensions between being attentive to the learning needs of the individual and the programmatic, administrative agenda of the organization (Cox, 2015).

The Case: Stepping into Leadership as a New Coach

Heather had been an elementary teacher for five years at Midway Hills Primary School (grades K–4), a small, predominantly White suburban school in the Midwest, when she first accepted the position of building-level instructional

DOI: 10.4324/9780429331503-13

104   *The Decisions of New Coaches*

coach. The school district administrative team adhered to a transformational model of leadership, including an active professional learning model in which teachers participated in regular workshops on a few targeted initiatives each month, and met in small learning communities (SLCs) to support instructional changes in response to the new initiatives for an hour every week. Heather was a member of her grade-level SLC in which teachers met to plan and reflect on instruction, design common assessments, and analyze student assessment and achievement data for all third graders at their school. The meetings were often facilitated by the grade level team lead or the building reading specialist. While Heather was not the most experienced teacher in the group, veteran colleagues often turned to her for support when implementing new technology or learning a new resource. She enjoyed being helpful, often sharing resources and ideas she garnered from her graduate courses in Reading Education. Her demeanor was friendly and open, and she was regarded as a valuable colleague to many across the school community.

At the end of the school year, Heather's administrator asked her if she would be interested in a new coaching position beginning in the fall. Among the many goals for the instructional coaching initiative, the principal hoped Heather could support teachers in implementing the new literacy curriculum. The selected curriculum emphasized repeated progress monitoring of literacy skills as well as implementing targeted, small group instruction. Flattered and eager to facilitate literacy instructional improvement, she accepted.

Over the summer, she attended a two-week coaching institute with her principal where they both received training by an external facilitator in the district's newly adopted coaching model. In August, she practiced her new coaching skills informally with a close friend and colleague on her grade-level team. Along with three other new coaches in the district, she received an additional two-day training led by the district curriculum coordinator who had experience with the coaching model. There were no additional plans for professional development for new coaches during the school year. By the end of August, Heather was eager to begin her new role and make a difference for students.

One of her first coaching assignments was to support a recently hired fourth grade teacher in learning the new literacy curriculum. Heather knew that Jenny had a few years of experience teaching in another district, but the literacy curriculum and assessment model would be new to her. In the first few weeks of the school year, Heather met individually with Jenny to build relational trust and rapport, which she knew to be an integral first step in any successful coaching relationship. Jenny was happy and eager to learn, and Heather provided helpful resources and tips with the curriculum that supported Jenny in establishing strong classroom routines for literacy. In early September, Heather and the reading specialist worked with Jenny to administer the initial literacy skills assessments. The three of them met several times to review and analyze data to establish initial small groups. By the end of September, Jenny and Heather were both feeling hopeful about their successes thus far in the school year, and Jenny invited

Heather in to observe her class to establish specific professional learning goals related to the literacy curriculum.

Heather was excited to "dive in" to coaching, spending considerable time preparing for their pre-observation conference. She planned to use the district-provided coaching protocol, along with a few pre-planned questions of her own, to help Jenny establish a learning goal and coaching plan. The protocol provided a general outline of questions and prompts to elicit professional goal-setting, but it was not specific to grade levels, content areas, or the literacy reform initiative in the building. One question on Heather's mind after working with Jenny thus far was about Jenny's use of the on-going formative literacy assessments to plan small-group instruction. The new literacy model encouraged fluid grouping of students, rather than static groups based on reading levels, as well as intentional, strategy-based instruction in response to weekly assessment results. She knew flexible grouping would be a big change for Jenny, so she hoped to be supportive; she was also aware her administrator expected all teachers to move away from homogenous ability grouping for reading instruction, which added a little pressure to Heather's coaching plans.

The pre-conference went quickly as some unexpected student concerns kept Jenny busy for the first half of her planning period. Heather was flexible and decided to omit her questions about assessment, determining that adhering to the district-provided protocol would be best. The conversation was comfortable, albeit brief, with Jenny sharing her goals for the upcoming lesson, reflecting that she was unsure if students were successfully applying the reading strategies she had taught during mini-lessons to their independent reading. Heather left the meeting with some ideas for what she might observe and felt confident in her ability to be supportive.

After observing in Jenny's class, Heather was surprised by her own concerns about how Jenny was monitoring student learning. She did not observe students applying any of the reading strategies from the new curriculum to their independent reading, and actually observed many students engaging in off-task behavior when they should have been reading. She also noticed that Jenny had not changed her groups since they were originally created at the beginning of the school year. Heather was nervous about presenting her concerns to Jenny. On the one hand, she didn't want to jeopardize the relationship she had worked so hard to establish; on the other hand, she felt it would be important for Jenny to make some real changes in her teaching. She also had her principal's concerns about leveled groups on the back of her mind. She spent a considerable amount of time preparing for the upcoming post-observation conference, and went into the meeting with anxious anticipation.

HEATHER: (coach): So, you shared with me that one of your objectives for the lesson was seeing how students took the reading strategy you taught in small groups and applied it to their independent reading. How did your students do with this?

106 *The Decisions of New Coaches*

JENNY: (teacher): Students really like the time to read in their independent choice books, and they seemed to really enjoy working with a partner, so I think they were really engaged!

HEATHER: [pause] I know you were planning to use observation to see if they understood the strategies, but what exactly were you looking for?

JENNY: Well, I walked around as they were working to see who got it and who didn't. I did work with a few students who were getting stuck, but most of them worked quietly or asked a partner if they needed help. It's good they were all on-task.

HEATHER: [pause] Okay, so what data were you able to collect during this lesson as evidence that students learned what you wanted them to?

JENNY: I guess I didn't really keep track... [trails off]

HEATHER: What is a system you could use for keeping track of which comprehension skill each student knows?

JENNY: [pause] I am thinking that once a month when we do the benchmark test, I can use it to show students their growth on literal, inferential, and vocabulary questions.

HEATHER: That sounds like a terrific system for your monthly checks. You know, what if you made a copy of that checklist with the dates for when you teach different strategies? During a lesson like this, would it work for you to be able to keep track of which students were able to apply the strategy?

JENNY: Oh yeah, I think that could work. Then I could ask students about the strategies when I have reading conferences with them.

HEATHER: Yes! Asking the students to self-monitor is a valuable way to help them gain independence with the strategies. I am also wondering about how you might use a system like this to rearrange your small groups? One of the goals of this curriculum is to move away from only using leveled groups for reading instruction.

JENNY: Yeah, that's right. But I am finding they are doing really well in their leveled groups, so I'm planning to keep them the same for a while.

HEATHER: I could see that, and I know when I was teaching it was difficult for me to shift to flexible groupings too. The nice thing about tracking student data is that you might start to see opportunities for new groupings that you haven't noticed before. Let's talk about groups again the next time we meet.

JENNY: Sure, we can do that.

Heather left this first coaching cycle with Jenny with mixed feelings. She was relieved that Jenny remained open to discussing her observations of the lesson and open to her suggestions. However, Jenny did not seem to share Heather's concerns or feel the same urgency about making changes to her teaching. Heather was most perplexed by Jenny's limited reflection on students' engagement and learning – she seemed unaware of the off-task behavior that was happening during the lesson. She wondered if there had been places in the conversation where she could have pushed Jenny with a more critical question or if she should have stated directly her observations of off-task student behavior. Unsure of how to proceed with these thoughts, she wished she had someone to talk to who could relate and offer suggestions. She was beginning to realize how much she had relied on her colleagues for support through difficult teaching decisions. Coaching was certainly turning out to be more challenging than she thought.

Discussion

Coaching for Transformation

Burns (1978) described leadership as either transactional or transformational. Transactional leadership focuses on the give-and-take of the leader-follower relationship, while transformational leaders are those who inspire followers to achieve at higher levels and develop their own leadership capacity. The transformational approach aims to create significant change in people's lives as well as within the culture of an organization. According to Burns (1978) transformational leadership relies on developing five leadership competencies of: 1) critical evaluation and problem detection, 2) envisioning creative responses to change, 3) communication skills for conveying a vision, 4) managing self-image, and 5) knowing how and when to empower followers (Conger & Benjamin, 1999, as cited in Bass & Riggio, 2006, p. 150–152). Coaching can be highly effective as a vehicle for developing these competencies at the individual and organizational levels.

Coaching makes use of Schon's (1983; 1987) adult learning theory of reflective practice, conceptualizing *reflection* as the essential component of professional knowledge, as opposed to theoretical knowledge. According to Schon (1983), professionals are dealing with divergent problems of practice that require critical in-the-moment decision-making, so building their capacity for reflection should be an integral part of professional training (p. 50). Since Schon's ground-breaking work in adult learning theory, reflective practice has been conceptualized as an experiential learning cycle, where coaches support client learning through a cycle of identifying a problem, observation of practice, completing analysis of data gathered during the observation, and supporting the client in dialogue and reflection (Osterman & Kottkamp, 2004).

Critics of Schon's work have argued that engaging in the full cycle can be time consuming, and does not capture the in-the-moment reflection that is happening at a much faster rate. Furthermore, the majority of learners are not ready for coaching until the familiarity of their everyday life is interrupted in some way. Mezirow (2000) explained these *disorienting dilemmas* as conflicts that occur and cause an adult to question their own effectiveness. Experiencing a *disorienting dilemma* can become the first phase of the transformation process, and can become an important opening for a coach. When discord between expectation and reality occurs, a client becomes coachable and the potential for some form of change becomes apparent (Cox, 2015). As middle-level

108   *The Decisions of New Coaches*

leaders, recognizing and capturing opportunities for the growth of followers, when they themselves have been followers for so long, can be difficult or uncomfortable. Consider the few possibilities for change that Heather observed in Jenny's classroom. How might she have transformed these observations into disorienting dilemmas for Jenny during the coaching conversation? Although Heather's teaching expertise was useful in identifying potential problems in Jenny's instruction, her knowledge of effective teaching does not directly translate into knowledge of effective coaching. Without opportunities for ongoing professional learning in the initial years of coaching, coaches may lack the means to develop effective facilitation practices in support of teacher transformation and change.

Moving Toward Critical Reflection

Mezirow (1997) argued that adult learning should respect adults' experiences but also offer opportunities to develop a "frame of reference that is more inclusive, discriminating, self-reflective, and integrative of experience" (p. 5). Central to this goal is guiding others through the process of critical reflection. Cranton (2013) described three different types of reflection to inform action: (a) content reflection, where individuals reflect on the description of a problem; (b) process reflection, which involves thinking about the strategies used to solve the problem; and (c) premise reflection, involving questioning the relevance of the problem and the assumptions underlying the problem. The last of these three, premise reflection, can lead to critical reflection and transformational learning. Working together to examine alternative points of view promotes premise reflection that allows the client, with support, to focus on his or her fundamental assumptions rather than to discuss content or process issues, which may not identify the underlying issues at hand. In the context of K–12 schools, Cox (2015) described the coach's role in supporting teacher transformation throughout a number of stages, including the goal of arriving at a "realization that the dilemma is a shared and potentially negotiable experience in the sense that it is a dilemma by interpretation – one that is instigated by outmoded frames of reference" (p. 34). After the teacher arrives at this conclusion, the work of the coach is to explore alternatives to replace the "lost" perspective, plan a course of action, and support reintegrating the new perspective into their work and lives.

In this case, Heather prompted Jenny to engage in *content reflection* first by asking, "How did your students do with this?" She then supported *process reflection* by asking, "What data were you able to provide…?" This question opened-up an opportunity for supporting teacher learning since Jenny acknowledged that she had not considered ways of collecting student learning data on this particular lesson. It makes sense that Heather then provided a suggestion: "What if you made a copy of a similar chart…" However, this could also be seen as an opportunity to dive deeper into the teacher's underlying beliefs and values of assessment with *premise reflection*. Consider if Heather had asked the question, "When you *do* track students' use of the reading strategies, what values about learning does that choice communicate to students?" A conversation about values and assumptions about the assessment of student learning can uncover hidden barriers to change in practice.

Coaching that seeks to support real teacher growth and change requires both careful planning and nimble, in-the-moment decision-making. These kinds of responsive coaching moves must be carefully balanced with any directive stances required by administration, leaders, or initiatives (Ippolito, 2010). As coaches cultivate the collegial relationships that serve as the context for meaningful professional learning, they face the tension of deciding when and how to challenge others to examine the beliefs or premises that may be holding them back from real change. For coaching to be a successful vehicle for transformational models of leadership, coaches will also need continued professional learning and support as they navigate the complexities of coaching practice.

Learning Activities

Discussion Questions

1. Coaches like Heather make many decisions throughout a coaching cycle that shape the dialogue and, hopefully, the teacher's thinking and practice.

    a   Consider the decisions Heather made *before* the coaching session. How did those decisions reflect her own professional learning goals? How did they reflect Jenny's goals? The school district's/administrator's goals? What is the outcome of coaching when those goals are in conflict?

    b   Look back at the transcript of the coaching conversation. What decisions did Heather make *during* the coaching session that provided Jenny an opportunity for reflection? What was the nature of the reflection that was achieved? Where do you see openings for reflection to move beyond a surface-level processing of the content of the lesson? Why might Heather have refrained from pushing for critical reflection?

    c   What decisions might Heather make *after* the coaching session to reconcile her uncertainty about the session? If you were Heather, what would be your next steps to coaching Jenny?

2. If the principal and curriculum coordinator are committed to transformational leadership, how can they continue to support Heather's capacities as a coach while also respecting her autonomy as a leader?

3. According to Cox (2015), learners require disruptions to their everyday life to be ready for coachable changes. What types of situations might lead to readiness for coaching for Jenny? What role (if any) should Heather play in helping Jenny recognize existing conditions that might disrupt Jenny's understanding of her practice?

110   *The Decisions of New Coaches*

Critical Reflection Activity

Have a practice coaching session where you are the coach supporting a peer's learning goal. Write out the questions you plan to ask and topics you want to address during the coaching. Video or audio record your conversation. After viewing/listening to the recording, reflect on the coaching you did. To what degree did you stay on track with your plan? How natural did the conversation sound and feel? How did it feel for your peer/colleague? Where did your peer/colleague cue for support? How did you respond? Were there places in the conversation where you felt you could have pushed for critical reflection but you chose not to? If so, what held you back?

References

Aguilar, E. (2013). *The art of coaching: Effective strategies for school transformation*. Wiley Publishers.

Bean, R. & Ippolito, J. (2016). *Cultivating coaching mindsets: An action guide for literacy leaders*, 1st ed. Learning Sciences International.

Knight, J. (2015). *Better conversations: Coaching ourselves and each other to be more credible, caring, and connected*. SAGE Publications.

Pletcher, B. C., Hudson, A. K., & Watson, K. (2019). "I want to learn from them as much as I want them to learn from me": Finding a balance of coaching and consulting through the analysis of a literacy coach's conversations. *Reading Horizons: A Journal of Literacy and Language Arts*, 58(1), 48–74.

Robertson, D. A., Padesky, L. B., Ford-Connors, E., & Paratore, J. R. (2020). What does it mean to say coaching is relational? *Journal of Literacy Research*, 52(1), 55–78.

Bass, B. M., & Riggio, R. E. (2006). *Transformational Leadership* (2nd ed.) Lawrence Erlbaum Associates.

Bates, C. C., & Morgan, D. N. (2018). Literacy leadership: The importance of soft skills. *The Reading Teacher*, 72(3), 412–415. doi:10.1002/trtr.1755

Burns, J. M. (1978). *Leadership*. Harper & Row.

Cox, E. (2015). Coaching and adult learning: Theory and practice. *New Directions for Adult and Continuing Education*, (148), 27–38. doi:10.1002/ace.20149

Cranton, P. (2013). Transformative learning. In P. Mayo (Ed.), *Learning with adults: A reader*, (pp. 267–274). Sense Publishers.

Ippolito, J. (2010). Three ways that literacy coaches balance responsive and directive relationships with teachers. *The Elementary School Journal*, 111(1), 164–190.

Mangin, M. M. (2016). Teacher leadership and high-stakes teacher evaluation: Complementary or conflicting approaches to improvement? *Journal of School Leadership*, 26, 938–974.

Mezirow, J. (1991). *Transformative dimensions of adult learning*. Jossey-Bass.

Mezirow, J. (1997). Transformative learning: Theory to practice. *New Directions for Adult and Continuing Education*, (74), 5–12. https://doi.org/10.1002/ace.7401.

Mezirow, J. (2000). *Learning as transformation: Critical perspectives on a theory in progress*. Jossey-Bass.

Osterman, K. F., & Kottkamp, R. B. (2004). *Reflective practice for educators: Professional development to improve student learning* (2nd ed.). Corwin Press.

Peterson, D. S., Taylor, B. M., Burnham, B., & Schock, R. (2009). Reflective coaching conversations: A missing piece. *The Reading Teacher, 62*(6), 500–509.

Schneider, A., & Ingram, H. (1990). Behavioral assumptions of policy tools. *The Journal of Politics, 52*(2), 510–529.

Schon, D. A. (1983). *The reflective practitioner: How professionals think in action.* Basic Books.

Schon, D. A. (1987). *Educating the reflective practitioner: Toward a new design for teaching and learning in the professions.* Jossey-Bass.

Showers, B. (1984). *Peer coaching: A strategy for facilitating transfer of training.* Center for Educational Policy and Management, University of Oregon.

Showers, B., & Joyce, B. (1996). The evolution of peer coaching. *Educational Leadership, 53*(6), 12–16.

Solansky, S. T. (2010). The evaluation of two key leadership development program components: Leadership skills assessment and leadership mentoring. *The Leadership Quarterly, 21*(4), 675–681.

11 We Can Do This!
Transformational Leadership for School Improvement

Jeremy D. Visone

Introduction

Transformational leadership, involving leaders' behaviors that inspire followers' intrinsic motivation to perform beyond expectations, has been studied for several decades (Bass, 1985; Mason et al., 2014; Northouse & Lee, 2019). This case explores the intersection of transformational leadership practices, professional learning, and social capital in a school setting. Transformative leaders engender trusting relationships with followers and help facilitate collective purpose (Northouse & Lee, 2019). Further, these leaders provide opportunities for intellectual stimulation (Bass, 1985). By focusing on trusting relationships and creating a foundation for collective learning, social capital – the totality of interactions among individuals in an organization – can be enhanced (Hargreaves & Fullan, 2012, 2013). Improvements in social capital, in turn, may positively impact student achievement (Leana, 2011; Learning Forward, 2020).

Case

Susan B. Anthony Elementary School[1] (SBA) was situated in an industrial zone and isolated from its suburban community's more affluent neighborhoods. Comparing SBA with another, similarly-sized school on the wealthier side of town, Riverside Elementary School (RS), SBA's students displayed greater need: children who were not yet proficient in English (35 students at SBA versus 3 at RS), families whose lower incomes qualified their children for free and reduced lunch rates (31 percent at SBA versus 20 percent at RS), and increased behavioral challenges (over 500 documented behavior incidents at SBA versus less than 200 at RS). Unlike RS, SBA was a Title I school, a federal designation that reflected its higher population of economically underprivileged students when compared with other district schools. The region of town serviced by SBA was adjacent to an economically depressed city, and a sizable SBA neighborhood (representing about 25 percent of SBA's population) was only accessible by driving through the neighboring urban area. Like its adjacent city, this SBA neighborhood consisted of duplex and multi-family homes clustered together. These homes typically sold for roughly

DOI: 10.4324/9780429331503-14

half the price of the single-family homes found in RS neighborhoods. Further, many families from the isolated SBA neighborhood rented their homes, as opposed to families in RS neighborhoods, who owned their homes, resulting in increased transience for families served by SBA. Additionally, SBA educated nearly 500 students, almost twice as many as RS's 270. Yet each district school was allotted the same number of support positions such as nurses, psychologists, and reading interventionists. Thus, SBA serviced its needier population with fewer resources per child.

On district- and state-wide academic assessments, RS scores would consistently top the district list, with 75–85 percent of students typically meeting proficiency. Conversely, SBA's scores were regularly last or second-to-last, at 60–70 percent students meeting proficiency levels. Further, RS kindergarten early literacy scores usually displayed about 80 percent student proficiency, whereas SBA scores typically demonstrated student proficiency rates of 50–60 percent. For SBA, the inability to escape lowered expectations and complacency with poor student outcomes seemed its destiny.

SBA teachers taught, and, with mixed success, students learned. From any outsider's perspective, the staff would have been described as caring and professional. Teachers collaborated formally during weekly grade level meetings where they discussed student data and curricular matters. Informally, teachers would share lesson ideas with each other.

Ann Knowles was a veteran educator, serving as principal of SBA for a decade. Ann was respected and well-liked by all. She recognized her teachers were hard working. She, in turn, provided teachers the structures they needed to run an efficient and organized operation. Ann was also a curricular leader, and engaged teachers in discussions on what they believed were effective strategies for SBA students. During grade level meetings, Ann shared student assessment data and facilitated analysis conversations. "Let's see how your students did on the reading benchmark," she would begin. "Where have your students succeeded? What do you need to adjust?" She would then suggest instructional strategies. "I think you should try this," she would advise. Teachers would implement Ann's suggestions. They generally trusted her judgment because she provided useful instructional strategies and ran an efficient school. The teachers rarely needed more than what Ann provided.

Jenn Turley was transferred from a middle school assistant principal position across town to become principal of SBA when Ann retired. Jenn had no elementary experience, which raised eyebrows, as SBA teachers wondered whether this "middle school person" would have the ability to lead their school. Additionally, Jenn's middle school was on the *wealthier* side of town, serving former students from RS and another lower-need school. Many SBA teachers wondered how Jenn would relate to challenges faced in *their* context.

In the summer following Ann's retirement, Jenn attempted to learn about her staff at SBA. She asked each teacher to respond to the following three prompts:

114 *Leadership for School Improvement*

1. What works well here?
2. What needs to change?
3. Recognize three colleagues for something they do well.

Teachers' feedback was helpful. First, Jenn found that staff members' dedication to their students "worked well." Second, the manner in which work was accomplished needed to change. Teachers were working too hard in isolation and wanted more opportunity to collaborate. The staff also did not believe they were included enough in decision making. Third, as Jenn hoped, every single teacher at SBA was recognized by at least one colleague; Jenn used this information to place a recognition note in each teacher's mailbox.

When Jenn examined student achievement data longitudinally, she quickly discerned the consistent pattern of SBA ranking last or second-to-last when compared to the district's other schools. District leaders frequently discussed these data with principals. During a summer meeting of the Administrative Council, Assistant Superintendent Janet Holliway asked all principals, "Given the spring scores we just examined, what are your plans for improvement?"

RS's principal, James Yessip, offered, "I will share these data with my teachers, and we will discuss what we did, curriculum-wise, that was successful. We will also discuss what didn't work. Then we will adjust accordingly." Jenn listened passively to the other principals' ideas, as she contemplated her improvement strategy.

To begin the new school year, Jenn shared the previous spring's data with staff during her first-ever faculty meeting as principal. Aggregate data were included in her presentation, and teachers received their individual student data. Like James Yessip's plan, Jenn asked teachers to reflect: "I would like you all to examine your individual and grade level datasets. Please find the treasures and areas for focus." After some small-group discussion and paper shuffling, a veteran Grade 2 teacher, Stephanie Childress, raised her hand.

"Jenn, I don't want to be disrespectful, but you just need to know … things are different here on *this* side of town. Our kids cannot do what they do over on the other side. Parents are not as supportive here, either. We barely get a majority of parents at conferences. We don't get kindergarteners that are already reading because parents can't – *or won't* – read to their kids at home. So many of our kids don't even know what school letters are when they start here. I have so many struggling readers to start each year, it is playing catch-up from the beginning, and I can tell these parents a thousand times what to do to help their kids at home, but they just don't. There is just so much more money and investment by the parents over there that we cannot compete with. Central office is always throwing it back at us that we don't get the scores that they get across town. Well, we shouldn't be expected to get the same results." As Stephanie finished speaking, Jenn could see a few other teachers' heads nodding in agreement. Most teachers, though, sat in stunned silence. Jenn inhaled deeply.

"Thanks for your perspective, Stephanie. It seems we have some work to do … "

Jenn's Solution

A few weeks later, at the next faculty meeting, Jenn shared her expectation that teachers consider themselves *leaders* and that their collective work should be guided by the following three principles: *empowerment, collegiality*, and *risk taking*. Teachers were already working together in some informal and formal ways, such as grade level meetings, but Jenn wanted to increase collaboration quality and quantity. For example, to provide more time for collaboration, she altered schedules to increase common planning time from once or twice a week to at least four times a week. Also, within weekly grade level meetings, she told teachers that they should not avoid reasonable instructional risks. "We will never get anywhere different from where we are if we do what we have always done" she told her faculty.

When having conversations about SBA data relative to other district schools, she politely, but consistently, asked teachers how SBA's own student achievement could improve. Rather than focusing on comparing SBA to other schools, she asked teachers to concentrate on "moving each child forward from where he or she is." Jenn asked for teachers' ideas, never hiding that her expertise was at the secondary level, and the *teachers* were the elementary experts. She called herself the "Number One Learner" at SBA, and manifested this disposition by regularly visiting classrooms, participating in book studies alongside staff, co-teaching lessons with teachers, and asking teachers how they accomplished their work. She referred to the staff as a "team" and frequently used the pronouns "we," "us," and "our."

To operationalize her "team," Jenn asked teachers to volunteer for teams designed to assist with leadership decision making. These included a School-Wide Data Team, Leadership Team, Teaching and Learning Team (TLT), Crisis Team, and Positive Behavioral Support Team. Each team drafted a purpose statement during its first meeting. See Figure 11.1 for a sample purpose statement.

As seen in Figure 11.1, the TLT outlined one of its main charges as leading the school's adult learning in order to improve SBA's student learning. Meanwhile, the School-Wide Data Team's purpose included crafting and monitoring the school improvement plan and its various student achievement goals and action steps. Jenn organized the relationships among different teams' functions into relatable visuals, such as the school improvement planning organizer shown in Figure 11.2, so all teachers would be able to visualize how their work within teams contributed to the school's larger purposes.

When Jenn's teams made suggestions, so long as the input was within reason and aligned with school goals, she listened and implemented the ideas. For example, the TLT launched a math problem solving initiative, which one of the team members had researched online, whereby all students in the school worked collaboratively over the course of a week on a common, challenging, and open-ended math problem that was differentiated by grade level. Thus, the entire school spoke about a common math experience several times

Purpose Statement: *Teaching and Learning Team*

In accordance with our *Mission Statement*:

- We help our students receive "rigorous and relevant learning experiences."
- We help our students obtain "the knowledge, skills, and attitudes necessary to succeed in a dynamic, competitive global society."
- We help ensure that our experiences "challenge students to become active problem solvers and creative, critical thinkers."

In support of our academic *School Improvement Goals*:

- By focusing on school improvement from an instructional/curricular perspective, we help to maximize our students' learning and growth.

To accomplish our *Purpose*, we:

- represent all grade levels in the school;
- use student data to make decisions about teaching and learning;
- help organize and facilitate professional learning experiences for staff;
- make decisions about instructional matters within the bounds of our curricula;
- provide feedback about curricula for the district to consider; and
- communicate our work back to the teams we represent.

Figure 11.1 Purpose statement for the Teaching and Learning Team at SBA.

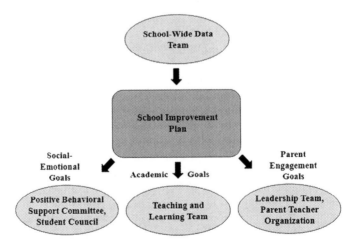

Figure 11.2 Team Relationship Organizer about School Improvement Planning

per year, and students could learn from one another's critical thinking and creativity. Work from these rigorous problems was displayed around the school and via the school's news network.

The TLT also requested a professional learning structure through which teachers could learn by observing one another's teaching practices. Thus, Jenn created *collegial visits*. Planning these visits began with the TLT examining the school improvement plan to determine an area of focus. For example, the math workshop method of instruction was an early focus. Next, one teacher in each grade level volunteered to host her colleagues to view a lesson, after a few weeks of experimenting with the selected focus area. The TLT also created guiding questions, which focused visiting teachers' attention while in their colleague's classroom. The questions helped guide the visiting team's debriefing session after the *collegial visit* to a peer's classroom. Jenn always participated in these classroom visits so she could learn alongside her teachers.

With regard to her guiding principle of risk taking, Jenn regularly shared the results of her own goals, which came from the school improvement plan and her evaluation from her supervisor, Janet Holliway. The results of these goals were often positive. Other times, however, Jenn did not meet her goals. She explained to teachers that it was acceptable to fail sometimes, and small setbacks helped improve her practice. When teachers did not meet their evaluation goals, Jenn did not chastise them. Rather, she asked teachers what these missed targets had taught them, as well as what next steps could be undertaken together to achieve improved future results.

During everyday interactions, Jenn listened thoughtfully and followed through on what she promised. When asked a question, Jenn wrote herself a note, which prompted her to communicate back to the inquiring teacher. Jenn was visible and connected with students, learning each student's name, as well as the majority of parents' names, and her warm style was evident in all interactions with parents, no matter the parents' dispositions. Consistently, Jenn modeled clear communication, a positive demeanor, humor, and humility.

Over time, teachers at SBA began to exhibit Jenn's values. For example, teachers would often speak about their teamwork and what they were achieving together, rather than their individual successes. At grade level meetings, teachers shared about grade-level successes and challenges, and teachers identified struggling students across a grade, often rearranging students among classrooms to create targeted intervention groups. Jenn's faculty began to take the habit of being first to volunteer during district-wide professional learning workshops offered by the district's central office. Jenn saw this as a way her teachers were manifesting their leadership. As teachers became more confident in Jenn's support of their room to experiment with instructional approaches, SVA teachers increasingly shared new and innovative ideas for how they might improve student learning.

As further evidence of the transformation at SBA – in terms of adult collaboration and collective learning – Jenn entered a classroom to observe, only to find a second teacher already there to observe. This situation was outside the formal collegial visits structure, and Jenn understood that this informal peer observation was an indicator that teachers viewed each other as

118 *Leadership for School Improvement*

resources. Most importantly, the children of SBA saw benefits, as well. SBA rose from second-to-last or last to first across many district assessments, eventually earning the distinction of a National Blue Ribbon School, within six years of Jenn taking over the principalship.

Supporting Literature Discussion

Transformational leadership has been of interest to scholars and leadership practitioners for decades. Transformational leaders inspire followers to exceed expectations and buy into larger organizational purposes, and there is evidence to suggest transformational leadership is associated with followers' intrinsic motivation (Bass, 1985; Mason et al., 2014; Northouse & Lee, 2019). To help followers realize their collective potential, transformational leaders exhibit qualities and behaviors to positively influence them. These include communicating clearly, empowering followers, possessing high expectations, engendering trust, modeling desired behaviors, and building collective purpose (Northouse & Lee, 2019). Bass (1985) shared an informative model that describes four factors of transformational leadership: idealized influence, inspirational motivation, intellectual stimulation, and individualized consideration. In the context of schools, transformational leaders provide space for teachers to learn and grow, particularly through creating intellectual safety and trust in leadership and each other (Zamarripa, 2014).

Many characteristics of transformational leadership are embedded within the case of SBA's turnaround. Jenn Turley communicated clearly to her teachers about her expectation that they view themselves as leaders, how individual efforts within the team system would contribute to larger purposes, and that teachers should focus more on moving individual students forward than comparing results with other schools. Teachers were empowered by Jenn's three guiding principles, participative team system, and her practice of listening to teachers' improvement ideas, which would also, potentially, increase teachers' trust in her leadership. High expectations were communicated when Jenn asserted that her teachers were to be leaders. Jenn modeled appropriate, constructive interactions with parents. She also displayed a learning disposition by participating in collegial visits and book clubs alongside staff and calling herself SBA's "Number One Learner." She built collective purpose through the guiding statements generated by each team.

Bass's (1985) four factors are more abstract, so asking her teachers about the factors' realization in Jenn's leadership might be necessary. However, one manifestation of inspirational motivation is leadership displayed by teachers outside of Jenn's presence. Also, she created a structure to provide intellectual stimulation via the TLT's work, including collegial visits. The implementation of this structure likely led to Jenn's finding a teacher observing a colleague on her own time.

To realize school transformation, adult learning and development are required. The juxtaposition of transformational leadership and adult learning and development is natural, given Bass's (1985) reference to intellectual stimulation. Further, Boydell's (2016) adult development continuum includes as its highest levels *connecting* and *dedicating*, which each include dispositions and actions consistent with both adult learning theory and transformational leadership. First, while *connecting*, Boydell stated that individuals seek to work with multiple stakeholders to solve complex problems using many perspectives. At this level, collaboration and collective purpose are evident, which were manifested in the case through Jenn's system of teams and their purpose statements. Second, in the *dedicating* mode, individuals again cooperate with many other stakeholders to solve problems, but individuals balance their own personal interests with those of others, again, displaying the collaboration and collective purpose of adult learning and transformational leadership. The case included the SBA teachers displaying leadership efforts without Jenn present to indicate their commitment to her vision of leadership expectations.

Adult learning, considered *professional learning* in PreK–12 education, is a key vehicle for improving teaching practices (Drago-Severson & Blum-DeStefano, 2014) and student achievement (Learning Forward, 2020). The *Standards for Professional Learning* (Standards; Learning Forward, 2020) call for opportunities for professional learning to be embedded throughout the school year, deeply connected to the daily work of teachers, driven by data, and requiring active participation. Consider here Jenn's plan for the TLT to use the School Improvement Plan to create learning experiences, including collegial visits, where teachers would learn from observing each other. The Standards indicate that independent learning of teachers is not enough for whole-school success. Thus, connecting with the need to build a collective purpose required for transformational leadership, professional learning for teachers should be collaborative and rely on the expertise of teachers (such as in the case of the TLT and collegial visits), who possess meaningful insights and have greater motivation to learn when their specific learning needs and preferences are considered (DeWitt, 2017; Learning Forward, 2020).

The need for teachers to work and learn together has been outlined by research about *social capital* in schools (Hargreaves & Fullan, 2012, 2013), which can be defined as the totality of interactions between an organization's individuals. Jenn attempted to increase both the frequency of teacher collaboration opportunities (through adding common planning time and creating a system of teams) and the quality of their interactions (through collegial visits and team purpose statements). Connecting to transformational leadership, social capital also involves trusting relationships and collaboration with one another, and these prerequisites are complex and take time and intentional leadership to develop (Drago-Severson & Blum-DeStefano, 2014; Zamarripa, 2014). Schools with higher degrees of social capital achieve better student results (Hargreaves & Fullan, 2012, 2013), so Jenn's efforts to improve collaboration and teamwork are consistent with research about improving school outcomes. Further, teachers whose students do not achieve as well as their colleagues' students, but work in schools with higher degrees of social capital, can improve to the level of their average-performing colleagues by nature of

120   *Leadership for School Improvement*

the learning they experience in a collegial and trusting environment (Leana, 2011). Thus, Jenn's strategies have the potential to improve the practice of her least effective teachers.

Discussion Questions

1. Think about your organization (i.e., school, business, health care organization, government agency, non-profit entity, etc.).

    a   What parallels can you draw among the leadership styles of Ann Knowles, Jenn Turley, and leaders you know?
    b   Further, what leadership styles have you found to be more effective in motivating people to improve?
    c   Why do you think some of these methods and strategies are more effective than others?

2. How would you articulate the underlying dilemma(s) in this case?

3. *Transformational leadership* was described above as a means to inspire followers and increase their intrinsic motivation, improving buy-in for collective purposes, often resulting in followers exceeding expectations. Did Jenn Turley inspire her teachers or increase their intrinsic motivation to address the underlying dilemma(s) you identified in Question 2? If so, in what specific ways did she do so? If not, what could she have done more effectively?

4. Predict what might happen if Jenn Turley were to leave SBA. In other words, extend the case to consider how her strategies might have impacted the school after her departure.

5. *Professional learning* for teachers is characterized in contemporary standards as embedded throughout the school year, deeply connected to the daily work of teachers, driven by data, and requiring active participation. Evaluate the quality of Jenn Turley's strategies to provide her teachers with professional learning that meets the expectations of these standards.

6. What leadership takeaways can you identify from this case? How can leadership in your context be altered to reflect your learning (i.e., what leadership strategies will you adopt, discontinue, modify, etc.)?

Note

1   All names are pseudonyms.

References

Hargreaves, A., & Fullan, M. (2012). *Professional capital: Transforming teaching in every school.* Teachers College Press.

Learning Forward. (2020). *Standards for professional learning.* https://learningforward.org/standards-for-professional-learning

Bass, B. M. (1985). *Leadership and performance beyond expectations.* Free Press.

Boydell, T. (2016). Facilitation of adult development. *Adult Learning*, 27(1), 7–15. doi:10.1177/1045159515615111

DeWitt, P. M. (2017). *Collaborative leadership: 6 influences that matter most.* Corwin Press.

Drago-Severson, E., & Blum-DeStefano, J. (2014). Leadership for transformational learning: A developmental approach to supporting leaders' thinking and practice. *Journal of Research on Leadership Education*, 9(2) 113–141.

Hargreaves, A., & Fullan, M. (2012). *Professional capital: Transforming teaching in every school.* Teachers College Press.

Hargreaves, A., & Fullan, M. (2013). The power of professional capital: With an investment in collaboration, teachers become nation builders. *Journal of Staff Development*, 34(3), 36–39.

Leana, C. R. (2011). The missing link in school reform. *Stanford Social Innovation Review*, 9(4), 30–35.

Learning Forward. (2020). *Standards for professional learning.* https://learningforward.org/standards-for-professional-learning

Mason, C., Griffin, M., & Parker, S. (2014). Transformational leadership development: Connecting psychological and behavioral change. *Leadership & Organization Development Journal*, 35(3), 174–194. doi:10.1108/LODJ-05-2012-0063

Northouse, P. G., & Lee, M. (2019). *Leadership case studies in education* (2nd ed.). Sage.

Zamarripa, G. G. (2015). *Creating transformational learning opportunities for teachers: How leadership affects adult learning on a school campus* [Doctoral dissertation, University of Southern California]. University of Southern California Digital Library. doi:10.25549/usctheses-c3-439860

12 Because They Are Worth It

Utilizing Servant Leadership to Increase First Generation College Persistence

Alexis N. Hartley and Sonya D. Hayes

Introduction

Although fictional, this case is based on a real-life experience of a university academic advisor and focuses on the challenges that academic advisors have as informal leaders working with students within higher education institutions. This case is relevant as it highlights the challenges that first generation college students (FGCS) face in pursuing a four-year degree and the realities that academic advisors have in helping FGCS overcome these challenges. The case also highlights the informal leadership role advisors have in working with students and the ethical dilemmas they face in balancing institutional pressure and time demands with the advising needs of their students. The case narrative illuminates an academic advising session between an overworked academic advisor and a FGCS on the verge of dropping out of college due to financial and family concerns. Drawing upon social capital theory (Coleman, 1988; Putnam, 1995) and servant leadership (Greenleaf, 1977), the reader is asked to analyze the case and determine whether or not the actions of the academic advisor exhibit the qualities of servant leadership and are in the best interest of the student.

Case Story

The University of Nashville is a large public university in the south and has historically faced public scrutiny for its lack of student support services for under-resourced students and for high dropout rates among low-income FGCS. In response, the new Chancellor has an aggressive goal of improving graduation rates for FGCS to 90 percent by 2025. Due to lack of funding by the state, the Chancellor has also reduced the student support services budget (i.e., tutoring services, academic advisors, admissions personnel, financial aid representatives, and student engagement program funding) by 20 percent and eliminated the career exploration and planning department. To combat the lack of funding and support for the new initiative to increase the graduation rate for under-resourced students, administrators implemented a new advising model to help ensure student success. This model focuses on all students attending the university and has three major components: student self-

DOI: 10.4324/9780429331503-15

discovery, academic planning, and career exploration. Advisors were given increased responsibility to assist their advisees with self-discovery through mechanisms such as personality tests, exploration of values and academic goals, career exploration, specialized one-on-one academic advising, and holistic support tailored to each student's individual needs.

Realities of Academic Advising

Jessa Jones is 35 years old and has been an advisor at the university for five years. She is under pressure from upper administration to increase student persistence and graduation rates for low-income FGCS. The new advising model has increased her advising caseload from 200 to 350 students, and with the increase of duties and number of students, she has reduced the amount of time allowed for each appointment to 30 minutes so she can have time to meet with each student. Unfortunately, Jessa has found 30 minutes to be an inadequate amount of time to effectively build the necessary relationship with each student to help them with personal details such as self-discovery.

Jessa became an advisor so she could help students feel as though they matter and belong so they can thrive and succeed in college. She recalls that at her own college graduation, her advisor of four years introduced himself to her as if they were complete strangers. Jessa does not want this experience for any of her advisees. Due to her frustration over the new advising model, she decided to attend a professional development conference conducted by the National Academic Advising Association (NACADA), where she learned that academic advising leadership is a unique type of servant leadership. Academic advising leadership is best utilized when the advisor prioritizes the needs of each student to promote the student's academic success above the self-interest of the institution. Jessa is excited by this idea and all the possible ways she can implement this leadership style in her advising practice.

Journey of a First Generation Student

Taylor is a 21-year-old FGCS. She began her college journey at the University of Nashville as a public relations major. The day she left for college her mother told her, "College is not for people like us. College will only leave you in debt you will have to pay back the rest of your life, for what? There is no guarantee you will even finish or get a job after. You should just take that job as a secretary with your cousin at the doctor's office. It is a good job with benefits. Don't waste your time with college."

Taylor knows what she wants, and she wants to work in dazzling New York City as part of the fashion industry. It is what she has dreamed of since she was a little girl watching *Project Runway* with all the chic clothes, fancy lights, and prestige. She is terrified to leave home without the support of her mother, but it is something she must do for herself.

124 *Because They Are Worth It*

Taylor was able to get a small scholarship to pay for her tuition, but it does not cover living expenses. She has to work full time as a waitress at a local sports bar to cover rent, car payment, and groceries. She is also helping to support her family because her mom is ill and cannot work. Taylor has the only car in the family and provides transportation for her mother to attend doctor's appointments, which always turns out to be two to three days a week because of her mother's illness. She also provides transportation for family errands like grocery shopping. If her family needs anything, Taylor is always right there to help. It is how she was raised: family first, always.

As a student, Taylor has a positive, down-to-earth attitude and has consistently maintained a grade point average of 2.9. She absolutely loves her public relations courses. She enjoys learning about how to write press releases, organize events, and talk to people in a professional setting. She was encouraged by her advisor to connect with the Public Relations Student Society of America (PRSSA) to help her achieve her career goal and make friends. She joined PRSSA in her second semester, and within the last year she has already received an invitation from PRSSA to be an intern during New York Fashion Week next year. Although she has not made many friends and often feels like an outsider, she is succeeding in her goals toward a career in the fashion industry.

However, lately she is contemplating leaving college. The stress of having to take care of her family and balance her school responsibilities is becoming too much to handle. It would be a dream come true to intern at New York Fashion Week, but she does not think this is a realistic opportunity for her. She cannot afford to travel to New York, and her family would struggle without her. She is heartbroken and feels like she must give up on this opportunity. Under the heartbreak, having to work full time, and stress of her responsibility to her family, Taylor's grades start to deteriorate, especially in her Spanish class. She hates having to learn a foreign language. "Why do I have to learn something I will never use?" Taylor asks herself. She is ready to give up on Spanish, on college, on her dreams.

Leadership Through Academic Advising

Taylor and Jessa are meeting today for their semi-annual academic advising appointment. When Taylor arrives for her routine appointment, Jessa greets her.

JESSA: Well good morning Taylor! What is going on? How can I help you today?

TAYLOR: Well Ms. Jessa, classes this semester are going okay, but I am really struggling in Spanish. Do I even really need this course to graduate?

JESSA: Unfortunately, you do. It is a degree requirement for your major. What about Spanish is giving you a hard time?

TAYLOR: Well, I just feel like no matter how much I study I never understand the material. Plus, the class is taught in Spanish. How am I supposed to understand what is going on if I can't even understand what the instructor is saying?

JESSA: Yes, I see how that would be tough. I can tell you several years ago the instructors for foreign languages determined that students learn and retain more of the language if it is taught through immersion. That means the instructors will always teach in the language you are taking. But, having taken a German course and two semesters of American sign language during my undergrad years, I do understand how difficult it can be to learn a language this way. Did you know about or have you tried the foreign language tutoring center or at my alma mater. They had a "coffee and conversation" for each language at a designated time once a week. Have you tried anything like that?

TESSA: Yeah, I saw flyers about the coffee hours. They are always on Wednesday and Friday nights at 6:00 PM. To pay for my tuition this year I had to pick up a second job waitressing. Nights and weekends are mandatory for me since I am only part-time and my boss will work around my school schedule during the weekdays. Financial aid just is not enough to pay my tuition and still be able to pay my rent and food.

JESSA: That is a hard situation, but I am glad your boss is willing to work around your school schedule. What about the foreign language tutoring center? They are open during the week. Any way you can stop in between other classes while you are on campus? That way you do not have to make a special trip.

TESSA: I mean, I can try. But I only have two breaks during the week. On Tuesday and Thursday, I have a break at 12:00–1:30 which is the only chance I have to eat on those days. Monday, Wednesdays, and Fridays I have a break between 2–4. But on Mondays and Fridays I have to take my mother to doctors' appointments and drive her for her weekly errands since I have the only car in the family. My mom is constantly on my case about wasting my time in college. If I do not help her during the week I am afraid she would just lecture me more about how I am abandoning the family and how college is a waste of time. Then on Wednesdays, I run the youth group at my church. Church is a very important part of who I am so I can't give that up.

JESSA: Okay, well this course is required for you to graduate so we need to come up with a plan to ensure you can have a successful semester. How can I help you? What are some other ways I can support you during this difficult time?

TAYLOR: I don't know what to do. You just don't understand. I am barely passing my classes, and I have so many things on my plate all the time. PRSSA offered me an internship during fashion week and I just can't afford that. I honestly just need to quit college so I can take care of my family and work a realistic job. My mom was right – this college thing is a waste of my time.

126 *Because They Are Worth It*

Discussion

In the United States, 33 percent of higher education students are FGCS (RTI International, 2019). Many FGCS face financial, psychological, and academic challenges in a university setting, and they need advising and support to stay in college and graduate. Academic advisors are called upon to increase the graduation rates of FGCS and support them through the barriers and challenges that first generation students encounter. This case examines the complexities academic advisors face when providing guidance to FGCS and encourages dialogue among students in leadership programs about social capital and servant leadership.

Supporting Literature

Earning a college degree continues to be a "critical pathway to economic and social mobility in the United States" (Garriott et al., 2015, p. 253). FGCS, commonly defined as students who do not have at least one parent with a Bachelor's degree (Nguyen & Nguyen, 2018), face different challenges pursuing higher education than their continuing-education peers. Generally speaking, FGCS come from lower-income families (Engle & Tinto, 2008), hold a job off-campus (Walpole, 2003), lack social capital (Pascarella et al., 2004), and have higher college dropout rates (DeAngelo et al., 2011). Additionally, FGCS report decreased levels of social support, life satisfaction, and increased levels of depression and traumatic stress (Jenkins et al., 2005). Despite these challenges FGCS pursue a college degree with hopes of achieving financial security and upward mobility (Lohfink & Paulsen, 2005). In the United States, 33 percent of higher education students are FGCS (RTI International, 2019), but the retention rate of FGCS is low. Six years after first entering post-secondary education, 56 percent of FGCS have not earned their degree (RTI International, 2019).

Academic Advising

With low completion rates nationwide, higher education institutions have focused on implementing high-impact practices to improve student perseverance, such as academic advising (Smith & Allen, 2006). Academic advising provides key support to FGCS along their pathways through the higher education system (Frost, 2003). Active student participation in academic advising is key to fostering successful outcomes such as graduation from the university and the successful pursuit of a career (Crookston, 1994). A well-functioning academic advising program can increase feelings of student self-efficacy, student commitment towards the university, and student retention rates (Vianden & Barlow, 2015). Moreover, an academic advisor can develop a positive relationship and provide additional support for FGCS through the use of interpersonal leadership skills such as: a) empathy during times of crisis; b) listening to understand the student's perspective; c) awareness of additional supports for the student as necessary; d) persuasion in an effort help the student achieve their goals; e) building of a community within the higher education system; and f) a commitment to assist the student grow and develop during their time in college.

Social Capital

Social capital is defined as the effective functioning of groups through interpersonal relationships, a shared sense of identity, a shared understanding, shared norms, and shared values (Coleman, 1988). In the context of higher education, social capital is considered the norms and knowledge of college. Higher education institutions promote specific values, norms, and language that are often unfamiliar to FGCS (Jury et al., 2015). Since first generation students have not experienced the university culture, it is foreign to them; consequently, they lack social capital and have greater difficulty adapting in a university setting than their continuing education peers. Additionally, parents of FGCS typically lack personal knowledge about the college environment and are unable to understand some of the stressors their children encounter while in college (Bryan & Simmons, 2009). Many FGCS report feeling as though they are living dual lives between their college life and their home life (Lohfink & Paulsen, 2005).

During the transition into higher education for FGCS, it is important for university personnel (e.g., academic advisors) to encourage social and academic integration that respects the background and experiences of FGCS (Jehangir et al., 2012). Braxton and Hirschy (2004) developed a model derived from Tinto's (1975) *interactionalist* model of student retention in college that includes the influence of integration (assimilation into college) for students. Braxton and Hirschy highlight that the university's commitment to student welfare (based on student perception) is a significant influence on social integration. Their findings suggest that universities should collaborate with students to support them in attaining academic and social integration, which in turn, supports student retention in the university setting. Integration allows for the accumulation of social capital, which improves academic achievement and predicts persistence (Strayhorn, 2010). By investing time and developing meaningful relationships with FGCS, academic advisors provide additional guidance and resources to support FGCS in developing and increasing their social capital within higher education.

Servant Leadership

Servant leadership is a leadership philosophy where leaders are called upon to serve others and prioritize the needs of others (Greenleaf, 1977). Servant leaders do not necessarily serve in formal leadership roles. Servant leadership occurs when an individual puts aside their own self-interest or the interest of

128 *Because They Are Worth It*

the organization and focuses on the needs of others. Spears (1995) argues that there are ten major attributes of servant leadership:

1. Listening
2. Empathy
3. Healing
4. Awareness
5. Persuasion
6. Conceptualization
7. Foresight
8. Stewardship
9. Commitment to the growth of people
10. Building community (p. 6)

Throughout his writings on higher education, Greenleaf asserted that "universities had lost sight of their purpose, which he believed was to serve the needs of students" (Frick, 2004, p. 14). Academic advisors exhibit servant leadership though constructs such as listening, awareness, foresight, and persuasion (Paul et al., 2012). Paul et al. (2012) explain that "[advisors] can empower students to become active learners and participants in their educational endeavors" (p. 55). As servant leaders, advisors are driven by a desire to serve students and a concern for their growth and development (McClellan, 2007). Advisors who genuinely care for students focus on their students' strengths and potential and engage students as partners in their academic journey (McClellan, 2007). Advisors who exhibit servant leadership are those who form a dyadic mentoring relationship with their students and partner with them to solve problems and address their students' concerns. In contrast, advisors who are not motivated by affection or concern for their students and perceive them in a negative light are more likely to be dismissive or prescriptive in their advisement (Rawlins & Rawlins, 2005).

Discussion Questions

1. In developing responsive academic advising programs, what does it mean to be a servant leader? What servant leadership attributes should Jessa employ in advising Taylor?
2. In developing programs and services for FGCS, how can advisors help students accumulate social capital in a university setting? How can academic advisors assist families of FGCS understand the challenges of obtaining a degree and the stressors their children face while in college?
3. Within the context of state budget cuts, limited time and resources, is it feasible for academic advisors to invest more time in supporting FGCS? What are some strategies that Jessa could implement to support Taylor and other FGCS in their college-tenure?

4. Jessa is under pressure to increase retention and graduation rates for FGCS; however, there are a variety of factors that influence a FGCS' decision to quit school. How can Jessa work with higher education administrators to understand the unique challenges that FGCS face? On an institutional level, what can be done to develop special programming and support for FGCS to help with student retention?
5. In partner pairs, continue the academic advising session between Jessa and Taylor. If you were Jessa, how would you advise Taylor? What would be the pros and cons of Taylor continuing with her college degree?

References

Braxton, J., & Hirschy, A. (2004). Modifying Tinto's theory of college student departure using constructs derived from inductive theory revision. In M. Yorke & B. Longden (Eds.), *Retention and student success in higher education* (pp. 89–101). Open University Press.

Bryan, E., & Simmons, L.A. (2009). Family involvement: Impacts on post-secondary educational success for first-generation Appalachian College students. *Journal of College Student Development* 50(4), 391–406.

Coleman, J. (1988). Social capital in the creation of human capital. *American Journal of Sociology* 94, 95–120.

Crookston, B. B. (1994). Classics revisited a developmental view of academic advising as teaching. *NACADA Journal*, 14(2), 5–9.

DeAngelo, L., Franke, R., Hurtado, S., Pryor, J. H., & Tran, S. (2011). *Completing college: Assessing graduation rates at four-year institutions.* Higher Education Research at UCLA.

Engle, J., & Tinto, J. (2008). *Moving beyond access: College success for low- income, first-generation students.* The Pell Institute.

Frick, D. M. (2004). *Robert K. Greenleaf: A life of servant leadership.* Berrett Koehler.

Frost, S. H. (2003). Academic advising in higher education. *Encyclopedia of Education*, 194 (1), 2–5.

Garriott. P. O., Hudyma, A., Keene, C., & Santiago, D. (2015). Social cognitive predictors of first and non-first generation college students' academic and life satisfaction. *Journal of Counseling Psychology*, 62(2), 253–263.

Greenleaf, R. (1977). *Servant leadership: A journey into the nature of legitimate power and greatness.* Paulist Press.

Jehangir, R., Williams, R., & Jeske, J. (2012). The influence of multicultural learning communities on the intrapersonal development of first-generation college students. *Journal of College Student Development*, 53(2), 267–284.

Jenkins, S., Belanger, A., Connally, M., Boals, A., & Durón, K. (2013). First-generation undergraduate students' social support, depression, and life satisfaction. *Journal of College Counseling*, 16(2), 129–142.

Jury, M., Smeding, A., & Darnon, C. (2015). First-generation students' underperformance at university: The impact of the function of selection. *Frontiers in Psychology*, 6(710), 1–11.

Lohfink, M. M., & Paulsen, M. B. (2005). Comparing the determinants of persistence for first-generation and continuing-generation students. *Journal of College Student Development*, 46(4), 409–428.

McClellan, J. L. (2007). The advisor as servant: The theoretical and philosophical relevance of servant leadership. *NACADA Journal*, 27(2), 41–49.

130 *Because They Are Worth It*

Nguyen, T. H., & Nguyen, B. M. D. (2018). Is the "first-generation student" term useful for understanding inequality? The role of intersectionality in illuminating the implications of an accepted—yet unchallenged—term. *Review of Research in Education,* 42(1), 146–176.

Pascarella, E. T., Pierson, C. T., Wolniak, G. C., & Terenzini, P. T. (2004). First-generation college students: additional evidence on college experiences and outcomes. *The Journal of Higher Education,* 75(3), 249–284.

Paul, W., Smith, K., & Dochney, B. (2012). Advising as servant leadership: Investigating the relationship. *NACADA Journal,* 32(1), 53–62.

Rawlins, W. K., & Rawlins, S. P. (2005). Academic advising as friendship. *NACADA Journal,* 25(2), 10–19.

RTI International. (2019). *First-generation college students: Demographic characteristics and postsecondary enrollment.* NASPA. https://firstgen.naspa.org/files/dmfile/FactSheet-01.pdf

Smith, C. L., & Allen, J. M. (2006). Essential functions of academic advising: What students want and get. *NACADA Journal,* 26(1), 56–66.

Spears, L. (1995). Servant leadership and the Greenleaf agency. In L. Spears, (Ed.), *Reflections on leadership: How Robert K. Greenleaf's theory of servant-leadership influenced today's top management thinkers* (pp. 1–14). Wiley & Sons.

Strayhorn, T. L. (2010). The influence of diversity on learning outcomes among African American college students: Measuring sex differences. *Journal of Student Affairs Research and Practice,* 47(3), 343–366.

Tinto, V. (1975). Dropout from higher education: A theoretical synthesis of recent research. *Review of Educational Research,* 45(1), 89–125.

Vianden, J., & Barlow, P. J. (2015). Strengthen the bond: Relationships between academic advising quality and undergraduate student loyalty. *NACADA Journal,* 35(2), 15–27.

Walpole, M. (2003). Socioeconomic status and college: How SES affects college experiences and outcomes. *The Review of Higher Education,* 27(1), 45–73.

13 Using a Feminist Approach to Leadership Education to Promote Coaction Among Women Collegiate Student-Athletes

Joanna Line

The Dominant Conceptualization of Leadership

The association of leadership with formal leadership roles and a narrow set of characteristics limits the conceptualization of who can be a leader and how they should lead. Traditional leadership discourse predominantly focuses on White, male, masculine, individuals (Batliwala, 2011; Chin, 2007; Fine, 2009; Lui, 2019; Regan et al., 2014; Suyemoto & Ballou, 2007; Wakefield, 2017). This discourse prevents people with numerous other social identities from being recognized as leaders. Furthermore, an individualistic understanding of leadership perpetuates a structure in which only those with formal leadership positions are recognized as leaders, while the contributions of those who support them and enable their success are diminished (Wakefield, 2017). If leadership is narrowly defined, and only a select few individuals get recognized for a team or organization's success, this creates an exclusive cycle in which only those who fit the mold of hegemonic leadership are recognized as leaders and offered formal leadership opportunities.

This cycle is exemplified by the persistent inequities in representation of people with minoritized identities in formal leadership positions in collegiate athletics. Title IX was passed nearly 50 years ago to prevent sex-based discrimination in federally funded educational programs and activities, including athletics. While this policy positively affected girls' and women's participation in sports, the number of women in leadership roles in sports dropped significantly and has remained low (Acosta & Carpenter, 2014). As of 2019, 25 percent of head coaches and 22 percent of athletic directors across all National Collegiate Athletic Association (NCAA) institutions were women (NCAA, 2020). When representation of women with multiple minoritized identities is examined, representation decreases. Women of color fulfill only 4 percent of head coach and 3 percent of athletic director positions. Furthermore, women college coaches with minoritized sexual identities are silenced about this aspect of themselves (Calhoun et al., 2011; Krane & Barber, 2005). This lack of people with minoritized identities represented in formal sports leadership positions is not due to lack of qualifications. Rather, the hegemonic conceptualization of leadership influences who is perceived to be a leader. To

DOI: 10.4324/9780429331503-16

132   *Using a Feminist Approach*

break this exclusive cycle, we must examine how leadership is learned, and create spaces in which diverse leaders and ways of leading are recognized and valued. Together, a feminist approach to leadership and feminist pedagogy offer a framework to explore how the conceptualization of leadership can be expanded.

Case: Cultivating Leaders on a Collegiate Cross Country Team

The following dialogue is a creative account inspired by my experience coaching women's collegiate cross country and facilitating a leadership program for women collegiate student-athletes. College student-athletes are emerging leaders in the field of sports. Understanding student-athletes' leadership development experiences provides insight into the systemic barriers they face in this process. This insight enables the creation of strategies to break down these barriers.

Case Context

This case takes place at Lake University, a mid-size public university in the Midwest. It is the beginning of the fall women's cross country team's season. This case presents a dialogue among several student-athletes on a university women's cross country team and their Assistant Coach, Coach Line (White heterosexual woman). This dialogue begins as one student-athlete, Valerie (Latina heterosexual woman, third-year student-athlete), discusses her role on her team with Coach Line after she was not selected to be a team captain for the upcoming season. The dialogue continues between Coach Line, Valerie, and additional team members Kimberly (White heterosexual woman, first-year student-athlete), Emma (White lesbian woman, second-year student-athlete), Carmen (Black heterosexual woman, fourth-year student-athlete), and Rachel (White heterosexual woman, fourth-year student-athlete) who discuss their perception of leadership on the team and who they perceive as leaders.

Scene 1: What Is the Purpose of a Title?

One afternoon at cross country practice, I could tell Valerie was upset because she had separated herself from the team during a group run and was running on her own. I fell into stride beside her.

COACH LINE: "Do you mind if I join you for your run today?"
VALERIE: Valerie nodded.
COACH LINE: "Is everything okay, Valerie?"
VALERIE: "I have been talking to Coach about being captain all summer. He knows I want to be captain. I've done all the right things. I've trained

hard, I've communicated with my teammates all summer to support them. Why didn't he choose me to be captain?"

COACH LINE: "Do you think that your teammates might see you as a leader even though you're not the captain? Do you need to have that title to continue to support your team?"

VALERIE: "I know I can support them without a title, but I think I've earned being the captain."

In sports, a team's success depends on every member's contributions, such as playing different positions, developing strategies, and providing motivation. As a coach, it was disheartening to hear that Valerie felt that she needed the title of captain to affirm her contributions. I wondered if her teammates felt the same way.

Scene 2: Leadership Challenges

I decided to ask additional members of the women's cross country team if they perceive themselves as leaders on the team, and how they think they contribute to the team. As the team was gathered to stretch after their run, several of the student-athletes responded.

KIMBERLY: I want to be a leader on the team but I'm shy, and this is my first year on the team, so I don't know how I can be a leader. Back in high school, my coach told me I was our team captain when I became a senior. Now that I'm a first-year in college, I'm one of the young ones again, so I'm still learning how to lead on the team.

CARMEN: Yeah, my high school coach picked me to be the team captain because I was the fastest on the team. Everyone on this team has been recruited because they were successful high school athletes. So, I'm not the fastest anymore.

COACH LINE: Can you be a leader in other ways?

CARMEN: I think the way you interact with the team is really important. Leaders also make sure everyone is doing what they need to do to be successful. I don't like to be the one up in front of everyone, telling everyone what to do though, so I don't want to be a captain. I'm more comfortable when I can be in the background.

EMMA: I like to speak up to encourage other people, but I'm not as comfortable speaking up if someone is doing something I don't agree with, or that is against our team rules. I don't want to cause any trouble on the team. Addressing issues on the team is the captain's responsibility, and I'm not a captain.

COACH LINE: Do you all think being a supportive teammate can be a form of leadership?

134 *Using a Feminist Approach*

VALERIE: Yeah, I guess it can be. I think we all try to support the team in our own ways, but I don't always know the best way to help. I work hard to achieve my athletic goals, and I hope that others see me as a leader by example.

COACH LINE: Rachel, you're the captain now, do you think you were a leader before you became a captain?

RACHEL: I always hoped I would be a captain when I became a fourth-year. I think I also was a leader by example before this year. I have always tried to be encouraging. Now that I'm the captain though, I've taken more ownership of holding other people accountable.

I thanked the student-athletes for sharing their perspectives with me and assured them that they each contribute to the team in their own ways, regardless of titles or years on the team. I knew that my encouragement was not enough to help them all recognize their impact on the team, and the value that each of them brings to their team. While several student-athletes discussed seniority and specific behaviors as factors contributing to leadership, it is important to contextualize their beliefs within the predominantly White, heteronormative leadership structure of the Athletic Department. I wondered how I could help them recognize their contributions to the team and to cultivate their leadership efficacy, regardless of their role.

The Dilemma

Team captains are perceived as role models and decision-makers for the team. Team members who aspire to be leaders but are not selected as captains may not perceive themselves as influential. Some team members may not perceive themselves as leaders because they do not relate to the captains they see. How can educators empower people who do not perceive themselves to be leaders to develop as leaders?

Discussion: A Feminist Approach to Leadership and Feminist Pedagogy

This case presents a feminist approach to leadership and cultivating leadership using feminist pedagogy, within the context of collegiate sports.

A Feminist Approach to Leadership

The following explanation of a feminist approach to leadership provides a conceptual framework to examine the concept of leadership, including who is perceived as a leader and how they are expected to lead. Feminist researchers agree that practicing a feminist approach to leadership requires engaging in a collaborative process in which power is shared equitably among community members (Batliwala, 2011; Chin, 2004; Christensen, 2011; Costello, 2015; Lazzari et al., 2009; Wakefield, 2017).

Batliwala's (2011) model of the *feminist leadership diamond* suggests that every person has the capacity for leadership, and their engagement as a leader is influenced by their individual qualities, experiences, and the systems of power within which they are enmeshed. The diamond includes four interrelated components: power, principles and values, politics and purpose, and practices. This highlights that power is inherent within leadership. It also illustrates that who is perceived to be a leader, why they lead, and how they lead within an organization is informed by a combination of how power functions in that organization, and the organization's ideology, goals, and cultural context.

While the interplay of these components may determine the dominant understanding of leadership and who is a leader, every person has the capacity to lead. Batliwala (2011) explains that the four components of leadership are affected by five aspects of the individual: *personality and self-esteem, history and experience, personal social capital, talents, abilities and inclinations,* and *identities. Personality and self-esteem* influence whether a person shares or withholds power in their interactions with others. *History and experience* inform a person's understanding of power, whereas *personal social capital* is developed through past experiences and may contribute to a person's leadership roles and how they lead. Additionally, a person's *talents* and *abilities and inclinations* contribute to the "unique package" (p. 58) they possess and can use to lead. Lastly, *identities* influence a person's experiences of privilege and oppression, and their possession and use of power. As a whole, Batliwala's feminist leadership diamond suggests that there is not one ideal way to lead. Rather, different individuals can contribute to a team or organization in different ways, but who is perceived as a leader, and the way that they lead are dependent upon the dominant understanding of leadership in that context (in this case, the White heteronormative context of the Athletic Department). Regardless of a person's leadership abilities, the way that people around them understand leadership influences how they are perceived.

In alignment with the feminist leadership diamond, Suyemoto and Ballou (2007) propose using the term *coaction* rather than *leadership*. An individualistic understanding of leadership is inherent in the language used to describe leadership; a person becomes a leader by gaining followers. This change in terminology shifts the hierarchical structure of a leader guiding their followers to a collaborative network of many leaders. Coaction also emphasizes engaging in a process rather than possessing specific characteristics (Suyemoto & Ballou, 2007) or obtaining a title or position within an organization. The understanding that every person has the capacity to lead enables this shift in the structure of leadership, through which many people can engage as co-actors contributing to a common goal. Suyemoto and Ballou (2007) explain:

> Coaction is a feminist understanding of "leadership" that aims to integrate intersections of multiple oppressions and resist the effects and enactments of these oppressions. Therefore, coaction must value the

136 *Using a Feminist Approach*

experience of relational mutuality and prioritize commitment to creating social change for liberation.

(p. 48)

The purpose of developing leadership skills and employing a feminist approach to leadership is to contribute to a shared goal, often to promote social change (Batliwala, 2011; Costello, 2015; Dentith & Peterlin, 2011; Lazzari et al., 2009). Each team member contributes their own experiences and expertise. Individuals who practice a feminist approach to leadership may provide resources and guidance to one another in similar pursuits, and develop solutions together to successfully navigate and address common barriers to leadership opportunities faced by people with minoritized identities (Costello, 2015; Lazzari et al., 2009). As such, coaction may be applied by any group in a variety of contexts. The goals and strategies employed to achieve them can be defined collectively, informed by the values, knowledge, and experiences of those involved.

Feminist Pedagogy

Feminist pedagogy offers a conceptual framework for examining how teaching practices employed for leadership education influence students' understanding of leadership. Hoffman and Stake (1998) proposed four components of feminist pedagogy: "*participatory learning, validation of personal experience, encouragement of social understanding and activism,* and *development of critical thinking and open-mindedness*" (p. 80). This collaborative approach to learning is fostered through modeling equitable relationships in the classroom. In contrast to the traditional teacher-student binary, power is shared among all members of the classroom community, who are encouraged to act as co-teachers and co-learners. Furthermore, feminist pedagogy necessitates particular attention to how systems of power function to marginalize people with minoritized identities. The classroom must be a space in which sharing diverse perspectives and ideas is encouraged and valued among students, through discussion of their own experiences as well as course materials (Carter & Prewitt-White, 2020). Incorporating discussion of lived experiences into classroom discussions validates experiential knowledge and encourages students to consider how their own identities and experiences shape their knowledge and perspectives. Creating a space in which they can share their knowledge with one another and encounter and raise questions about different ways of thinking enables students to engage in co-construction of new knowledge that affects personal growth and social change (Hoffman & Stake, 1998).

Putting a Feminist Approach to Leadership into Practice

Teaching about leadership guided by feminist pedagogy puts a feminist approach to leadership into practice. Feminist pedagogy encourages critical thinking about power dynamics, which students are challenged to critique, implicitly or explicitly, through the following activity, Leadership Illustration. Engaging in a collaborative learning process to explore understandings of leaders challenges the binary of leader and follower to empower students to recognize their own strengths and knowledge and seek opportunities to learn from others with different perspectives. Drawing upon participants' identities and experiences can enable participants to examine how they have developed their own understanding of leadership. Providing a space for sharing diverse experiences and understandings of leadership offers validation of the many ways in which a person can lead and encourages critical thinking about the limitations of the dominant conceptualization of leadership. It can also inspire students to evaluate the leadership structure within their own teams and organizations, and consider how they can apply coaction to work toward collective goals.

Activity: Leadership Illustration

Supplies: Paper, magazines, scissors, glue, colored markers, post-its (optional: computers)

1. Each participant will make an illustration depicting their definition of leadership. This may involve collage, drawing, writing, or digital art if computers are available. (45 minutes)
2. Place completed illustrations on tables or walls around the classroom.
3. Participants take a viewing tour of the classroom to observe each other's illustrations. (15 minutes)
4. Group discussion. (30 minutes)

Questions to consider:

1. Among your group, share about how your illustration depicts leadership.
2. Who is the intended audience for your illustration and why?
3. How do you relate to the definition of leadership that you depicted?
4. Are there images or words that were similar among the group?
5. Did everyone attribute the same meaning to these words or images?
6. What images or words did you observe on other people's illustrations that describe leadership differently from your understanding?
7. What aspects of leadership were most prominent (e.g., values, behaviors, characteristics, roles, contexts)?
8. How are the leadership roles and behaviors that you discussed similar or different to your reflection about what determines whether a person is a leader? Provide an example.
9. How do the leadership role models you included in your illustration demonstrate or differ from the leadership roles and behaviors that you discussed? Provide an example.
10. How can you apply what you have learned from your classmates' explanations of leadership to your own leadership practices and development?

138 *Using a Feminist Approach*

This activity applies tenets of feminist pedagogy to support the concepts of the feminist leadership diamond and coaction. This activity validates students' personal experiences in several ways. The act of creating leadership illustrations enables students to take a personal approach to explaining their understanding of this concept. Students choose the method with which they are most comfortable to express themselves and may include writing, drawing, collage-making, or digital art. They may incorporate images to symbolize concepts they associate with leadership, or they may choose words to describe a leader. These options enable students to draw from their experiences and express themselves and their ideas in ways that they may not otherwise communicate in a class discussion or written reflection. Providing the opportunity for each student to share their own understanding of leadership in the form of an illustration engages them in participatory learning that invites different perspectives. This is furthered by class discussion about the illustrations, which encourages them to share their personal understanding of leadership with one another. Students learn about different ways of explaining leadership, as well as how their classmates express themselves through how they have designed their illustration.

Conversation prompts encourage students to identify commonalities as well as differences among their approaches and explanations of leadership. This may challenge them to consider new aspects of leadership that contrast with their own, or raise questions about leadership definitions or practices they have observed in other contexts. In doing so, this activity promotes development of critical thinking and open-mindedness. It encourages students to reflect on how their experiences have shaped their own perspective and provides an opportunity to learn and grow through considering different perspectives. This approach to teaching about leadership encourages students to recognize their own leadership capacity, and to envision a broader understanding of who can be a leader and how they can lead.

References

Batliwala, S. (2011). *Feminist leadership for social transformation: Clearing the conceptual cloud* [pdf]. Crea. http://www.creaworld.org/publications/feminist-leadership-social-tra nsformation-clearing-conceptual-cloud-2011-0

Carter, L., & Prewitt-White, T. (2020). Teaching with feminist pedagogy. In J. E. Coumbe-Lilley, & A. M. Shipherd (Eds.), *High impact teaching for sport and exercise psychology educators* (pp. 217–225). Routledge.

Chin, J. L. (2007). Overview: Women and Leadership: Transforming visions and diverse voices. In J. L. Chin, B. Lott, J. K. Rice, & J. Sanchez-Hucles (Eds.), *Women and leadership: Transforming visions and diverse voices* (pp. 1–17). Blackwell Publishing Ltd.

Acosta, R. V., & Carpenter, L. J. (2014). *Women in intercollegiate sport: A longitudinal, national study, thirty seven year update. 1977–2014.* Unpublished manuscript. http://a costacarpenter.org/

Batliwala, S. (2011). *Feminist leadership for social transformation: Clearing the conceptual cloud* [pdf]. Crea. http://www.creaworld.org/publications/feminist-leadership-social-tra nsformation-clearing-conceptual-cloud-2011-0

Calhoun, A. S., LaVoi, N. M., & Johnson, A. (2011). Framing with family: Examining online coaches' biographies for heteronormative and heterosexist narratives. *International Journal of Sport Communication*, 4(3), 300–316.

Carter, L., & Prewitt-White, T. (2020). Teaching with feminist pedagogy. In J. E. Coumbe-Lilley, & A. M. Shipherd (Eds.), *High impact teaching for sport and exercise psychology educators* (pp. 217–225). Routledge.

Chin, J. L. (2004). 2003 Division 35 presidential address: Feminist leadership: Feminist visions and diverse voices . *Psychology of Women Quarterly*, 28, 1–8.

Chin, J. L. (2007). Overview: Women and leadership: Transforming visions and diverse voices. In J. L. Chin, B. Lott, J. K. Rice, & J. Sanchez-Hucles (Eds.), *Women and leadership: Transforming visions and diverse voices* (pp. 1–17). Blackwell Publishing Ltd.

Christensen, M. C. (2011). Using feminist leadership to build a performance-based, peer education program. *Qualitative Social Work* 12(3), 254–269.

Costello, L. A. (2015). Standing up and standing together: Feminist teaching and collaborative mentoring. *Feminist Teacher*, 26(1), 1–28.

Dentith, A. M., & Peterlin, B. (2011). Leadership education from within a feminist ethos. *Journal of Research on Leadership Education*, 6(2), 36–58.

Fine, M. G. (2009). Women leaders' discursive constructions of leadership. *Women's Studies in Communication*, 32(2), 180–202.

Hoffmann, F. L., & Stake, J. E. (1998). Feminist pedagogy in theory and practice: An empirical investigation. *NWSA Journal*, 10(1), 79–97.

Krane, V., & Barber, H. (2005) Identity tensions in lesbian intercollegiate coaches. *Research Quarterly for Exercise and Sport*, 76(1), 67–81.

Lazzari, M. M., Colarossi, L., & Collins, K. S. (2009). Feminists in social work: Where have all the leaders gone? *Affilia: Journal of Women and Social Work*, 24(4), 348–359.

Liu, H. (2019). Redoing and abolishing whiteness in leadership. In B. Carroll, S. Wilson & J. Firth (Eds.), *After leadership* (pp. 101–114). Routledge.

National Collegiate Athletic Association. (2020). NCAA demographics database [Data visualization dashboard]. http://www.ncaa.org/about/resources/research/ncaa-demographics-database

Regan, M., Carter-Francique, A. R., & Feagin, J. R. (2014). Systemic racism theory: Critically examining college sport leadership. In L. L. Martin (Ed.) *Out of bounds: Racism and the Black athlete Out of bounds: Racism and the Black athlete* (pp. 29–53). Praeger.

Suyemoto, K. L. & Ballou, M. B. (2007). Conducted monotones to coacted harmonies: A feminist (re)conceptualization of leadership addressing race, class, and gender. In J. L. Chin, B. Lott, J. K. Rice, & J. Sanchez-Hucles (Eds.), *Women and leadership: Transforming visions and diverse voices* (pp. 35–54). Blackwell Publishing Ltd.

Wakefield, S. (2017). Transformative and feminist leadership for women's rights [pdf]. Oxfam. https://www.oxfamamerica.org/explore/research-publications/transformative-feminist-leadership-womens-rights/

14 Visionary and Mission-Minded School Leadership Grounded in Adult Learning Theory

Tyrone Bynoe

Context

Columbia Central School District is a large school community with two high schools. Three junior high schools feed into both high schools: Paul Revere Junior High School (JHS), Sojourner Truth JHS, and Alexander Hamilton JHS (Hamilton JHS). Eighty percent of the students in Hamilton JHS chose to enroll in Eagle Mills High School, one of the district's two high schools. Hamilton JHS has been a school with an unusually large number of student problems, and administrator turnover is high. Teachers with 1–5 years of experience form 19.8 percent of the staff; those with 6–10 years of experience form 32.1 percent of the instructional staff; those with 11–20 years form 17.9 percent, and those with over 20 years of experience form 14.8 percent. There are 600 students in Hamilton JHS; students' ethnic breakdown is 65 percent White, 25 percent Afro-American, 9 percent Latino-American, and 1 percent American Indian. The special education population is 20 percent. Most Special Education students are classified as emotionally disturbed and are in an inclusion classroom setting. Hamilton JHS is classified as a Title I School, and 93 percent of students qualify for free and reduced lunch.

Introduction

The case reading exposes the behavior that key school actors must avoid when seeking to author a vision statement and mission statement for an individual school. In fact, the case emphasizes that effective school leadership must thrive on a human-relations model of harnessing buy-in and co-authorship from organizational actors for both vision and mission. This case contains two parts. In the first part, Dr. Stephen Matthews has served as principal of Hamilton JHS for a year, and has started his second year. His assistant principals, Martha Spieler and Bob Perez, are sharing impressions during a weekly meeting with Dr. Matthews about the vision statement and mission statement that the school has adopted. During the previous spring, the superintendent charged each school to develop a campus vision and mission to support the broad school district vision of *quality for all* and the district mission of *productive citizenship*.

DOI: 10.4324/9780429331503-17

During the second part of the case reading, assistant principals Martha Spieler and Bob Perez are sharing reflections about the recent retreat held by their school. With the goal of refining the vision and mission statements, the entire faculty and administration participated in a two-day professional learning community (PLC) retreat at the start of the new school year. This retreat was held sometime *after* the meeting that Dr. Matthews had with his assistant principals described in the first part of this scenario, and *before* this discussion between the two assistant principals. Martha missed a portion of the retreat due to an emergency appendectomy; so, in the second part of this scenario, Bob is explaining his experience of the retreat during the time of Martha's absence.

Case Reading

Part I

During their weekly meeting, Dr. Matthews and members of the school's shared decision-making team were reviewing the school's vision and mission statements. There appeared to be consensus among shared decision-making team members on these statements. But five minutes before this meeting was scheduled to end, Mrs. Mulligan, one of the team's teacher representatives, expressed some apprehension with the vision statement's expectation that teachers "ensure that students would become life-long learners." Note: As an outcome of transformational learning (Bennetts, 2003), life-long learning refers to the journey of ongoing and self-directed learning that occurs after formal education, while using reflectively some of the skills and processes of learning during formal education.

Mrs. Mulligan also expressed concerns over the school's mission statement, which called for the school "to provide students with a world-class education to compete in a global economy." Mrs. Mulligan insisted that teachers could not ensure that students will develop critical thinking skills to become life-long learners or global competitors. Dr. Matthews countered and voiced that Hamilton JHS must adopt high teacher quality, and that the high teacher quality would improve student performance and set students on the path of life-long learning so that students could become worldwide citizens.

Mr. Holden, an English teacher and a representative in the shared decision-making team, then defended Mrs. Mulligan, and he sought to discredit Dr. Matthews' claim that teachers could ensure that students become life-long learners and global competitors. Mr. Holden insisted that the teachers could only provide quality instruction, and that this would not lead to all students being ready for life-long learning and global participation. Further exchanges between Dr. Matthews and the teacher representatives followed.

Suddenly, the parent and student representatives gave their opinions about the phrases of teachers "ensuring that students would become life-long

142 *Visionary and Mission-Minded Leadership*

learners ... and global competitors," and their views differed markedly from those of Dr. Matthews. Parent representatives voiced that the only education preparation their children needed was to become functioning members of the local community, and they were not ready to embrace the idea of students' preparation for global competitiveness. Student representatives voiced bewilderment with the idea of becoming life-long learners and expressed preference for schooling that would allow them to overcome trauma and challenges that many of the Hamilton JHS students have experienced.

Dr. Matthews became frustrated and raised his voice. In an authoritative tone, he stated: "I am the principal in this building, and the buck stops with me. The council will keep the vision statement that teachers 'will ensure that all students will become lifelong learners,' as well as adopt the mission statement of the school to prepare students 'with a world-class education to compete in a global economy." Overall, the meeting took approximately 30 minutes, and the different stakeholder groups left the meeting feeling very frustrated and dissatisfied. In fact, the resolution for the vision and mission statements was postponed to the next shared-decision team meeting due to the intractable and divergent views that surfaced regarding the school's vision and mission statements.

Part II

BOB: What a time we had at the PLC retreat! All the teachers were at this professional development conference for both days. We reviewed the very broad district vision of *quality for all* and the district mission of *productive citizenship*; we talked about what that meant for each of our roles. We shared how we might see the vision and mission in place at our campus. It was very exciting to see people who have not spoken up in years perk up and add to the conversation. Being in small groups probably helped with the flow of discussion. Maybe Dr. Matthews' emphasis on the learning principles of andragogy is helping to make a difference because of the emphasis on building trust and listening. People felt valued. In particular, they felt comfortable sharing their views and their own more specific visions for individual classrooms. But we really had a difficult time coming up with a vision statement and a mission statement for our campus. You know how secondary teachers usually are – their focus is usually the content of their courses. We made great progress, but we still don't have vision and mission statements that everyone supports.

MARTHA: I heard that the meetings moved along smoothly most of the time. However, there were noticeable sticking points. What happened when Language Arts teacher Ms. Kerner decided to speak out about what nonsense this was? Did you hear that? I'm beginning to think she has a difficult time finding anything positive to say about anything or anyone at any time. I know she's been around for 35 years, but does that give her carte blanche in her speech and actions? And then there was Mr. Cousins [a Foreign Language teacher] who said all this talk would lead nowhere. He thought the process was a waste of time! I thought just getting all that student performance data in front of the teachers would be very helpful. How can someone argue with the student performance data or the recent climate inventories? The social studies' teachers and math teachers conclude that 50 percent of the students simply cannot learn. So, a good part of the school's core staff does not feel that the students are capable of high performance, and they maintain that the administration has not been a help in supporting teachers to raise student performance expectations.

BOB: I was wondering why Dr. Matthews didn't respond. Maybe he was just trying to let all viewpoints be expressed. I really don't know.

MARTHA: So, Bob, where are we now with the process of developing our vision and mission? What do we have to do next? Let's talk to Dr. Matthew and see how we can help.

Later that afternoon, Martha and Bob asked to visit with Dr. Matthews. He invited them into his office.

DR. MATTHEWS: How can I help you two?

BOB: We really want to help you if we can. Or perhaps it's better to say we want to help everyone at this school. We want to know what we can do to help the campus complete the development of both the vision statement and mission statement. How do we proceed?

DR. MATTHEWS: A vision is really a picture of the future that can be shared by the entire PLC. This means that the best vision must incorporate input from parents, students, and staff as well as the administration. The mission states explicitly how the school will actualize the vision. We have heard from the teachers in several ways. First, there was my initial meeting with them last January when they listed the perceived strengths and weaknesses of the school. Secondly, we have climate inventories. These questionnaires were administered to gather feedback on how the teachers have approved or disapproved the quality of the current school's instructional program. Now we have a pretty good idea about the predominant beliefs, values, and attitudes that most of them share. We need to elicit the views of other people in our community too. We must have a collaboratively developed vision and mission if these statements are to be effective as a unifying force. So, you ask, what must we do next? Again, and always, we must listen. This time we'll bring in teacher representatives to meet with some parents and share the teachers' thoughts as revealed in the two-day PLC retreat. The parents will be those who have responded to our campus survey indicating a desire to serve on some committee. We'll also select some student representatives from each class – freshman, sophomore, junior, and senior – to meet with all of us. We'll go through a process similar to the

144 *Visionary and Mission-Minded Leadership*

one you experienced at the PLC retreat. However, I think we have to break the process into smaller units. We'll have to hold some night meetings for a while because most parents cannot give up entire days to be part of this. Also, we don't want students missing lots of classes. That would reflect badly on the administration and the planning. This entire process might appear challenging, but it is very important to listen to the reflections from teachers who participated in the PLC retreat as well as others in our school community.

MARTHA: Is the student performance data needed for these meetings readily available? I'm not sure what else we might need, but I can see that if we get a grandparent like Colonel Stephenson, we'll certainly need the most up-to-date information. Otherwise, he'll be criticizing us in *The Town Crier* [the town's newspaper]. I know he wants to be helpful, but he seems to want to take charge and dictate what's needed as well as how the process will go.

DR. MATTHEWS: You're right. We need everything up to date. I think the data we provided the teachers are fine. We'll plan to use that set of data again with the parent group. If we find that the process takes so long that the data shifts, we'll note that. I'm not anticipating a lengthy process. I do recognize that the vision and mission statements will change over time as the issue and attitudes and emphasis on certain values change.

BOB: I've heard in some of my Master's courses that it's helpful when the principal can share stories from the past about beliefs that have been instrumental in making the school what it is today. Although we've had some difficulties with turnover more recently, we have had some great teachers and principals. I do not remember hearing about these during the retreat days. Do you think we could give some of that information to parents and students? Could we get some of the teacher representatives who have been here a long time to share? What do you think, Dr. Matthews?

DR. MATTHEWS: I think that's a very good idea, Bob. Will you research that for me, please? We'll need stories to emphasize the values highlighted in the teacher discussions. We talked about the meaning of the district vision of *quality for all* and the district mission of *productive citizenship*, but we didn't clarify it with examples from the past. Let's see what we can come up with for the next steps. I am sorry I didn't think of this earlier. I guess that goes to show you that anyone can get so busy they forget to sound out others. We should have had this session much earlier. Well, I am learning too. I'm counting on you both to help throughout the process. Come to think of it, perhaps the district superintendent could shed some light on these stories, Bob. Superintendent Dr. Mary Petrovsky has been here for 20 years, and I am sure she would have some ideas for us. Please include her too. She certainly is on our team.

Discussion of Supporting Research/Literature

The supporting literature below contains one notable publication on the developmental model of school supervision, two publications on the process of skillful process of how organizations adopt vision and mission statements, and two additional publications clarifying the principles of adult learning featuring transformational learning, life-long learning, and andragogy.

Suggested Reading as a Support for This Case

Bennetts, C. (September-October, 2003). The impact of transformational learning individuals, families and communities. *International Journal of Lifelong Education, 22*(5), 457–480.

David, F. & David, F. (2015). *Strategic management: Concepts and cases* (15th ed.). Pearson, Inc. (Suggested for further inquiry: Chapters 1, 3, and 4).

Glickman, C., Gordon, S., & Ross-Gordon, J. (2018). *Supervision and instructional leadership: A developmental approach*, 10th Ed. Pearson, Inc.

Nelson, M. (2014). Engaging adults in professional development environments. *Research Gate*, 1–7. file:///D:/Nelson EngagingAdultLearnersinProfessionalDevelopmentEnvironments%20(2).pdf

Orhan, G., Erodgan, D., & Durmaz, V. (2014). Adopting mission and vision statements by employees: The case of TAV airports. *Procedia – Social and Behavioral Sciences, 150*, 251–262.

Learning Activities

Discussion Questions for Part I of the Case Reading

1. Do you believe Dr. Matthews is exhibiting exemplary leadership in Part I of the case? Explain your answer and use the concepts covered (e.g., transformational leadership and andragogy) to justify your answer.
2. Using your knowledge of leadership theory and adult development with respect to vision and mission building, how would you characterize and explain the school and learning organization that Dr. Matthews supervises?
3. When working with institutional leaders, what professional development and dispositions must different stakeholder groups (e.g., teachers, students, parents) in this scenario demonstrate to develop vision and mission for a positive learning organization? And what dispositions in this scenario must leaders demonstrate, such as Dr. Matthews?

Discussion Questions for Part II of the Case Reading

1. Do you see any change in Dr. Matthew's leadership style between Part I and Part II? If so, describe this change in leadership style.

146 *Visionary and Mission-Minded Leadership*

2. When using the principles of andragogy and transformational learning, describe how three of the four actors contribute to the formation of vision and mission in Hamilton JHS:

   a   Teachers
   b   Shared decision-making team representatives
   c   School principal
   d   Assistant principals

3. During the PLC retreat, did teachers participate in self-directed learning, cooperative inquiry, critical reflection, or any combination of the three aspects of adult learning when developing the vision and mission statements? Which details are you using to justify your answer?
4. During the PLC, did administrators participate in self-directed learning, cooperative inquiry, critical reflection, or any combination of the three aspects of adult learning when developing Hamilton JHS's vision and mission statements? Which details are you using to justify your answer?
5. When working with institutional leaders, which professional development and dispositions represented in this scenario might support the organization's success? How?
6. Which dispositions were lacking in the case as presented? Based on your knowledge of professional standards for educators, what would you expect to see that differed from the scenarios described? Why?

Reflection Questions for Both Parts of Case Reading

1. Discuss the andragogical and transformational learning challenges that prevent stakeholder groups in your organization/workplace from developing a shared vision statement and/or mission statement.
2. Discuss the andragogical and transformational learning strengths that can enable stakeholder groups in your organization to successfully collaborate on authoring vision and/or mission statements.

References

Works Cited References on Vision and Mission Emphasizing the Science of Leadership
David, F., & David, F. (2015). *Strategic management: Concepts and cases* (15th ed.). Pearson, Inc.
Fuller, J., & Green, J. (2005). The leader's role in strategy, *Graziadio Business Review* 8(2).
Gabriel, J., & Farmer, P. (2009). *How to help your school thrive*. Association of School and Curriculum Development.
Glickman, C., Gordon, S., & Ross-Gordon, J. (2018). *Supervision and instructional leadership: A developmental approach*, 10th Ed. Pearson, Inc.
Orhan, G., Erodgan, D., & Durmaz, V. (2014), Adopting mission and vision statements by employees: The case of TAV airports. *Procedia – Social and Behavioral Sciences*, 150, 251–262.
Works Cited References on the Topics of Adult Leadership and Adult Learning

Bennetts, C. (September-October 2003). The impact of transformational learning individuals, families and communities. *International Journal of Lifelong Education, 22*(5), 457–480.

Carroll, M. (2009). Supervision: Critical reflection for transformational learning (Part 1). *The Clinical Supervisor, 28,* 210–220.

Carroll, M. (2010). Supervision: Critical reflection for transformational learning (Part 2). *The Clinical Supervisor, 29,* 1–19.

Christie, M., Simon, S., Graham, W., Call, K., & Farragher, Y. (2019). Bungee jumping and rocket launching: Transformative learning for today's transformational school leaders. *International Journal of Educational Management, 33*(7), 1–15.

Merriam, S. B. (1996). Updating our knowledge of adult learning. *Journal of Continuing Education in the Health Professions, 16,* 136–143.

Nelson, M. (2014). Engaging adults in professional development environments. *Research Gate,* 1–7. file:///D:/Nelson EngagingAdultLearnersinProfessionalDevelopmentEnvironments%20(2).pdf

Rodman, A. (2019). *Personalized professional learning.* Association of School and Curriculum Development.

Weinstein, M. (2004). *An Investigation of CEO's learning experiences: Implications for leadership training,* Paper presented at the Academy of Human Resource Development International Conference, Austin, TX. 363–372. https://eric.ed.gov/?id=ED492286

15 Curriculum and Pedagogy Considerations for Connecting Personal Growth and Leadership Development

Ronald S. Glickman and Max H. Glickman

Introduction

This case discusses the nexus between authentic leadership theory (Northouse, 2016) and self-authorship theory (Magolda, 2004), and examines *what* is required for college students to become authentic leaders and *how* universities can tailor instruction to support their personal growth and leadership development. It draws from the existing literature on theoretical understandings of authentic leadership and self-authorship, as well as pedagogy and curriculum considerations for exemplary leadership development programs in higher education.

California is facing a serious shortage of college educated workers with the leadership competencies to support the fifth largest economy in the world. If current labor market trends persist, the state will have a shortage of 1.1 million college educated workers by 2030 (Johnson et al., 2015). Therefore, California's higher education system is a critical driver of the state's economic progress. While college graduates are more likely to be employed and earn higher wages than non-graduates, which increases state tax revenues and reduces social services costs, "California's higher education system is not keeping up with the changing economy" (Jackson & Johnson, 2018, p. 1). This problem is exacerbated by the imminent retirement of the Baby Boomers in California (8.4 million people born between 1945 and 1964), which represents the first time in the state's history that such a large, well-educated generation will be exiting the workforce (Johnson et al., 2015).

The Baby Boomer generation was influenced by an industrial leadership paradigm that was largely transactional, where leadership was experienced as an individual, hierarchical, and operational activity (Eich, 2008). In the post-industrial leadership paradigm of the 21st century, leadership is more transformative and experienced as a collaborative partnership between leaders and followers (Dugan, 2006). Komives et al. (2013) define this paradigm as "a relational and ethical process of people together attempting to accomplish positive change" (p. vii), whereas Northouse (2016) describes it as "a process whereby an individual influences a group of individuals to achieve a common goal" (p. 6). In this context, an individual can engage formally or informally as a leader, follower, subordinate, or committed member of a group or team

DOI: 10.4324/9780429331503-18

(Komives et al., 2013). This paradigm shift means that the generation of college graduates who replace the Baby Boomers must develop modern leadership skills to succeed in the workforce. The shift from transactional leadership where leaders are born, to transformative leadership where leaders are made, means that 21st century leadership competencies can be taught, and college students who involve themselves in leadership education have the potential to increase their leadership know-how (Eich, 2008; Northouse, 2016). With this in mind, the search committee for Southern California State University (SCSU), hired President Susan Belinda to position the university for preparing the next generation of leaders for the California workforce.

Case: Leveraging Developmentally Effective Experiences in Postsecondary Leadership Education

In this case, we share the story of President Susan Belinda, who, after gaining approval of her strategic plan, engages two trusted advisors to plan a new leadership development course for the university. We follow Belinda as she considers divergent perspectives on the most appropriate pedagogies and curricula for the course, as well as the positioning most likely to support the university's vision to prepare the next generation of leaders for the California workforce.

Case Context

Founded in 1947, SCSU is a regional public comprehensive university offering 60 undergraduate majors, 55 Master's degree programs, and three Doctoral programs to more than 28,000 students, almost 75 percent of whom are the first in their families to pursue a university degree. In their vision statement, SCSU claims to deliver cutting-edge academic programs that prepare students to be innovative leaders in both their professional and civic lives, while serving the public good through community initiatives and strategic partnerships.

Key Individuals

President Susan Belinda was recently appointed president of SCSU. First in her family to earn a college degree, Susan is deeply committed to providing opportunities for students to achieve academic, personal, and professional success, and helping them to develop a high regard for the intellectual and cultural diversity that distinguishes SCSU and its surrounding community.

   Dr. Rachel Perry is Dean of the College of Business and Economics (CBE) at SCSU. She is a leadership scholar who has published numerous articles and presented her research at academic conferences nationwide. In addition to overseeing the CBE, Dr. Perry teaches an undergraduate leadership course based on an academically robust account of the major leadership theories from the 20th century. She typically scores lower than average on

150 *Curriculum and Pedagogy Considerations*

student satisfaction surveys because she "teaches to the test" and the "information is not applicable outside of the classroom."

Max Herschel is a seasoned executive who has been developing high potential talent and motivating culturally diverse teams to deliver breakthrough results for 30 years. He is an SCSU alumni and a member of the President's advisory board. As a part-time lecturer, Max teaches an undergraduate leadership course based on a combination of readings, lectures, expert presentations, and action learning exercises. Max typically scores higher than average on student satisfaction surveys because "he shares stories of real-life experiences... the things people need to hear because you can't get that from books."

Scene 1: The SCSU Board of Trustee's Meeting

President Belinda was relieved that her strategic plan was finally approved. One strategy to make SCSU's vision statement a reality was the creation of a world class leadership development program, anchored by a brand new leadership course. As she explained to the Trustee's, the desired outcomes for the program and the course were based on best practices. The program aims to influence how learners think about leadership, while increasing their level of self-knowledge and capacity to engage others in collaborative work. For this reason, the course will employ pedagogies that facilitate the integration of theory and practice, and curriculum to link classroom learning to the real world. Susan decided to plan the leadership course first, so she scheduled a meeting with her trusted advisors Mr. Herschel and Dean Perry to get started.

Scene 2: The Leadership Course Planning Meeting

President Belinda was not prepared for the divergent perspectives she encountered in the meeting. Dean Perry believed strongly that leadership is best defined as a collection of theories, supported by scholarly research, and taught by leadership academics within the CBE. She argued that part-time lecturers diminish the prestige of the university. Moreover, not all students can learn to lead, therefore, an exemplary leadership course should not be included in the general education curriculum. Conversely, Mr. Herschel believed wholeheartedly that all students can learn to lead. He argued that leadership is best taught by experienced practitioners who model effective leadership practices in the classroom, share stories of real-life experiences, and advance student learning with a robust combination of readings, lectures, guest speakers, and action learning exercises.

The Dilemma

President Belinda's initial excitement about the prospects of the new leadership course was quickly curtailed by the contentious discourse in the planning meeting. She believed that a well-designed, properly positioned leadership course could be the cornerstone of a leadership development program to help prepare the next generation of leaders for the California workforce. After the meeting, she was conflicted. Where should she position the new course within the university's overall curriculum? What role, if any, should adjunct lecturers (i.e., experienced practitioners) play in designing and teaching leadership courses at SCSU?

Discussion: Authentic Leadership and Self-Authorship

Authentic Leadership

In the early 21st century, terrorist attacks, widespread corporate corruption, and a troubled economy in the United States created a sense of uncertainty and anxiety in people about their leaders (Northouse, 2016). As a result, authentic leadership emerged as a new area of leadership research in response to societal demands for genuine, trustworthy, and constructive leaders to serve the common good (Fry & Whittington, 2005; Walumbwa et al., 2008). Although a commonly agreed upon definition of authentic leadership has yet to emerge in the literature, Northouse (2016) claims that authentic leadership can be defined by three sets of competencies: intrapersonal, interpersonal, and developmental.

Intrapersonal leadership focuses on the leader's knowledge, self-regulation, and self-concept. People perceive leaders with greater self-awareness as more authentic (Northouse, 2016). Developing self-awareness is a process of reflecting on one's core values, motives, feelings, and goals that helps leaders understand themselves, including their strengths and weaknesses, and the impact that they have on others (Northouse, 2016). Self-aware leaders display authentic behaviors that reflect consistency between their values, beliefs, and actions (Walumbwa et al., 2008). Moreover, their leadership conduct is guided by internal values as opposed to external influences, such as threats, inducements, or social expectations (Ryan & Deci, 2003). When individuals come to know themselves and what they stand for, they have a stronger foundation for their leadership decisions and actions (Avolio et al., 2004).

Interpersonal leadership is a collective process that is characterized by two key concepts: relational transparency and balanced processing (Walumbwa et al., 2008). Relational transparency is a reciprocal process for developing authentic relationships between leaders and followers, where individuals share both positive and negative aspects of themselves with one another to build rapport (Northouse, 2016). Balanced processing refers to a leader's ability to analyze information objectively and explore divergent points of view without bias before making important decisions (Gardner et al., 2005). Leaders who adopt this approach are seen as authentic because they are open about their own perspectives, while remaining objective when considering other points of view. Interpersonal authentic leadership focuses on communicating openly and

152 *Curriculum and Pedagogy Considerations*

being trustworthy in relationships with others, leading to greater loyalty and commitment between leaders and followers (George, 2003; Northouse, 2016).

Developmental leadership supports the important notion that authentic leaders learn from their experiences and improve their intrapersonal and interpersonal leadership competencies over time (Northouse, 2016). In fact, authentic leadership development is based largely on the insights gained and lessons learned from difficult life experiences that help individuals grow into stronger, more authentic leaders (Luthans & Avolio, 2003; Northouse, 2016). Leadership is a goal oriented process that can be learned, rather than a trait that is inherited (Komives et al., 2013; Northouse, 2016). Therefore, college students who participate in leadership education can learn the competencies necessary to become authentic leaders who serve the common good (Dugan et al., 2012; Eich, 2008). While authentic leadership outlines *what* characteristics are important to develop authentic leadership skills and know-how, it does not address *how* best to develop them (Glickman, 2020).

Self-Authorship

While research examining authentic leadership in higher education is relatively sparse, self-authorship is a theoretical framework that has been used extensively to describe how college students grow and change (Barber et al., 2013; Carpenter & Peña, 2017; Cohen et al., 2013; Magolda, 2004; Pizzolato, 2005). Self-authorship is based on the work of early developmental researchers, including Jean Piaget and Robert Kegan. Kegan (1994) leveraged Piaget's (1972) theory of constructive-developmentalism, an individual's perception of reality that is actively constructed and continuously evolving, to describe how human consciousness develops over a lifetime. Kegan's (1994) constructive development framework consists of five phases that people move through as their thinking about the world, themselves, and their relationships with others develop over time. More specifically, "complex epistemological, intrapersonal, and interpersonal development is necessary for adults to build complex belief systems, to form a coherent sense of identity, and to develop authentic, mature relations with diverse others" (Magolda, 2008, p. 269). The term "self-authorship" was created by Kegan (1994) to describe the fourth phase of his framework, where individuals begin to act based upon internal beliefs and values rather than external expectations and approval.

In her seminal 21-year longitudinal study of young adults age 18 to 39, Magolda (2004) drew on Kegan's (1994) framework to develop the concept of self-authorship, which she defines as "the internal capacity to define one's beliefs, identity, and relationships" (Magolda, 2009, p. 631). In this context, self-authorship consists of three developmental dimensions: intrapersonal (i.e., how one defines their identity); interpersonal (i.e., how one constructs relationships with others), and epistemological (i.e., how one makes meaning of their knowledge and experiences). Developing the capacity to think contextually and behave in ways that are congruent with one's belief system are key outcomes of self-authorship

(Magolda, 2008). To realize these outcomes, individuals move through and between four phases of self-authorship, where forward movement involves a shift in meaning-making as individuals transition from a reliance on externally derived ways of thinking to more internally constructed perspectives (Carpenter & Peña, 2017; Magolda, 2004).

The first phase of self-authorship, *external formulas*, depicts an individual's lack of self-directive behavior and a heavy reliance on external authorities (i.e., parents, family, teachers, and mentors) for knowledge construction (Magolda & King, 2012). The next phase, *crossroads*, involves the development of a nascent internal voice by questioning external authorities and resolving conflicts that arise from the cognitive dissonance associated with challenges to epistemologies construed in the external formulas phase of self-authorship (Carpenter & Peña, 2017). The third phase, *self-authoring*, is characterized by a more independent process of meaning-making and a stronger, more mature, internal voice. In the final phase, *internal formulas*, individuals develop a profound commitment to using and trusting their internal voice as a basis to make sense of the external world and understand their role in life (Magolda & King, 2012). Individuals who reach the internal formulas state of self-authorship "consider multiple perspectives, reflect on their own values and motivations, and utilize goals and perspectives that are internally grounded and evaluated as a foundation for meaning-making" (Barber et al., 2013, p. 870).

Bringing the Theories Together

Authentic leadership theory asserts that leaders possess self-awareness, clear beliefs and values, and the desire to serve others (George et al., 2007; Komives et al., 2013). Self-authorship theory provides a framework for understanding how college students develop a strong sense of self (Magolda, 2004). College students must be able to develop and define a set of core values that define a strong sense of self in order to develop into authentic leaders (Eriksen, 2009). Together, these two theories form a College Student Leadership Development Framework (see Figure 15.1) that takes into account *what* is required for college students to become authentic leaders and *how* postsecondary institutions can tailor instruction to support their personal growth and leadership development. In the framework, developmentally effective experiences, defined as learning experiences that fundamentally change a student's beliefs, values or behaviors (Barber et al., 2013), are an important catalyst for growth across the developmental dimensions of self-authorship and authentic leadership. These experiences aim to surface the interconnectivity of how students view the world, how they see themselves, and how they view social relations, fostering cognitive dissonance and prompting exploration, reflection, and, ultimately, developmental growth (Carpenter & Peña, 2017).

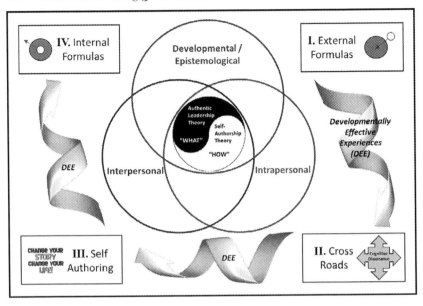

Figure 15.1 College Student Development Framework
Note. Adapted from Preparing Latinx College Students for Leadership in California, by R. S. Glickman, 2020. North America Business Press. Copyright 2020 by Journal of Leadership, Accountability and Ethics.

Developmentally Effective Learning Activities

DiSC® Profile: The DiSC® is a non-judgmental tool used for discussion of individual behavioral differences. Participants answer a series of questions that produce a detailed report about their personality and behavior. The report provides a common language that people can use to better understand themselves and adapt their behaviors with others.

1. Purchase and complete the DiSC® Profile: https://www.discprofile.com/products/disc-classic-2-0/.
2. Review your report.
3. What were your biggest intrapersonal and interpersonal developmental insights?
4. How will you make meaning from this experience and apply what you learned?

Leadership Style Analysis (Lestan): The Lestan exercise distinguishes five levels of participation and 11 situational factors that influence the effects of teamwork on decision quality, implementation time, and team development. The experience enables learners to examine their implicit assumptions about the consequences of sharing their decision-making power (Vroom, 2003).

1. Download and complete the Lestan assignment: https://www.decisionma
   kingforleaders.com/dmfl/cases-english.pdf.
2. Analyze your answers and identify patterns in your decision making style.
3. What were your biggest intrapersonal and interpersonal developmental
   insights?
4. How will you make meaning from this experience and apply what you learned?

DEE Lesson Plan: Design a classroom exercise to foster a DEE. Align the
desired student learning outcomes with the developmental dimensions of
authentic leadership and self-authorship. Aim to stimulate cognitive dissonance
and prompt exploration, reflection, and, ultimately, developmental growth.

1. Seek student feedback on the new DEE.
2. What were their biggest intrapersonal and interpersonal developmental
   insights?
3. How did they make meaning from this experience?
4. How do they intend to apply what they learned?

Discussion Questions

1. Do you think the new leadership course at SCSU should remain in the
   CBE or be positioned elsewhere? Why?
2. In what ways can President Belinda leverage DEEs to encourage a deeper
   level of student learning across curriculums and departments?
3. How might the faculty at SCSU effectively transition DEEs from physical
   to virtual classrooms in the aftermath of the Covid-19 pandemic?

References

Bradberry, T., & Greaves, J. (2009). *Emotional intelligence 2.0.* TalentSmart.

Sharma, R. (2011). *The leader who had no title.* Free Press.

Wheatley, M. (2006). *Leadership and the new science.* Berrett-Kochler Publishers.

Avolio, B. J., Gardner, W. L., Walumbwa, F. O., Luthans, F., & May, D. R. (2004).
Unlocking the mask: A look at the process by which authentic leaders impact follower attitudes and behaviors. *The Leadership Quarterly*, 15(6), 801–823. https://doi.
org/10.1016/j.leaqua.2004.09.003.

Barber, J. P., King, P. M., & Magolda, M. B. B. (2013). Long strides on the journey toward
self-authorship: Substantial developmental shifts in college students' meaning making .
The Journal of Higher Education, 84(6), 866–896. https://doi.org/10.1353/jhe.2013.0033.

Carpenter, A. M., & Peña, E. V. (2017). Self-authorship among first-generation
undergraduate students: A qualitative study of experiences and catalysts . *Journal of
Diversity in Higher Education*, 10(1), 86–100. doi:10.1037/a0040026

Cohen, J., Cook-Sather, A., Lesnick, A., Alter, Z., Awkward, R., Decius, F., & Men-
gesha, L. (2013). Students as leaders and learners: Towards self-authorship and
social change on a college campus . *Innovations in Education and Teaching International*,
50(1), 3–13. doi:10.1080/14703297.2012.746511

156 *Curriculum and Pedagogy Considerations*

Darling-Hammond, L., LaPointe, M., Meyerson, D., Orr, M. T., & Cohen, C. (2007). *Preparing school leaders for a changing world: Lessons from exemplary leadership development programs*. Stanford Educational Leadership Institute, Stanford University.

Dugan, J. P. (2006). Explorations using the social change model: Leadership development among college men and women . *Journal of College Student Development, 47*(2), 217–225. doi:10.1353/csd.2006.0015

Dugan, J. P., Kodama, C. M., & Gebhardt, M. C. (2012). Race and leadership development among college students: The additive value of collective racial esteem. *Journal of Diversity in Higher Education, 5*(3), 174–189. doi:10.1037/a0029133

Eich, D. (2008). A grounded theory of high-quality leadership programs: Perspectives from student leadership development programs in higher education . *Journal of Leadership & Organizational Studies, 15*(2), 176–187. doi:10.1177/1548051808324099

Eriksen, M. (2009). Authentic leadership: Practical reflexivity, self-awareness, and self-authorship. *Journal of Management Education, 33*(6), 747–771. doi:10.1177/1052562909339307

Fry, L. W., & Whittington, J. L. (2005). In search of authenticity: Spiritual leadership theory as a source for future theory, research, and practice on authentic leadership. In B. Avolio, W. Gardner, & F. Walumbwa, F. (Eds.), *Authentic leadership theory and practice: Origins, effects, and development*. Monographs in leadership and management, Vol. 3, 183–200.

Gardner, W. L., Avolio, B. J., Luthans, F., May, D. R., & Walumbwa, F. O. (2005). Can you see the real me? A self-based model of authentic leader and follower development. *The Leadership Quarterly, 16*(3), 343–372. doi:10.1016/j.leaqua.2005.03.003

George, B. (2003). *Authentic leadership: Rediscovering the secrets to creating lasting value*. Jossey-Bass.

George, B., Sims, P., McLean, A. N., & Mayer, D. (2007). Discovering your authentic leadership . *Harvard Business Review, 85*(2), 129. https://hbr.org/2007/02/discovering-your-authentic-leadership

Glickman, R. S. (2020). Preparing Latinx college students for leadership in California. *Journal of Leadership, Accountability and Ethics, 17*(4). doi:10.33423/jlae.v17i4.3094

Jackson, J., & Johnson, H. (2018). California is facing a shortfall of college-educated workers. http://www.ppic.org/publication/californias-future-higher-education/

Johnson, H., Mejia, M. C., & Bohn, S. (2015). *Will California run out of college graduates?* http://www.ppic.org/publication/will-california-run-out-of-college-graduates/

Kegan, R. (1994). *In over our heads: The mental demands of modern life*. Cambridge, MA: Harvard University Press.

Komives, S. R., Lucas, N., & McMahon, T. R. (2013). *Exploring leadership: For college students who want to make a difference* (3rd ed.). Jossey-Bass.

Luthans, F., & Avolio, B. J. (2003). Authentic leadership development. In K. S. Cameron, J. E. Dutton, & R. E. Quinn (Eds.), *Positive Organizational Scholarship* (pp. 241–258). Berrett-Koehler.

Magolda, M. B. B. (2004). *Making their own way: Narratives for transforming higher education to promote self-development*. Stylus Publishing, LLC.

Magolda, M. B. B. (2008). Three elements of self-authorship. *Journal of College Student Development, 49*(4), 269–284. doi:10.1353/csd.0.0016

Magolda, M. B. B. (2009). The activity of meaning making: A holistic perspective on college student development . *Journal of College Student Development, 50*(6), 621–639. doi:10.1353/csd.0.0106

Magolda, M. B. B., & King, P. M. (2012). Special issue: Assessing meaning making and self-authorship: Theory, research, and application. *ASHE Higher Education Report, 38*(3), 1–138. doi:10.1002/aehe.20003

Northouse, P. G. (2016). *Leadership: Theory and practice* (7th ed.). SAGE Publications.

Piaget, J. (1972). A structural foundation for tomorrow's education. *Prospects*, 2(1), 12–27. doi:10.1007/BF02195648

Pizzolato, J. E. (2005). Creating crossroads for self-authorship: Investigating the provocative moment . *Journal of College Student Development*, 46(6), 624–641. doi:10.1353/csd.2005.0064

Ryan, R. M., & Deci, E. L. (2003). On assimilating identities to the self: A self-determination theory perspective on internalization and integrity within cultures. In M. R. Leary & J. P. Tangney (Eds.), *Handbook of self and identity* (pp. 253–272). The Guilford Press.

Shamir, B., & Eilam, G. (2005). "What's your story?": A life-stories approach to authentic leadership development. *The Leadership Quarterly*, 16(3), 395–417. doi:10.1016/j.leaqua.2005.03.005

Vroom, V. H. (2003). Educating managers for decision making and leadership . *Management Decision*, 41(10), 968–978. doi:10.1108/00251740310509490

Walumbwa, F. O., Avolio, B. J., Gardner, W. L., Wernsing, T. S., & Peterson, S. J. (2008). Authentic leadership: Development and validation of a theory-based measure. *Journal of Management*, 34(1), 89–126. doi:10.1177/0149206307308913

16 Preparing Educators to Lead Professional Learning in P–12 Schools

Applying Research on Leadership Development and Adult Learning

Dustin Miller and Anika Ball Anthony

Introduction

This case study is designed to familiarize future and current school leaders with collaboration and adult learning and their applicability in developing professional learning plans (PLP). Through the use of PLPs, educators grow in their thinking as they work to improve school conditions, teaching practice, and student learning outcomes. Although this case study supports a school leader designing adult professional learning for teachers, the tenets can be naturally transferred to growth opportunities in other professions.

Case Study

Imagine that you are the principal of a large high school consisting of grades 9–12 in a large Midwestern city. Prior to the start of the school year, you received a call from the chief academic officer who was very concerned about declining state test scores. Based on state data, math scores have been steadily declining in your building over the past four years and she expects you to put a PLP in place to correct this negative trend.

Upon reflecting on the conversation with your chief academic officer, you felt declining scores were a factor of climate and instructional practice as opposed to student motivation or ability. To assess your feelings, you asked the teachers in the math department to share their impressions as educators directly involved with student learning. Based on their perspectives, they believed there was a lack of professional learning when new state standards were released five years earlier, and there had been no training or opportunities for purposeful implementation. They also felt the absence of a clear instructional vision hindered their planning and student learning. Lastly, they stated a belief in your leadership as the principal, but voiced concerns that you had not intentionally encouraged teachers to work together.

Based on information shared by faculty in the math department, you agreed collaboration is likely the biggest contributor to declining scores. If a clear vision and supporting goals were developed by the faculty, intentional collaboration around instructional practice could be prioritized and

DOI: 10.4324/9780429331503-19

conversely have a positive impact on student learning. With this in mind, teacher collaboration was identified as a problem of practice for the upcoming academic year.

In order to facilitate this change, you knew teachers needed ownership of their growth, and framing this work in the context of a PLP was best positioned to deliver positive results. You charged the math faculty to come together as a data team to develop a PLP. A data team is an intentional approach to bring educators together to engage in the process of analyzing student data to ultimately reflect and grow in instructional practice (Anderson et al., 2010). The result of the data team's work is:

- *Problem of Practice* – Teachers will have time, resources, and structures for collaborating with colleagues around matters of instruction.
- *Goals* – Based on a review of pertinent data and supporting best practice literature, teachers will utilize weekly planning time to analyze student data, create common instructional lessons, and participate in instructional rounds to enrich their own instructional practice.
- *Timeline* – Through the use of weekly team meetings and instructional rounds, teachers will make collaboration a priority focus for the upcoming academic year with a continued secondary focus over the following three years.
- *Evaluation* – Survey, focus groups, and student achievement data will be collected at the end of each quarter, analyzed, and recommendations for adjustments implemented.

Unfortunately, the group was unable to come up with appropriate *instructional strategies* to make adequate progress toward their goals surrounding teacher collaboration. This is where the PLP work needs to commence.

Literature Review

Given the importance of collaboration and social interaction for how principals and teachers partner to lead schools and support learning (Anthony et al., 2019; Printy et al., 2009), this case is framed from a leadership development perspective, while also applying principles of collaboration and adult learning. The sections below explain how leadership development, collaboration, and adult learning will be applied toward helping school leaders learn to work collaboratively with teachers as they identify and address problems of practice.

Leadership Development

Leadership development focuses on developing all organizational members with respect to leadership, specifically concerning their interactions, relationships, and ability to set visions, make decisions, and navigate change. On the

160 *Professional Learning in P–12 Schools*

contrary, leader development is focused on individual growth concerning the knowledge and skills to perform a formal leadership role (Day, 2000). From an organizational perspective, leadership development not only improves social processes and shared meanings within organizations, but also overall organizational capacity to address organizational needs and goals, as well as the development of individual leaders (Riggio, 2008). Leadership development learning activities should be a collaborative undertaking that involves multiple stakeholders in identifying needs, setting learning goals, and aligning leadership development efforts with organizational priorities (Hrivnak et al., 2009). Such learning activities may include dialogue, reflection, critical thinking, mentoring, and problem-solving (Turner et al., 2018).

Collaboration

Collaboration is a process of two or more individuals interacting to create shared understandings and collectively solve problems (Graesser et al., 2018). Collaboration includes, yet extends beyond, related terms such as communication, coordination, and cooperation. For example, although individuals may use cooperation to exchange resources with one another in pursuit of a common goal, collaboration entails sharing and co-constructing beliefs, values, and understandings (Twidale et al., 1997). Collaboration in organizations has been positively associated with trust, productivity, and efficiency (Bolman & Deal, 2017). As previously noted, collaboration is an essential precursor to all members of an organization developing as leaders who are able to work together to co-construct understandings, identify organizational needs, set visions, make decisions, and advance organizational goals (Turner et al., 2018).

Collaboration among educators contributes to their collective efforts to improve instruction (Goddard et al., 2015), increase teacher efficacy to engage in new instructional practices (Goddard & Kim, 2018), and raise student achievement (Goddard et al., 2007). Indicators of collaboration among educators include practices such as sharing stories and resources, assisting one another, and engaging in joint work (Little, 1990). Schools in which there is collaboration among staff also increase trust as they develop shared understandings, beliefs, and values, thus resulting in positive changes in organizational culture (Hoy & Miskel, 2013). Structures and resources that enable collaboration in schools include common planning time, teacher teams, release time for teachers, and systems for sharing co-developed lessons (Voogt et al., 2016). However, structures and resources fall short of improving collaboration in practice if such efforts are disjointed and not supported by professional learning experiences that enable educators to develop social norms and routines for collaboration (Bray, 2000; Darling-Hammond, 1994).

Adult Learning

The way adults learn is different from that of children. It is critical that those charged with shifting adults in their thinking understand these unique characteristics of adult learners and how to plan professional learning accordingly. Adult learning, often referred to as andragogy, focuses on the understanding and support of the lifelong education of adults (Merriam, 2001; Courtney, 2018). Adults are best motivated to learn if they 1) understand why learning is necessary, 2) can connect past experiences to new learning, 3) have mutual control over the decision-making, 4) see immediate relevance, 5) are exposed to problem-centered learning versus content-oriented learning, and 6) can create internal motivators over external motivators (Knowles, 1978; Merriam & Bierema, 2018). Although each of these principles is important to adult learning, when connected together in a thoughtful manner, the outcomes of professional learning are more robust (Merriam, 2018).

Structuring professional development on the principles of adult learning enables educators to maximize understanding of new information through a practical lens (Mirriam & Bierema, 2014). The ability for educators to use past teaching experiences to construct new meaning not only values their work as professionals but provides a level of control over their learning (Merriam et al., 2007; Knowles, 1978). In this teaching case, students will use understanding of adult learning to incorporate appropriate instructional strategies into a PLP that strengthens teacher collaboration.

Professional Learning Instructional Strategies

Understanding that school-related factors such as academic emphasis (Hoy et al., 1990) and effective teaching (Hattie, 2009) significantly impact student growth and achievement, it is important that teachers approach their work with coherence and in coordination with colleagues. This intentional work requires ongoing growth and a thoughtful way to capture this process is often reflected in a PLP.

A PLP helps address a problem of practice through clarifying goals for professional learning and developing a plan to achieve the goals (Guskey, 2014). Traditionally, PLPs consist of the following components: school context, data analysis, goals, rationale, instructional strategies, reflective practices, and evaluation (Killion, 2013). For the purpose of this case, the work of participants will focus on implementing instructional strategies that support the growth of teacher collaboration. Examples of instructional strategies that align with collaboration initiatives are instructional rounds, lesson study, and critical friends (City et al., 2011; Zepeda, 2014).

- **Instructional Rounds** – a collaborative approach involving a team watching a colleague teach. Instructional rounds are comprised of the following seven embedded principles to support teachers' growth: 1) learning occurs when change happens to the level of content, teachers'

162 *Professional Learning in P–12 Schools*

knowledge and skill, and student engagement; 2) change to the three-tiered instructional core involves changing the other two; 3) if you cannot see it in the instructional core, it is not there; 4) instructional task predicts performance; 5) accountability lies in the tasks students are asked to do; 6) we learn by doing; and 7) description before analysis, analysis before prediction, prediction before evaluation (City et al., 2011).

- ***Lesson Study*** – an approach combining collaboration, reflection, and professional development into one structured experience for teachers to engage in constructing new meaning around instructional practices (Lewis et al., 2006; Zepeda et al., 2014). Viewed as a four-part cycle, lesson study involves 1) study of the curriculum and formulation of goals, 2) instructional planning, 3) conducting research, and 4) reflection (Collet, 2019).
- ***Critical Friends*** – an individual or group of colleagues where trust is paramount. These trusted friends ask provocative questions, provide data, offer feedback, take time to understand the context of the work, and advocate for the success of each other (Costa & Kallick, 1993). Trust and collaboration work in concert to strengthen relationships among colleagues.

Although there is no one right model, the strategies used should stem from an understanding of the adults involved and the confines of the operational aspects, and should complement the overarching goals.

Applicability of Literature to the Case Study

State boards of education and school districts have increasingly demonstrated an expectation that P–12 leaders are well-versed in supporting teachers in developing PLPs that address professional learning goals, strategies, and evaluation (Killion, 2013). Professional learning is informed by research indicating that meaningful and effective professional development is situated, content-focused, collaborative, sustained, and reflective (Darling-Hammond et al., 2017; Putnam & Borko, 2000). Similar to leadership development, professional learning arguably adds value to both individuals and the organizations in which they work (Hirsh & Hord, 2012; Killion, 2013). Related to collaboration and adult learning, professional learning views teachers as partners in their professional growth (Calvert, 2016, p. 4). Given that PLPs are developed with varying input from stakeholders, the work of identifying problems of practice and determining PLP instructional strategies necessitates teacher involvement and in-turn collaborative problem solving.

Discussion Questions and Learning Activities

Effective questioning should be used to support leader development and complement the creation of PLPs (Pagliaro, 2017; Stokhof et al., 2017). Listed below are example questions that instructors can use to facilitate whole or small group discussions in addition to individual reflection outside of class.

These questions are designed to assist participants in their reflection and sensemaking:

1. Teachers' lack of collaboration has been suggested as the main issue impacting declining math scores in this case study. How might better collaboration influence student learning outcomes?

   - ***Facilitator tip:*** *Encourage participants to consider how collaboration may impact teaching practice, as well as administrative and organizational supports for teacher collaboration.*

2. Lack of clarity around the school's instructional vision was articulated as a concern. What initial steps should the principal and teachers take to begin this work?

   - ***Facilitator tip:*** *Participation from the entire faculty will be beneficial to setting a vision that is embraced by the individuals in the school. Encourage participants to consider the use of a survey or focus groups to afford teachers an opportunity to stress beliefs and hopes for the school. Draft language should be created and shared with the faculty for input prior to finalizing.*

3. Purposeful instructional practice is a key driver for academic success. What steps should the principal and teachers take to identify appropriate instructional strategies to improve teacher collaboration throughout the building?

   - ***Facilitator tip:*** *Participants should look for strategies designed to foster teacher collaboration. For example, how might instructional rounds assist teachers to feel more comfortable collaborating with each other? What features could be added to the traditional instructional rounds framework to bolster collaboration opportunities?*

4. A willingness to collaborate hinges on trust. What steps should be taken to embed trust building exercises into a PLP designed to increase teacher collaboration capacity?

   - ***Facilitator tip:*** *Encourage participants to think about culture and climate prior to reflecting on effective instructional strategies. For example, step one of lesson study might entail a "getting to know each other" exercise before analyzing student data.*

5. Collaborative efforts take time. What opportunities exist during the teacher workday to increase time for collaboration among colleagues?

   - ***Facilitator tip:*** *Understanding that time is a valuable asset, participants should reflect on creative opportunities the principal and teachers have to rethink duty assignments in a way that provides more time for collaboration? For example, could a teacher's duty be shared with a colleague to permit additional planning time? Could a lunch duty be reassigned to other personnel allowing for more teacher collaboration time?*

After participants have reflected on and discussed these questions, additional learning activities should be used to deepen understanding. Due to varying

164 *Professional Learning in P–12 Schools*

degrees of experience, the following activities could involve dividing participants into future school leaders and current school leaders.

Learning Activities for School Leaders

Literature on leadership development (Hrivnak et al., 2009), instructional data use (Coburn & Turner, 2011), PLP development (Killion 2013), and collaborative problem solving (Graesser et al., 2018) support school leaders in facilitating interactions among stakeholders to gather background knowledge, notice data, raise questions, and negotiate problem identification. Drawing on adult learning, educators have the capacity as well to apply past professional experiences to help resolve current issues pertaining to their craft (Zepeda et al., 2014).

Whether a school leader is new or experienced, they should reflect on how they will prioritize collaboration efforts among teachers. Instructors could consider the following activities to engage participants in the work of developing a PLP around teacher collaboration:

1. Use the jigsaw strategy (Aronson, 2000) for participants to cooperatively research and to select appropriate instructional strategies to support teacher collaboration.
2. Divide participants into teams to collaboratively develop an implementation timeline to execute selected instructional strategies.
3. Invite a practicing school leader and/or educator to offer input on the quality and practicality of the team's teacher collaboration PLP.
4. Review a current master schedule and analyze embedded teacher collaboration time. Are teachers given the opportunity to meet as teams to grapple with issues impacting instruction? Are teachers provided time to plan with same subject colleagues? How can collaboration time be increased if not present?
5. Design a survey to provide baseline data on the levels of trust among faculty to assist in scaffolding collaboration efforts. Reflect on the impact trust (or lack thereof) has on teacher collaboration. How might a collective approach to increasing trust be established?

References

Anderson, S., Leithwood, K., & Strauss, T. (2010). Leading data use in schools: Organizational conditions and practices at the school and district levels. *Leadership and Policy in Schools*, 9(3), 292–327.

Anthony, A. B., Gimbert, B. G., Luke, J. B., & Hurt, M. H. (2019). Distributed leadership in context: Teacher leaders' contributions to novice teacher support. *Journal of School Leadership*, 29(1), 54–83.

Aronson, E. (2000). The jigsaw classroom. https://www.jigsaw.org/

D. Miller & A. Anthony   165

Bellanca, J. A., & Brandt, R. (2010). *21st century skills: Rethinking how students learn.* Solution Tree Press.

Bolman, L. G., & Deal, T. E. (2017). *Reframing organizations: Artistry, choice, and leadership.* John Wiley & Sons.

Bray, J. N. (2000). *Collaborative inquiry in practice: Action, reflection, and making meaning.* Sage.

Calvert, L. (2016). *Moving from compliance to agency: What teachers need to make professional learning work.* Learning Forward.

City, E. A., Elmore, R. F., Fiarman, S. E., & Teitel, L. (2011). *Instructional rounds in education: A network approach to improving teaching and learning.* Harvard Education Press.

Coburn, C. E., & Turner, E. O. (2011). Research on data use: A framework and analysis. *Measurement, 9,* 173–206.

Collet, V. S. (2019). *Collaborative lesson study: ReVisioning teacher professional development.* Teachers College Press.

Costa, A. L., & Kallick, B. (1993). Through the lens of a critical friend. *Educational Leadership, 51,* 49–49.

Courtney, S. (2018). *Why adults learn: Towards a theory of participation in adult education.* Routledge.

Darling-Hammond, L. (1994). *Professional development schools: Schools for developing a profession.* Teachers College Press.

Darling-Hammond, L., Hyler, M. E., & Gardner, M. (2017). *Effective teacher professional development.* Learning Policy Institute.

Day, D. V. (2000). Leadership development: A review in context. *The Leadership Quarterly, 11*(4), 581–613.

Donovan, S., & Bransford, J. (Eds.). (2005). *How students learn.* The National Academies Press.

Goddard, R. D., Goddard, Y., Kim, E. S., & Miller, R. (2015). A theoretical and empirical analysis of the roles of instructional leadership, teacher collaboration, and collective efficacy beliefs in support of student learning. *American Journal of Education, 121,* 501–530.

Goddard, Y. L., Goddard, R. D., & Tschannen-Moran, M. (2007). A theoretical and empirical investigation of teacher collaboration for school improvement and student achievement in public elementary schools. *Teachers College Record, 109*(4), 877–896.

Goddard, Y. L., & Kim, M. (2018). Examining connections between teacher perceptions of collaboration, differentiated instruction, and teacher efficacy. *Teachers College Record, 120*(1), 90–103.

Graesser, A. C., Fiore, S. M., Greiff, S., Andrews-Todd, J., Foltz, P. W., & Hess, F. W. (2018). Advancing the science of collaborative problem solving. *Psychological Science in the Public Interest, 19*(2), 59–92.

Guskey, T. R. (2014). Planning professional development. *Educational Leadership, 71*(8), 10–16.

Hattie, J. (2009). *Visible learning: A synthesis of over 800 meta-analyses relating to achievement.* Routledge.

Hirsh, S., & Hord, S. M. (2012). *A playbook for professional learning: Putting the standards into action.* Learning Forward.

Hoy, W. K., & Miskel, C. G. (2013). *Educational administration: Theory, research and practice* (9th ed.). McGraw-Hill.

Hoy, W. K., Tarter, C. J., & Bliss, J. R. (1990). Organizational climate, school health, and effectiveness: A comparative analysis. *Educational Administration Quarterly, 26*(3), 260–279.

166 *Professional Learning in P–12 Schools*

Hrivnak, G. A., Reichard, R. J., & Riggio, R. E. (2009). A framework for leadership development. In S. J. Armstrong & C. V. Fukami (Eds.), *The SAGE handbook of management learning, education, and development* (pp. 456–475). Sage.

Killion, J. (2013). *Professional learning plans: A workbook for states, districts, and schools.* Learning Forward.

Knowles, M. S. (1978). Andragogy: Adult learning theory in perspective. *Community College Review,* 5(3), 9–20.

Lewis, C., Perry, R., & Murata, A. (2006). How should research contribute to instructional improvement? The case of lesson study. *Educational Researcher,* 35(3), 3–14.

Little, J. W. (1990). The persistence of privacy: Autonomy and initiative in teachers' professional relations. *Teachers college record,* 91(4), 509–536.

Marzano, R. J. (2007). *The art and science of teaching: A comprehensive framework for effective instruction.* ASCD.

Merriam, S. B. (2001). Andragogy and self-directed learning: Pillars of adult learning theory. *New Directions for Adult and Continuing Education* (89), 3–14.

Merriam, S. B. (Ed.) (2018). *Adult learning theory: Evolution and future directions* (2nd ed.). Routledge.

Merriam, S. B., & Bierema, L. L. (2014). Andragogy: The art and science of helping adults learn. *Adult Learning: Linking Theory and Practice,* 42–60.

Merriam, S. B., & Bierema, L. L. (2018). *Adult learning theory: Linking theory and practice.* Jossey-Bass.

Merriam, S. B., Caffarella, R. S., & Baumgartner, L. (2007). *Learning in adulthood: A comprehensive guide.* John Wiley.

Pagliaro, M. M. (2017). *Questioning, instructional strategies, and classroom management: A Compendium of criteria for best teaching practices.* Rowman & Littlefield.

Printy, S. M., Marks, H. M., & Bowers, A. J. (2009). Integrated leadership: How principals and teachers share instructional influence. *Journal of School Leadership,* 19(5), 504–532.

Putnam, R. T., & Borko, H. (2000). What do new views of knowledge and thinking have to say about research on teacher learning? *Educational Researcher,* 29(1), 4–15.

Riggio, R. E. (2008). Leadership development: The current state and future expectations. *Counseling Psychology Journal: Practice and Research,* 60(4), 383–392.

Stokhof, H. J., De Vries, B., Martens, R. L., & Bastiaens, T. J. (2017). How to guide effective student questioning: a review of teacher guidance in primary education. *Review of Education,* 5(2), 123–165.

Turner, J. R., Baker, R., Schroeder, J., & Johnson, K. R. (2018). Leadership development techniques: Mapping leadership development techniques with leadership capabilities using a typology of development. *European Journal of Training and Development,* 42(9), 538–557.

Twidale, M. B., Nichols, D. M., & Paice, C. D. (1997). Browsing is a collaborative process. *Information Processing & Management,* 33(6), 761–783.

Voogt, J. M., Pieters, J. M., & Handelzalts, A. (2016). Teacher collaboration in curriculum design teams: effects, mechanisms, and conditions. *Educational Research and Evaluation,* 22(3–4),121–140.

Zepeda, S. J., Parylo, O., & Bengtson, E. (2014). Analyzing principal professional development practices through the lens of adult learning theory. *Professional Development in Education,* 40(2), 295–315.

17 The Gap between Theory and Practice

A Scenario from Higher Education

Viktor Wang and Geraldine Torrisi-Steele

Introduction

In higher education, leadership positions are occupied by academics, who often have very little, if any, experience or training in leadership practices, decision-making processes, and even of ethical decision-making in their capacity as leaders (Torrisi-Steele, 2020). Their "ascension" to positions of "power" typically takes place through their academic achievements or other circumstance. These positions often call for new leaders to engage in the evaluation of other faculty, make policy decisions, and even facilitate what teaching and research might look like across their universities.

This case focuses on the gap between theory and practice of higher education leadership and on the consequences of that gap. The case provides an opportunity to explore leadership styles and reflect on the interaction of those styles with the context in which leadership is being enacted. Wang and Russo's model (Wang & Torrisi-Steele, 2015) can serve as the basis of teaching leadership theory and practice in higher education and provides part of the conceptual framework for the study.

Case: Leadership in Question

The case presented is fictitious. The central character is Dr. John Doe, a tenure track faculty member in a "typical" large multicultural university, who takes up the offer of an acting leadership position and is later appointed to a higher leadership position.

Context

Dr. John Doe is a tenure track faculty member in a large public university that we will refer to as FOU. Dr. Doe's teaching and scholarship did not meet the necessary level of performance. Student evaluations of his courses conveyed much less than "stellar performance" and never resulted in a status of exceeding expectations. Dr. Doe's research activities were satisfactory, although he was not highly active in collaborations across other institutions.

DOI: 10.4324/9780429331503-20

168   *Gap between Theory & Practice*

Dr. Doe demonstrated outstanding service in his administrative service to the university. Dr. Doe was very much a "home grown" academic with all his degrees coming from FOU and never having taught anywhere else.

The Dean for Dr. John Doe's college departed on relatively short notice. In these circumstances, it was common practice at FOU to nominate an acting Dean from the faculty members, allowing the search committee time to find a permanent replacement. Dr. Doe was nominated as acting Dean. He was pleased with his ascension from faculty member to acting Dean. Quite often, occupying acting positions of leadership proved to be the first step in a longer administrative trajectory. Dr. Doe felt that the opportunity to be in the acting Dean's role held potential for securing a tenured, full professor position in the future, and he expected that the role would not be too difficult to manage. Besides, accepting the role freed him up from some teaching duties. He wouldn't miss having to deal with student complaints about his teaching.

The Story as It Unfolded

Dr. Doe was flattered by his nomination to be acting Dean, but his nomination had little to do with his leadership skills and occurred more by default. No one else wanted the position. They were well aware of the challenges of the position, and there had been periods of financial stress during which some difficult decisions needed to be made. Dr. Doe's colleagues felt comfortable in more familiar roles of teaching and research rather than in administrative positions in which they had no experience.

Dr. Doe's mastery of administrative procedures and his knowledge of bureaucracy served him well. He efficiently signed off on documents, chaired, and attended the usual meetings for the committees as expected. During a quiet period, there was little significant decision-making to be made. No one expected that he would chart any new pathways for the future of the college – he was simply filling the position, keeping administrative cogs moving. As he expected, he expended little effort. But the position would likely play a role in his future plans for promotion. When a permanent replacement was found, he readily stepped down.

Dr. Doe was seen by most of his colleagues as inflexible, "sticking to the policy" type of person. From his perspective, the solution to every problem could be solved by adhering to established procedures and policy. During his time as acting Dean, faculty certainly did not feel invited to approach him with any grievances or innovative ideas for the future. But he was only an interim Dean. Little attention was paid to his leadership style.

A year later, Dr. Doe was appointed to the higher position of associate provost who shaped leadership positions as he saw fit. At FOU, it was common for assistant Deans to be removed and replaced with individuals with relatively little knowledge of the leadership content or college academics. Dr. Doe's modus operandi appeared to some observers as ad hoc. From the perspective of faculty, there were no obvious reasons for the changes he made, and there seemed to be no strategic vision. Notably, changes he made involved no consultation. He saw his leadership position as important and took it seriously, but he did not have strong interpersonal skills and struggled to see the perspective of others. Others felt strongly that Dr. Doe was acting on his personal biases. Two of the four positions that he had made changes to were filled by faculty who were either former collaborators, co-authors, or his avid supporters. What happened next was that Dr. Doe's lack of awareness of issues related to faculty and students fed into a problem of racial tension on FOU's campus.

It started with students from a particular cultural group feeling that they were being unfairly graded by a junior faculty member because of their race. Other students from the same cultural group expressed that they too had been unfairly treated and had been targeted on cases of academic misconduct simply because of their cultural group. Unfortunately, the junior faculty member failed to deal well with the complaints within the course. Dr. Doe had avoided involvement or guidance for the faculty member. The incident snowballed when some students from the college group began to vocalize their views actively with protests. As the views from these groups of students became known to those outside the college, other students became involved and brought forward their own perspectives. On occasion, the various groups clashed, and the campus, at times, seemed on the brink of violence.

Despite rising tensions, Dr. Doe did not provide any support to either students or faculty. He elected to ignore the situation, even when he personally witnessed a verbal attack between a pair of students that, in the already volatile atmosphere, nearly led to physical violence among two groups of students with opposing views. Dr. Doe was concerned about the situation but having difficult conversations and resolving conflict was never one of his personal strengths. He hoped the situation would self-resolve. University policies and procedures lead to a requirement for some decision-making on the various incidents that took place. Decisions were made behind closed doors, and no faculty members were asked to verify any facts leading to these decisions. Dr. Doe engaged in his usual process: follow the procedure and sign documents. Faculty members approaching him with their concerns left those conversations feeling that their concerns were not heard, not valued, and not welcome.

Budget complicated matters for Dr. Doe. Budget was always a concern, but there were some highly lucrative programs which his personal faculty friends were now teaching. Many of these friends did not have the required degrees or publications as required by accreditation standards. In the hands of Dr. Doe's appointed program leaders, the programs did not thrive. The enrollments in the programs decreased. One of the contributing factors was the lack of agility in the programs. The previous program leaders continually monitored the programs, maintained connection with demands of industry, and continually modified their programs in order to keep them strong. Some faculty approached Dr. Doe with ideas for new or improved programs, but he

170   *Gap between Theory & Practice*

saw no merit in the proposals and keenly maintained the status quo. Soon, faculty saw approaching him as a waste of time and stopped generating ideas.

Faculty had tolerated Dr. Doe as interim Dean, but in the position of Associate Provost, faculty and students expected "leadership" from him, which didn't materialize. This led to growing dissatisfaction with his performance and calls for his resignation. Government and economic circumstances meant a tight budget, but a highly successful sports program had been able to absorb some of the budgetary pressures, keeping the institution afloat. By way of protest, to force the resignation, faculty and staff put pressure where it would hurt most – on the sports program. With staff and students refusing to participate in the sports program, income suffered as a result of inability to host events – they effectively held Dr. Doe "to ransom."

Dr. Doe, seeing himself as a victim of circumstance, resigned from the position. The senior administration of the university now had the difficult task of appointing another Provost, who through good leadership, could repair the damage and set the university back on course for success. Given the current conditions, even an Interim Provost must be someone capable of at least beginning to set a new, more positive direction for the college and the university. With Dr. Doe's resignation in hand, the senior administrators pondered what kind of person they really needed for the now vacant position.

Conceptual Framework

There are beautifully well-reasoned theories regarding leadership, but the gap between leadership practice and theory in higher education remains. Lack of leadership success will likely have demoralizing effects and result in low satisfaction and high turnover. Universities educate a nation's workforce, and adverse effects in universities are reflected in the well-being of the whole nation (Wang, 2010).

Leadership is a process whereby one individual is able to influence a group of individuals to achieve a common goal (Northouse, 2007). The "best" leaders have honesty, integrity, communication, and empathy (Gayle et al., 2011; Sadeghi & Pihie, 2012; Salahuddin, 2011; Schick, 2014; Siddique, 2011), and must possess technical skills, communication skills, and conceptual skills (Katz, 1955). Weak or destructive leaders (Johnson, 2011) are in contrast incompetent, rigid, and unyielding; closed to new ideas; lacking in self-control; callous and uncaring for the needs of others; corrupt; and possess insular ways that may cause severe physical or psychological harm on others.

A classic study of leadership style or teaching style highlighted a threefold typology (Lippitt & White, 1952) with institutions of higher education: authoritarian (create a sense of group dependence on the leader), laissez-faire, and democratic (achieve group cohesion and working relationships whether the leader is present or not) (as cited by Jarvis, 2002, p. 27). In "shared governance," a faculty member is considered a leader and a leader is considered a faculty member. Although McGregor (1960) and Knowles (1978) developed

Theory X and Y assumptions to explain avoidance and engagement with work, Knowles et al. (2005) posited that leaders can become creative, make things happen, and release the energy of others. We posit that expertise in teaching, research, and service should be in place for any university faculty member wishing to enter the arena of administration. The late Chinese Chairman Mao Zedong used to encourage the Chinese people to "unite theory with practice," and "walk on two legs" (Kaplan et al., 1979); there seems to be wisdom in these ideas that university leaders would benefit from embracing.

Leaders, regardless of rank or title must know their field of study (Taylor's principles as cited in Wang, 2011, p. 15). Without being experts in their fields, leaders may not be able to ferret out inefficiencies in the system (systems thinking) and which leadership practices will work with their followers. Universities have a variety of institutionally specific standards, policies, and procedures, and although they may seem to be set in stone, the university is a dynamic environment where flexibility within leadership and faculty is essential for positive organization evolution. Higher education institutions consciously build their reputations on the basis of having experts in their fields. Leaders of these institutions are experts in their discipline and have the potential to model teaching, research, and scholarship to define expectations of their faculty.

Most leaders do not have a degree in business management or leadership but have expertise in their respective content area and are valued for either their expert or referent power, perhaps both (Northouse, 2010). Sometimes university leaders are chosen based on seniority, irrespective of teaching, scholarship, and service, or due to interpersonal connections with already seeded administrators. These "puppet" administrators may not have demonstrated either expert power or referent power but were considered based on similar thinking patterns and/or "moldability" to fit current administrative beliefs.

Institutions of higher education must be classified as a learning organization, not static organizations, if they are truly working toward their mission. A learning organization is one that "is continually expanding its capacity to create its future" (Senge, 1990, p. 14). And the learning organization is continually adjusting and allowing for flexibility (Wang & Bain, 2014). Table 17.1, adapted from Wang and Bain, (2014) outlines characteristics of both static and learning organizations.

In a learning organization, change is the norm, and trust is particularly important for overall employee motivation and commitment (Griffith et al., 2011). Conversely, broken trust likely leads to employee turnover, draining the workforce's intellectual capability. Trust is broken when leaders choose to abuse power and make decisions based on faulty premises or organizational politics in order to maintain position power. Resentment may build but faculty, for fear of repercussion, often can't "rock the boat."

172   *Gap between Theory & Practice*

Table 17.1 Static Organizations Versus Learning Organizations

Dimensions	*Characteristics*	
	Static Organizations	Learning Organizations
Structure	Rigid	Flexible
Atmosphere	Task-oriented	People-centered
Management Philosophy and Attitudes	Use of coercive power	Use of supportive power
Decision-making and Policy Making	High participation and top; low participation at bottom	High participation at all levels
Communication	Top-down; one-way	Multidirectional

A Framework for Change in Connection with the Aforementioned Scenario

The following conceptual framework offers a useful lens for considering the scenario and examines: (1) the inter-action of one's teaching philosophies and teaching theories; (2) the interaction of one's teaching philosophies and leadership theories; and (3) behaviors and interactions of leaders and followers to prevent leaders acting together as a group in a way that disempowers followers or even creates a culture of fear or hopelessness among followers. Wang-Russo's Higher Education Model of Theory and Practice is a synthesis of these three concepts, with theory leading to practice within the higher education arena. The Higher Education Model of Theory and Practice model can serve as the basis of teaching leadership theory and practice in higher education. The utilization of this framework potentially translates into a professional and social web within the organization, further helping with the need to adapt to change.

Teacher philosophy is how one thinks or conceptualizes beliefs, values, and truth, which inevitably shapes a sense of justice within the sphere of an educational environment – it is the reason why professors do what they do, and one would assume these beliefs are altruistic and humanistic when the professoriate interfaces with students and administration. The way in which the teaching philosophy is grounded will have a direct impact on which teaching theories are utilized by faculty and what should be acceptable to administration. Perhaps, when administrators interface with faculty, the administrators should do just as educators do as in assessing student learning. In this way, and using this kind of teaching theory formulation, we can pass a wide variety of information to stakeholders that they can understand and apply in their own natural frame. If faculty are legitimately included and listened to within a shared decision-making process then they will be empowered to offer suggestions and ideas to make the organization more efficient and effective.

Top-down management is an approach that assumes and designates power by position on a tiered management hierarchy; this is a model that is ineffective in a learning organization that is to be built on shared governance. To flatten the organization, the hierarchy itself may not need to change, but the value of functional roles needs to be altered. Value should be determined by behavior exhibited as defined by functional role definition of leadership, management, and other as needed. Karl Marx said, "from each, according to his ability; to each, according to his work" (as cited in Pena, 2011). In a learning organization, value is based on one's contributions, not the position held.

Collaboration is essential to effective working relationships between faculty and administration. For collaboration, collegiality is not crucial but is desirable. The "top" often sets the tone for collegiality. Congeniality naturally builds stakeholder rapport, and will foster a shared sense of community, thereby meeting the relational psychological need as outlined by self-determination theory (Deci & Ryan, 2000).

The final main point in Wang-Russo's model is termed, "no fear." In this model, fear is seen as a negative emotion that stifles production and employee ability to contribute to the organization. In universities, fear is often the result of a controlled environment in which faculty fear for their jobs if they do not comply with the vision or task set by leadership. Fear diminishes the trust needed for flatter organizational structure. In a "no fear" environment, people are authentic. Faculty and leaders should hold fast to the three components of the Wang-Russo model to stay in control of their teaching, scholarship, and above all, leading others in higher education.

Conclusion

Implementing leadership theory requires critical thinking, the challenging of presuppositions (Brookfield, 1995, 2005), and the ability for ethical decision-making. As illustrated in the scenario, lack of practice of theory of leadership can have serious negative implications. Faculty who aspire to leadership roles need the components of scholarship, teaching, and service, as well as technical skills, human skills, and conceptual fluency, to be "qualified leaders" who engender trust and can work within an organizational structure where shared governance and shared ideas are the norm.

Questions/Learning Activities

Advertise for a new university Dean: Collaboratively develop a concept map for the characteristics of good leadership. Write a call for an expression of interest for a Deanship, which lists and explains the leadership competencies that the applicant must demonstrate.

Discussion Questions

1. How might authoritarian, laissez-faire, and/or democratic behaviors be demonstrated in a higher education environment, and how might followers respond to each? Explain with scenarios to illustrate.

174 *Gap between Theory & Practice*

2. What role does trust serve in learning organizations? How might a leader, in a position such as Dr. Doe's, create a culture of trust in a higher education organization?
3. What is meant by a flat organization? Was Dr. Doe's approach consistent with a flat organizational model? Explain your reasoning.
4. Do you believe Dr. Doe's behavior was ethical in his actions as Associate Provost during the period of racial tensions? Explain your views.

Role-Play

In groups of three to five, conduct a brief review of literature (five to ten articles) around leadership in higher education. According to the literature, which leadership styles would be most appropriate to the higher education setting?

Using this knowledge, in a group of three to five, adopt a leadership style that you believe would have been more effective than Dr. Doe's approach, role-playing the scene where the faculty members approach Dr. Doe as Associate Provost with ideas for improving a program of study. Try on different leadership styles. How might leadership in the scenario play out with different styles?

References

Northouse, P. (2018). *Leadership theory and practice* (8th ed.). Sage.

Wang, V. (Ed.) (2020). *Handbook of research on ethical challenges in higher education leadership and administration.* Information Science Reference.

Brookfield, S. D. (2005). *The power of critical theory.* Jossey-Bass.

Deci, E. L., & Ryan, R. M. (2000). The "what" and "why" of goal pursuits: Human needs and the self- determination theory of behaviour. *Psychological Inquiry*, 11(4), 227–268.

Gayle, D. J., Tewarie, B., & White Jr, A. Q. (2011). *Governance in the twenty-first- century university: Approaches to effective leadership and strategic management: ASHE-ERIC Higher Education Report* (Vol.14). John Wiley & Sons.

Jarvis, P. (Ed.). (2002). *The theory & practice of teaching.* Kogan Page.

Johnson, C. (2011). *Meeting the ethical challenges of leadership: Casting light or shadow.* Sage.

Kaplan, F. M., Sobin, J. M., & Andors, S. (1979). *Encyclopedia of China today.* Harper & Row.

Katz, R. L. (1955). Skills of an effective administrator. *Harvard Business Review*, 33(1), 33–42.

Knowles, M. S. (1978). *The adult learner: A neglected species* (2nd ed.). Gulf.

Knowles, M. S., Holton, E. F., & Swanson, R. A. (2005). *The adult learner: The definitive classic in adult education and human resource development* (6th ed.). Elsevier.

Lippitt, R., & White, R. K. (1952). An experimental study of leadership and group life. In G. E. Swanson, T. M. Newcomb, & E. L. Hartley (Eds.), *Readings in social psychology* (3rd ed.) (pp. 340–355). Holt.

McGregor, D. (1960). *The human side of enterprise.* McGraw-Hill.

Northouse, P. G. (2007). *Leadership theory and practice* (4th ed.). SAGE Publications.

Northouse, P. G. (2010). *Leadership: Theory and Practice* (5th ed.). SAGE Publications.

Pena, D.S. (2011). You might be a Marxist if...you believe in from each according to their abilities, to each according to their needs. http://www.politicalaffairs.net/you-might-be-a-marxist-if-you-believe-in-from-each-according-to-their-abilities-to-ea ch-according-to-their-needs/

Sadeghi, A., & Pihie, Z. A. L. (2012). Transformational leadership and its predictive effects on leadership effectiveness. *International Journal of Business and Social Science*, 3(7), 186–197.

Salahuddin, M. M. (2011). Generational differences impact on leadership style and organizational success. *Journal of Diversity Management (JDM)*, 5(2), 1–6.

Schick, E. B. (2014). Shared visions of public higher education governance: Structures and leadership styles that work. http://repositorio.ub.edu.ar:8080/xmlui/bitstream/handle/123456789/2136/ED353948.pdf?sequence=1

Senge, P. (1990). *The fifth discipline: The art and practice of the learning organization* Doubleday Dell.

Sharif, M. M., & Scandura, T. A. (2014). Do perceptions of ethical conduct matter during organizational change? Ethical leadership and employee involvement. *Journal of Business Ethics*, 124(2), 185–196.

Siddique, A., Aslam, H. D., Khan, M., & Fatima, U. (2011). Impact of academic leadership on faculty's motivation, and organizational effectiveness in higher education system. *International Journal of Business and Social Science*, 2(8), 184–191.

Taylor, F. W. (1911). *The principles of scientific management*. Harper & Brothers Publishers.

Torrisi-Steele, G. (2020). Ethics in higher education leadership: Current themes and trends. In V. Wang, *Handbook of research on ethical challenges in higher education leadership and administration* (pp. 1–17). IGI Global.

Wang, V. (2010). Editorial preface. *International Journal of Adult Vocational Education and Technology*, 1(2), i–iii.

Wang, V. (2011). Principles of scientific management and occupational analysis. In V. Wang (Ed.), *Definitive readings in the history, philosophy, theories and practice of career and technical education* (pp. 15–26). Information Science Reference and Zhejiang University Press.

Wang, V., & Bain, B. (2014). Comparing learning organizations with static organizations. In V. Wang (Ed.), *Handbook of research on education and technology in a changing society* (pp. 165–177). Information Science Reference.

Wang, V., & Torrisi-Steele, G. (2015). Online teaching, change, and critical theory. *New Horizons in Adult Education & Human Resource Development*, 27(3), 18–26.

18 "I Can't Hear You"

Incorporating Developmentally Appropriate Feedback for Adults in Balkor Elementary Charter School

Patricia M. Virella

Balkor Elementary Case Study

Background

Balkor Elementary Charter School is located in New York City, with 462 students and serves Kindergarten through fourth grades. Most students within the school are Latino or African American. Approximately half of the school qualifies for free and reduced lunch, which means the school is designated as a Title I school. Title I funding provides federal supplemental aid for schools with concentrated poverty populations to meet educational achievement. Established in 2004, Balkor Elementary has enjoyed over a decade of high student enrollment and achievement. Despite past successes, Balkor Elementary has experienced high leadership turnover, lower student enrollments, increased absenteeism, and lackluster student achievement over the past three years. Balkor Elementary became a school in need of improvement in 2017, according to the New York State Department's Charter School Oversight Office. The superintendent hired Jasmine Ellis as principal of Balkor Elementary to improve student achievement, increase enrollment, and reduce absenteeism. In this case, I explore how Principal Ellis aimed to increase student achievement by implementing developmentally appropriate feedback cycles for teachers.

Entry Plan and Findings

Before her tenure as principal of Balkor Elementary Charter School, Principal Ellis investigated the school's standing, the organizational practices, and teacher beliefs that might contribute to the problems she was tasked with solving. To start, she created an entry plan to inform her theory of action for strategic change. Jentz and Wofford (2008) described entry plans as strategic plans of action created by the entering school leader, which require leaders to first interview multiple stakeholders of an organization; secondly, review data of the organization; and then pull together a plan of action. This is designed to be completed as soon as the new leader enters the organization. Entry plans

DOI: 10.4324/9780429331503-21

are created often shared with various stakeholders. Principal Ellis's entry plan included activities such as interviews, data dives, and meetings with key stakeholders. She also reviewed the previous year's feedback surveys given to teachers to understand their needs for improvement, and worked to identify trends in student achievement data. Finally, she studied the outgoing principal's teacher observation feedback notes, triangulating student achievement data, and teacher evaluations.

After six weeks of inquiry, Principal Ellis concluded her entry plan and generated initial findings. She found that teachers wanted better feedback to increase their instructional delivery. However, teachers felt coaching only happened punitively to correct poor teaching resulting in a lack of trust in the instructional leadership team. Principal Ellis also learned from her entry plan initial findings that teachers at Balkor were motivated to achieve better results for their students and the school community. She identified the following two key goals and began to draft some potential strategies to implement.

Goal 1: Create a learner's culture by honoring diverse adult learning styles tied to goals that support growth in practice.

Principal Ellis believed the creation of short-term and long-term goals would develop teachers' capacity to improve instruction and become more autonomous, reflective thinkers around their pedagogy. She thought these goals could help teachers to take more responsibility for instructional outcomes. To accomplish this first goal, she drew on adult learning theorists such as Drago-Severson (2011) as a foundation for her work. For example, Drago-Severson (2011) stated, "learning designs that invite adult learners to experience the processes they are learning about as they are learning about them are often most effective" (p. 12). Principal Ellis believed by bringing her teachers into the learning experience, they would feel that they had goals that would meet their professional expectations and increase their desire to learn. Principal Ellis thought this strategy's success rate would be limited if there wasn't a clear objective or goal identified at the beginning of the learning cycle and a lens to observe in. She was committed to helping teachers outline personalized goals and provide a supportive space for reflection, learning, and growth.

Goal 2: Self-reflection of teaching and instructional strategies by teachers to discuss efficacy in instruction and the learner (teacher).

This goal entails teachers having to think deeply about what they felt would help push their practice and support their students. Principal Ellis was concerned with the statement from one of the Kindergarten teachers in reference to students, that "the low ones cannot do anything." This statement was indicative of limited self-reflection on the part of the teacher, and a problem with deficit thinking being applied to student learning. Are the teachers able to reflect on their narratives and biases that manifest in their teaching?

178 *"I Can't Hear You"*

Principal Ellis was convinced that reflection is at the heart of effective teaching. To her, reflection is the mirror to both the educator's practice, as well as the students' experience.

Teachers would need their instructional leadership team to give them precise and relevant feedback to challenge deficit thinking and any beliefs that students at Balkor were not capable of high academic achievement. Principal Ellis expected that teachers would welcome a tailored approach to feedback, based on her entry plan information gathering; feedback from previous years' teacher survey responses indicated that they wanted more specific and constructive feedback. Finally, she believed her plan would be beneficial for her instructional leadership team members' own professional growth as they began to learn principles on adult development's "way of knowing" (Drago-Severson & Blum-DeStefano, 2016, p. 2). Principal Ellis saw several potential opportunities afforded by enacting her plan. She met with the superintendent to describe how she planned to use adult developmentally appropriate feedback as a lever to support growth.

Creating a Plan of Action

Based on these findings, Principal Ellis decided the best starting point for meeting these challenges was to improve feedback cycles. She determined that a new approach centered around developmentally appropriate feedback would accelerate the teachers' capacity to deliver effective instruction to support improved student achievement. Furthermore, Principal Ellis presumed implementing adult developmentally appropriate feedback would build trust and ultimately meet academic achievement goals. It was clear from the entry plan findings that trust was also depleted in the school. Teachers did not trust the school leadership team to have integrity in their feedback, believing that the leadership team only sought to advance their own agendas.

Principal Ellis focused on her theory of action, which would shape her strategic plan. She believed that if teachers receive developmentally appropriate feedback, this would accelerate the development of their instructional delivery, and student achievement would improve. Principal Ellis paid close attention to her instructional leadership team, which included an assistant principal, literacy coach, math coach, and director of special education; she wanted to better understand how they could assist her in the turnaround process. Her strategic plan included opportunities for learning with her leadership team to prepare them for this new approach and successful implementation of the instructional feedback cycles.

Over the school year, Principal Ellis and her instructional leadership team implemented feedback that was designed to be developmentally appropriate for adult learners, using the book *Tell me so I can hear you* (Drago-Severson & Blum-DeStefano, 2016) as the foundation for their work. She used this text to base feedback conversations and monitor the progress of change. In this book, Drago-Severson and Blum-DeStefano (2016) described how adults learn, affecting how they receive feedback. They assert that we must pay careful attention and understand the adult learner's way of knowing if we are going to give effective feedback.

Principal Ellis drew on this framework in particular because feedback from her entry plan interviews revealed that the teachers at Balkor did not understand, internalize, or use the feedback given by their instructional leadership team. The participants in the interviews described that the feedback was ineffective. However, Principal Ellis believed the feedback problem was actually due, at least in part, to the different ways people internalize feedback.

Beginning the Work

Principal Ellis began her work in the early fall, immediately meeting with the instructional leadership team and modeling coaching cycles. Her biggest goal was to build a culture of trust that allowed for effective feedback across the school. Following the text, she began to set the preconditions for growth in order to build the leaders' capacity on her team. She focused her plan on the guiding question: "What has to happen *first* – after one learns about constructive-developmental theory and its implications for individual mean-ing-making – in order to offer the most meaningful feedback for growth and improvement?" (Drago-Severson & Blum-DeStefano, 2016, p. 95). She decided she would have to conduct regular meetings to engage her team in learning about a developmental approach to feedback. She decided to structure the meetings to focus in part on learning and book study, and also action plans.

Principal Ellis began the first meeting by posing questions such as, "What feels most exciting to you about building a culture of feedback?" (Drago-Severson & Blum-DeStefano, 2016, p. 114) in order to build support for this approach from her team. She then asked, "What feels most challenging to you about building a culture of feedback?" (Drago-Severson & Blum-DeStefano, 2016, p. 114) to get her instructional team members to reflect on the challenges they had experienced with the teaching staff and building motivation for developing skills that would deepen teachers' instructional practice.

Principal Ellis listened to the team's concerns and shared her plan. She delivered the books to the leadership team and asked them to read the first chapter to orient them to the learning styles and assess their own individual learning styles. She also asked team members to journal, using the reflective questions at the end of the chapter to shape discussions at their next meeting. After this initial meeting, the instructional leadership team walked away feel-ing good about the next steps to jumpstart their work. In the second meeting, leaders came back and described their way of knowing based on the reflective work Principal Ellis had them complete. Some leaders were more candid, while others did not share as readily. Principal Ellis kept this in mind as a point to work on as the year progressed. She then began to ask leaders to identify where they thought their teachers were with regard to ways of

180 *"I Can't Hear You"*

knowing. It was at this point that the Principal saw what the teachers had described. Leaders began to use their own personal problems to frame their sensemaking of teachers' ways of knowing. Principal Ellis asked for evidence connected to observations, data, and student learning in order to develop and strengthen the conversation.

Once this lens was applied, the instructional team began to dialogue and began to debate the teachers' classifications in order to reach a consensus. By the fourth meeting, in mid-October, the first round of observations would occur. Principal Ellis asked her instructional leadership team to prepare a pre-observation meeting script designed with the teacher's developmentally appropriate stage based on the adult development readings. The instructional team shared their writings and gave each other feedback while Principal Ellis facilitated. After this meeting, she brought the team members back to the point of reflection on the process before releasing them to have their meetings. As the instructional leadership team met with their supervisees, she observed them in practice giving feedback to teachers. She also modeled giving developmentally appropriate feedback to the teachers and staff in order to build a culture of growth across the building.

Opportunities and Tradeoffs

Principal Ellis faced several opportunities and challenges in implementing this approach. For example, although there is no hierarchical structure in the adult learning framework created by Drago-Severson and Blum-DeStefano (2016) some members of the leadership team did have a tendency to impose hierarchy in the "ways of knowing," referring to some teachers as "limited" because of their adult development style. In contrast, some teachers had the opportunity to be seen in a new and positive light. Despite Principal Ellis's success with improved student achievement at the end of the school year, she did experience high teacher and leader turnover, as well as mixed reviews about this initiative from staff.

Supporting Literature

Adult development theory (Drago-Severson and Blum-DeStefano, 2016) allows educators to understand the significance of adult growth and how school leaders engage in adult education to promote that growth. This case draws on two bodies of literature: a) educational leadership literature to understand the varied tasks and priorities that principals take on; and b) andragogy-pedagogy literature to understand how to establish a learning orientation with adult learners. Oxford (1996) states, "individuals instigate, direct, and sustain activity to satisfy certain needs that are hierarchical in nature, beginning with biological needs and progressing upward to psychological ones" (p. 43)

Patricia M. Virella 181

Leadership

Principals carry out many types of work while addressing a wide range of problems. A principal's primary job within the school setting is to be an instructional leader (Fullan, 2014). Principals are also responsible for community relations and school finances, and are accountable to families and board members. I use the leadership literature to understand how the principalship is a complex interplay of types of leadership. Stentz et al. (2012) summarized leadership as the relationships between several parties, and "the leader as a person, the behavior of the leader, the effects of the leader, and the interaction process between the leader and followers" (p. 1176).

Additionally, the principalship presents as technically intuitive (i.e., instructional leadership, data-driven decision-maker), empath, mentor, and inspiration for their staff (Hess et al., 2007). These complex narratives of the principalship provide many avenues for principals to strategize to meet school improvement aims. Coupled with the notion that teacher leadership is a strong way to implement school improvement (Harris & Jones, 2019; Wenner & Campbell, 2016), principals need to develop their understanding and exercise methods to establish adult-learning opportunities. Andragogy-pedagogy offers a technique to enact change by working with adult learners.

Andragogy

Malcom Knowles (1970) popularized the theory of andragogy, referred to as "the art and science of helping adults learn" (McGuire, 2011, p. 1). Knowles contrasted this theory with pedagogy, which is considered the art and science of teaching children. As school leaders, principals are expected to create learning experiences for adults who teach children through their own experiences, curricula, and learning styles. Well-designed professional learning, which directly relates to teachers' work, further accommodates teachers' individual learning needs (Guskey, 2002). As a result, teachers can connect their andragogical learning experiences to their pedagogy in order to advance their skills in multiple ways (Hunzicker, 2012). Principals who are tasked with creating and conducting professional development sessions for adults can benefit from implementing andragogical principles in their learning activities; this will require moving deeper than merely focusing on professional development content and structure (e.g., half-day workshop vs. self-paced online). Difficulties in adult learning initiatives can arise when pedagogical methods are applied without considering andragogical dynamics (Knowles, 1970; Pew, 2007). Andragogy is defined as:

> the art and science of helping adults learn. In the andragogical model, there are five assertions: 1) The learner's need to know why something is important to learn, 2) showing learners how to direct themselves through information, 3) relating the topic to the learner's experiences, 4) people

182 *"I Can't Hear You"*

will not learn until they are ready and motivated to learn. This requires helping overcome inhibitions, behaviors, and beliefs about learning.

(Conner, 2004, p. 12)

Andragogy draws on how leaders can instruct adults, while also considering that adults have unique learning continuum needs. Further, the use of andragogical principles supports the learner's motivation to successfully meet the learning objectives. Thus, school leaders who are working to improve student outcomes via teacher and/or staff professional development need to consider andragogy and the unique demands of adult learners as they work toward the more distal goal of strong pedagogy and students' success.

Conclusion

Principals tasked with school improvement must consider teachers' professional development needs as part of the approach to change, especially in school turnaround scenarios. In addition, the fact that most principals hired for turnaround are expected to make school improvements happen quickly; this demand for quick improvement creates added pressure on school leaders and their leadership teams. There are multiple pathways to school improvement, and one of the most promising is improved teaching. In the case presented here, Principal Ellis worked to understand teachers' perceptions of their needs and how school leadership could help. At Balkor Elementary, it seemed that effective feedback on instructional practice should be a priority for school improvement. By working to address broad issues such as the need to develop a culture of feedback that empowers teachers to grow, Principal Ellis hoped to see results in student outcomes. We encourage readers to consider how the adult development literature, especially that focused on andragogical principles of adult learning, might support school leaders facing similar demands.

Discussion

This can be completed either independently or in small groups.

1. Would you describe Principal Ellis's way of knowing as beneficial or problematic to school improvement? How could Principal Ellis have leveraged her own way of knowing?
2. What adult learning theories could be considered alongside Principal Ellis's approach? How would this theory help to meet school improvement goals?
3. How did moving toward developmentally appropriate feedback for adult learners (Drago-Severson & Blum-DeStefano, 2016) prove useful in promoting school improvement? Prove ineffective in developing school improvement?
4. How could a focus on developmentally appropriate feedback for adult learners impede building trust between the instructional leadership team

and teachers? How might this feedback support trust building between the instructional leadership team and teachers?

5. Analyze the leadership provided by Principal Ellis and think about how she might better support the turnaround effort for Balkor Elementary Charter School. What challenges did Principal Ellis face, which she did not consider in her theory of action? Which aspects of leadership is she currently ignoring?

References

Conner, M. (2004). An introduction to andragogy + pedagogy. ttps://marciaconner.com/resources/andragogy-pedagogy/

Drago-Severson, E. (2011). How adults learn forms the foundation of the learning designs standards. *Leaning Forward, 32*(5), 10–12.

Drago-Severson, E., & Blum-DeStefano, J. (2016). *Tell me so I can hear you: A developmental approach to feedback for educators.* Harvard Education Press.

Fullan, M. (2014). *The principal: Three keys to maximizing impact.* Josey-Bass.

Guskey, T. R. (2002). Professional development and teacher change. *Teachers and Teaching: Theory and Practice, 8*(3), 381–391. doi:10.1080/135406002100000512

Harris, A., & Jones, M. (2019). Teacher leadership and educational change. *School Leadership and Management, 39*(2), 123–126. doi:10.1080/13632434.2019.1574964

Hess, F. M., & Kelly, A. P. (2007). Learning to lead: What gets taught in principal-preparation programs. *Teachers College Record, 109*(1), 221–243.

Horng, E. L., Klasik, D., & Loeb, S. (2010). Principal's time use and school effectiveness. *American Journal of Education, 116*(4), 491–523.

Hunzicker, J. L. (2012). Professional development and job-embedded collaboration: How teachers learn to exercise leadership. *Professional Development in Education, 38*(2), 267–289.

Jentz, B. C., & Wofford, J. (2008). The entry plan approach: How to begin a leadership position successfully. Leadership & Learning, Inc.

Jones, M. (2006). Teaching empowered students. *Teaching Exceptional Children,* 12–17.

Knowles, M. (1970). *Andragogy: An Emerging Technology for Adult Learning,* 53–70. http://ccomentor.itee.radom.pl/file_course/adult_learning_knowles.pdf

Leithwood, K. (2005). Understanding successful principal leadership: Progress on a broken front. *Journal of Educational Administration, 43*(6), 619–629. doi:10.1108/09578230510625719

McGuire, D. (2011). Adult learning theories. *Human Resource Development: Theory and Practice,* (11), 64–78. doi:10.4135/9781446251065.n7

Mezirow, J. (1997). *Transformative learning: Theory to practice.* New Directions for Adult and Continuing Education.

Oxford, R. L. (1999). *Language learning motivation: pathways to the new century.* University of Hawaii Press.

Pew, S. (2007). Andragogy and pedagogy as foundational theory for student motivation in higher education. *InSight: A Collection of Faculty Scholarship, 2,* 14–25.

Ryan, R. M., & Deci, E. L. (2000). Intrinsic and extrinsic motivations: Classic definitions and new directions. *Contemporary Educational Psychology, 25*(1), 54. doi:10.1006/ceps.1999.1020

Ryan, R. M., & Deci, E. L. (2000). Self-determination theory and the facilitation of intrinsic motivation, social development, and well-being. *American Psychologist, 55*(1), 68–78.

184 *"I Can't Hear You"*

Stentz, J. E., Plano Clark, V. L., & Matkin, G. S. (2012). Applying mixed methods to leadership research: A review of current practices. *Leadership Quarterly*, 23(6), 1173–1183. doi:10.1016/j.leaqua.2012.10.00

Wenner, J. A., & Campbell, T. (2016). The theoretical and empirical basis of teacher leadership: A review of the literature. *Review of Educational Research*, 87(1), 134–171. doi:10.3102/0034654316653478

19 The Sharpie Incident

Coloring in the Lines and School Policing of Black Hair

Jennifer L. Martin

Introduction

According to Cooper (2018) the racial empathy gap occurs when "… people, regardless of race, believe that Black people experience less physical pain than White people experience. This racial empathy gap influences everything from harsher sentences for crime to differential prescribing practices for pain medication based on race" (p. 93). Likewise, as Goff et al. (2014) found, children of color are in general perceived as older and thus more culpable for their actions than their White peers. Accordingly, such belief systems have substantial implications for school-based discipline and punishment. Warikoo et al. (2016) assert that teachers treat students differently based on race, and this differential treatment contributes to disparities in achievement based on race. "Explicit attitudes are beliefs and evaluations about people and things that individuals knowingly endorse and have complete discretion over whether they disclose" (p. 508). If left unaddressed, implicit biases lead to profoundly rooted and debilitating cycles of inequities within schools (Jones et al., 2012).

Many teachers have lower expectations both behaviorally and academically for students different from them, which leads to classroom microaggressions (Kohli & Solórzano, 2012). Microaggressions are inconspicuous racial affronts aimed at Students of Color conveyed with action or language. These insinuations serve to make students feel inferior and promote the maintenance of existing power structures. The consistent barrage of cultural slurs disparages and demeans students, and affects self-esteem and achievement. Similarly, stereotypical beliefs and implicit biases lead educators to consciously or unconsciously act on the deficit theory. This perspective supposes that students from different cultures underperform academically because of cultural deficits. Teachers who succumb to the deficit theory hold lower academic and behavioral expectations for students and summarily provide substandard instruction, care, and social support. If students subsequently fail to achieve, their underachievement is blamed on their lack of intelligence and motivation, which is attributed to their cultural deficit (May, 2020).

DOI: 10.4324/9780429331503-22

186   *The Sharpie Incident*

The Case

Dress Code Violation?

On a Monday in October, Devonte Moore, a 13-year-old African American male in seventh grade, came to school at George Washington Middle School, a predominantly White institution. A successful student and athlete, he had a new haircut that was close cropped with lines shaved into the back of his head, similar to the letter W. When Devonte entered his homeroom, Ms. Hines, his teacher looked at him quizzically. A White woman in her fifth year as a math teacher, Ms. Hines asked him to turn around, as she inspected his new haircut.

"Devonte, go to the office," she directed. "You are out of compliance with the dress code."

Devonte did not argue. He simply backed out of the room and walked directly to the principal's office. Devonte had never been sent to the office before. As he entered the outer office, the secretary looked at him disapprovingly, and before he had a chance to speak she nodded her head toward the three chairs lined up against the wall. He assumed they were designated for students who were "in trouble" and he sat down and waited. The secretary returned to her work, and very shortly Mr. Brickman's door opened, and a student walked out of his office. Devonte stared at the boy and recognized him as one of the few eighth grade Black guys in the school. They exchanged a brief glance as he walked past him heading to the door leading to the hallway. Devonte then moved his gaze at the principal. Mr. Brickman, a White male with 20 years of administrative experience, narrowed his eyes as he examined Devonte and said, "What is it?" Devonte felt momentarily frozen and sheepishly dropped his head saying, "I was sent out of class by Ms. Hines," he replied.

"For what?" Mr. Brickman asked.

"My hair." Devonte stood up and turned to reveal the shaved lines in the back of his head.

Mr. Brickman lifted his arm and motioned for Devonte to come into his office. Devonte rose and walked to the door. The secretary lifted her eyes from her work and peered at him as he walked to the door. Once in the office, Mr. Brickman closed the door slightly and Devonte turned so he could see the back of his head.

"I'm calling your coach," Mr. Brickman stated as he walked to his desk to pick up the phone.

Devonte backed up slowly and sat down in one of the two available chairs near a small conference table to wait for his coach to enter the office.

Approximately five minutes later, Devonte heard the familiar sound of Coach Johansen's keys dangling as he approached the office. Coach Johansen was a White social studies teacher as well as the track and football coach with 10 years of teaching and coaching experience.

When Mr. Johansen entered the office, Mr. Brickman asked Devonte to stand, and the two men examined his hair. They then asked Devonte to wait outside. Devonte left and sat down in the same chair in the outer office across from the secretary, who did not look up from her work. Mr. Brickman closed the door, and the two men talked for approximately three minutes. They then opened the door and invited Devonte back into the office.

As Devonte entered the office once more, Mr. Brickman began, "Devonte, we are very disappointed in your hair *choice*. Your *choice* is a violation of the school's dress code. But we are going to give you another *choice*. You can either take an in-school suspension until your hair grows back, which will also affect your position on the track team, or we can take care of this today." Coach Johansen held up a marker.

Devonte looked from one man to the other, confused.

Coach Johansen went on, "This color," holding up the marker, "is very similar to the color of your hair. We'll just color in the lines. As you may or may not know, this school has a zero-tolerance policy regarding dress code nonsense."

The Aftermath

Mr. Brickman and Coach Johansen did indeed color in the lines that were shaved into Devonte's scalp. Ms. Hines also entered the office and watched as men colored in Devonte's head. All of this occurred and no one in the school called Devonte Moore's parents. Upon learning of the "Sharpie Incident," the Moore's immediately filed suit against the district for the mental distress the administration and staff caused their son. The parents argued that it took almost a week for the permanent marker to fade from their son's scalp, and that he was subject to teasing and bullying because of the incident. They also expressed outrage that their son, who had never been in trouble before, would be treated in such a manner.

As Mrs. Moore stated on the local news, "Our son is not a trouble maker. We are outraged that he is being treated this way. The school basically coerced him by threatening his position on the track team if he did not consent to having his head colored with permanent marker. It's an outrage. This design has nothing to do with gangs, drugs, instruction, or anything inappropriate. How a haircut can violate a dress code is beyond me." Mr. Moore then indicated that their son informed his parents that the three adults in the office laughed as they colored in the lines on his head.

The Moore's also argued that the marker did nothing to "hide" the haircut and or any part of the design lines that were shaved on their son's head. Instead, the marker made the lines more prominent. Moore's suit indicated that Devonte suffered anxiety and depression after the incident. Mrs. Moore told the press that before filing the lawsuit, she contacted the superintendent several times but received no response. A lawsuit, she felt, was their only recourse. District representatives did not respond to requests from the press for a statement.

The local news reported the district's dress code policy which they obtained from the district website. The policy read, "Hair must be neat, clean and well-

188 *The Sharpie Incident*

groomed. Extreme hairstyles such as carvings, mohawks, spikes, etc., are not allowed."

After this story was released in the press, national civil rights organizations converged on the school. Mr. Brickman was reassigned as head principal of the high school, and the district dress code was changed to allow for natural hairstyles and more culturally responsive dress code policies in general. The Moore's have not received an apology from the school district, and their lawsuit is in progress.

Discussion

Cultural Mismatch and Inequitable Discipline Practices

The education system in the United States has a history of institutional racism, which is revealed in differential discipline favoring White students and disadvantaging Students of Color (Black, 2016). Research indicates that Students of Color are still consistently under surveillance in schools (Ancy Annamma et al., 2019, 2018). Students of Color are often criminalized before they make a mistake. More specifically, racially coded dress codes place a spotlight on Students of Color in anticipation of any supposed infractions (AAPF, 2015; Ancy Annamma et al., 2019; Morris, 2016). Moreover, zero-tolerance guidelines, which impose punishments for each infraction that breaches specific policies are more common in schools with larger historically marginalized populations. In keeping with zero-tolerance policies, school districts have employed a discipline model that holds students responsible, at times criminally so, for infractions running the gamut from low level to violent (Perry & Morris, 2014).

Zero tolerance policies remove common sense and discretionary decision-making from "serious offenses." However, Students of Color are found to violate "serious offenses" more often and are more likely subject to suspension, expulsion, and criminal prosecution. A 2008 American Psychological Zero Tolerance Task Force Report highlighted devastating policy implementation where aspirin could be labeled as a drug offense, and a bobby pin could be marked as a weapon, and both would warrant expulsion. As research indicates, sanctions of preventative detention levied against Black males have been lodged at higher levels than are utilized against all other population groups (Lewis et al., 2010; Monroe, 2005). However, these supposed infractions are often subjective misinterpretations of critical cultural, linguistic, and behavioral patterns exhibited by young men in the African American community (Zion & Blanchett, 2011), exacerbated by implicit bias lack of racial empathy. Inequitable disciplinary techniques are negatively associated with educational outcomes and are inequitably levied toward Students of Color (Lewis et al., 2010; Perry & Morris, 2014).

Cultural mismatch impacts differential school discipline (Darling-Hammond, 2013). Cultural mismatches between students and teachers contribute to misunderstandings that harm students. For example, differences in responses may be misunderstood, misinterpreted, and viewed negatively, leading to more significant percentages of Students of Color receiving more behavioral referrals and referrals for special education services from White teachers (Milner, 2013). Schools with the highest populations of historically marginalized students refer more students for special education services; this mislabeling affects African American children twice as much as White children (Smitherman, 2006; U.S. Department of Education Office for Civil Rights, 2014). Students of Color are often perceived by White adults as criminals, "thugs," loud, and disrespectful. Thus, by their very existence, Students of Color are often perceived as already doing something wrong and are first to be targeted in terms of dress code violations and other subjective discipline infractions such as "disrespect" (Goff et al., 2014).

Influence of Implicit Bias

Research shows that racial bias strongly impacts the educational environment. Educators should acknowledge and understand that the expectations they hold for their students can be influenced by their own racial bias (Kirwin Institute, 2012; Steele & Cohn-Vargas, 2013). Aversive racist and stereotypical attitudes activated unconsciously or involuntarily are also known as implicit bias (Cohn-Vargas, 2015). Implicit racial bias "… can affect a student's self-esteem, motivation, and academic performance" (Kirwin Institute, 2012, p. 15).

Implicit or "hidden" biases are socially learned, pervasive, and held by everyone in society. Because our biases are often developed over time and held as "truths," many do not recognize they exist. Persons who are unaware of their hidden biases are still guided by them, even though they may perceive themselves as unprejudiced, non-discriminatory, and fair, and just in their interactions. This is especially problematic behavior in persons who hold positions of authority and/or power.

Implicit and explicit biases are related to each other in that our thoughts and actions relative to how we interact with others are rooted in deep-seeded stereotypical beliefs about them.

Explicit biases are those deep-seeded notions that we actively acknowledge, and implicit biases are those that we either do not recognize or do not understand that we hold. Because we are unaware of our beliefs, we sometimes take action based on them without realizing it. A teacher may state and believe that they hold equal expectations for all students but in truth, "… implicit bias lowers expectations for Students of Color and stimulates subtle differences in the way the teacher behaves toward these students for example less praise and recognition and more discipline" (Kirwin Institute, 2012, p. 15). Implicit racial bias fuels racial stereotypes. There is evidence of systematic bias in the use of exclusionary discipline. Black students are disproportionately represented in office referrals, suspensions, and expulsions, and for less serious and more subjective reasons than White students who commit the same offenses (Lewin, 2012).

190　*The Sharpie Incident*

Implicit biases actually may be entirely different than our stated positions. We may *say* that we believe that certain persons are "good" or "equal"; however, our internalized understandings of them and subsequent internalized belief systems about them (implicit bias) do not reinforce our stated beliefs. Once we are able to analyze and reflect on our own beliefs, we can understand the truly negative impact they have on others, and we can take steps to change those beliefs into something more constructive.

Questions for Reflection

1. What is the purpose of zero-tolerance policies, and what are considered to be the advantages and disadvantages in implementation?
2. Did the leaders, in this case, follow the dress code policy faithfully? Is there ever room for deviating from policy when leading a school and dealing with dress code issues and other discipline issues?
3. Would you describe the "Sharpie Incident" as representative of a zero-tolerance policy? How can zero-tolerance policies be harmful to students?
4. Does the "Sharpie Incident" discipline decision violate any laws or best practice norms? As a school leader, what would you do differently?
5. Where is the appropriate line between school dress code policy enforcement and student freedom of expression?

Case Background and Additional Information

The Real Story

On April 17, 2019, a 13-year-old middle school student in the seventh grade named J. T., got a "fade haircut with a design line" resembling the letter M (Fieldstadt, 2019, para, 3). According to Fieldstadt, "The haircut did not depict anything violent, gang-related, obscene or otherwise offensive or inappropriate in any manner. J. T. did not believe the haircut violated any school policy" (para. 4). Despite this, then Assistant Principal of Berry Miller Junior High School, Tony Barcelona, informed J. T. that he was to report to the discipline office for being "out of dress code" (Fieldstadt, 2019). The discipline clerk, Helen Day, gave J. T. the choice of in-school suspension, which would result in him missing class and potentially jeopardizing his position on the track team, or having the line design "colored in." J. T. had never been in trouble at school before and felt pressured to comply with school officials. School administrators made no attempt to contact J. T.'s parents.

Three White educators, Tony Barcelona (assistant principal), Helen Day (discipline clerk), and Jeanette Peterson (teacher) participated in this "discipline action" (Fieldstadt, 2019). While Assistant Principal Barcelona stood by, Day colored in the shaved line in J. T.'s hair with a permanent black Sharpie marker. Peterson eventually finished the job. It was reported that all three educators laughed as the incident occurred (Fieldstadt, 2019). According to Fieldstadt, "The jet-black markings did not cover the haircut design line but made the design more prominent and such was obvious to those present at the very beginning of the scalp blackening process" (para. 10). The black ink was visible on J. T.'s head for days after, which contributed to bullying and furthering J. T.'s anxiety. The parents subsequently filed a lawsuit citing "mental anguish."

The district released a statement after J. T.'s parents filed their lawsuit indicating that "the incident" was not condoned by the district, and "the administrator in question" was placed on leave. However, Barcelona was promoted to school principal at the end of the 2018–2019 school year. The school district ultimately changed their dress code at the end of the school year to "identify and remove any perceived racial, cultural and religious insensitivities." Restrictions on fade haircuts were also removed (see Fieldstadt, 2019, para. 20).

The CROWN (Creating a Respectful and Open World for Natural Hair) Act

The CROWN Act protects individuals from discrimination based on hairstyle, extending

"… statutory protection to hair texture and protective styles in the Fair Employment and Housing Act (FEHA) and state Education Codes" (The CROWN Coalition, n.d.). This Act was introduced in California (January, 2019) by Senator Holly Mitchell, which "… expanded the definition of race in the Fair Employment and Housing Act (FEHA) and Education Code, to ensure protection in workplaces and in K–12 public and charter schools" (The CROWN Coalition, n.d., para. 2). The CROWN Act took effect in California on January 1, 2020, enacted by Governor Gavin Newsom.

On December 5, 2019, Senator Cory Booker (D-NJ) and Congressman Cedric Richmond (D-LA) introduced The CROWN Act of 2019 in both chambers of Congress, which would if successful, offer federal protections. Twenty-two additional states are currently considering the CROWN Act and are in progress of introducing their own anti-discrimination of natural hair bills. These states are Colorado, Delaware, Florida, Georgia, Illinois, Kansas, Kentucky, Louisiana, Maryland, Massachusetts, Michigan, Minnesota, Missouri, Nebraska, Oregon, Pennsylvania, South Carolina, Tennessee, Virginia, Washington, West Virginia, and Wisconsin. The cities of Cincinnati, Ohio, and Montgomery County, Maryland, have also passed The CROWN Act on local levels.

Critical Reflection for Group Discussion

1. What is the major conflict of the case and what are the root causes?
2. What assumptions may be guiding the adult behaviors in the case?
3. How should school leaders address implicit biases that result in differential student treatment?

192 *The Sharpie Incident*

4. Is racial empathy necessary to address cultural differences?
5. What role, if any, does the community play in addressing the impact of implicit bias in schools?
6. Read the real case and associated news article and videos. Find additional instances of racial discrimination in school dress codes. Discuss and debrief. Ask:

    - Did your perceptions of the "Sharpie Incident" match your feelings about the real case? Explain.
    - What are some commonalities in racist dress code policies? How can the CROWN Act assist in making school dress codes more equitable and culturally inclusive?
    - What struggles might leaders have in leading culturally responsive and anti-racist work?

7. How does the Crown Act inform the state of race relations in America?
8. Intersectionality is the study of intersections between various forms or systems of oppression. Intersectionality includes individuals who may identify with more than one group, such as Black female, and experience multiple forms of oppression simultaneously. What intersections and forms of oppression are represented in the case?
9. Stereotype threat is an unconscious response to a prevailing negative stereotype about an identifiable group by a member of that group (Rudd, 2012). Research the concept of stereotype threat and discuss how it may contribute to how Students of Color perform in academic settings.

Activities and Resources

1. Search for additional stories on discrimination against African American natural hair styles. What were the similarities and differences in how the cases were handled? In hindsight, what leadership lessons can be drawn from the cases?
2. Could the CROWN Act apply to issues in your own school context? From a leadership perspective, what significant components should be included in a plan to address school-based cultural mismatches? Provide a rationale for the component selections.
3. Read more about the Racial Empathy Gap: https://www.ncbi.nlm.nih.gov/pmc/articles/PMC3108582/. What are the ramifications of engaging this concept?
4. Although this case dealt primarily with racial bias, examine the intersection of bias based on race and sex. Reflect on the concept of intersectionality using the resources listed below: Kimberlé Crenshaw on Intersectionality: https://www.ted.com/talks/kimberle_crenshaw_the_urgency_of_intersectionality?language=en
5. African American Policy Forum (n.d.). *Intersectionality matters podcast*. https://aapf.org/podcast

6. Take a few of the Harvard Implicit Bias Tests, particularly Race IAT: https://implicit.harvard.edu/implicit/takeatest.html

Reflect on your results, taking note on how the results made you feel. Take notes reflecting on what you may need to change within your own life. These steps could include reading relevant texts and attending professional development sessions.

References

African American Policy Forum. (2015). *Black girls matter: Pushed out, overpoliced, and underprotected.* Center for Intersectionality and Social Policy Studies.

American Psychological Association (2008, December) *Are zero tolerance policies effective in the schools? American Psychologist,* 63(9), 852–862. doi:10.1037/0003-066X.63.9.852.

Ancy Annamma, S., Anyon, Y., Joseph, N. M., Farrar, J., Greer, E., Downing, B., & Simmons, J. (2019). Black girls and school discipline: The complexities of being overrepresented and understudied. *Urban Education,* 54(2), 211–242.

Black, D. W. (2016). *Ending zero tolerance: The crisis of absolute school discipline.* New York University Press.

Cohn-Vargas, B. E. (2015). Tackling implicit bias. *Teaching Tolerance.* http://www.tolerance.org/blog/tackling-implicit-bias

Cooper, B. (2018). *Eloquent rage: A black feminist discovers her superpower.* Picador.

Crenshaw, K. (1993). Mapping the margins: Intersectionality, identity politics, and violence against women of color. *Stanford Law Review,* 43, 1241–1299.

The CROWN Coalition. (n.d.). The official campaign of the CROWN act. https://www.thecrownact.com/

Darling-Hammond, L. (2013). Diversity, equity, and education in a globalized world. *Kappa Delta Pi Record,* 49, 113–115.

Fieldstadt, E. (2019, August 19). Texas school staffers colored in black teen's haircut with a Sharpie, lawsuit claims. *NBC News.* https://www.nbcnews.com/news/us-news/texas-school-staffers-colored-black-teen-s-haircut-sharpie-lawsuit-n1043956.

Goff, P. A., Jackson, M. C., Di Leone, B. A., Culotta, C. M., & DiTomasso, N. A. (2014). The essence of innocence: Consequences of dehumanizing black children. *Journal of Personality and Social Psychology,* 106(4), 526–545.

Jones, J. M., Cochran, S. D., Fine, M., Gaertner, S., Mendoza-Denton, R., Shih, M., & Sue, D. W. (2012). *Dual pathways to a better America: Preventing discrimination and promoting diversity.* American Psychological Association, Presidential Task Force on Preventing Discrimination and Promoting Diversity.

Kirwin Institute. (2012). Implicit racial bias: Implications for education and other critical opportunity domains. *Kirwin Institute for the Study of Race and Ethnicity.* http://kirwaninstitute.osu.edu/docs/AACLD_implicit_bias_and_education.pdf

Kohli, R., & Solórzano, D. G. (2012). Teachers, please learn our names! Racial microaggressions and the K-12 classroom. *Race, Ethnicity & Education,* 15, 441–462.

Lewin, T. (2012). Black students face more discipline, data suggest. *The New York Times,* March 6. http://www.nytimes.com/2012/03/06/education/black-students-face-more-harsh-disciplinedata-shows.html

Lewis, C. W., Butler, B. R., Bonner, I. I., Fred, A., & Joubert, M. (2010). African American male discipline patterns and school district responses resulting impact on

194   *The Sharpie Incident*

academic achievement: Implications for urban educators and policy makers. *Journal of African American Males in Education*, 1(1), 7–25.

May, J.J. (2020). *Teacher talk: A 21st century guide for beginning educators.* Linus Learning.

Milner, H. R. (2013). *Start where you are, but don't stay there: Understanding diversity, opportunity gaps and teaching in today's classrooms.* Harvard Education Press.

Monroe, C. R. (2005). Why are "bad boys" always black? Causes of disproportionality in school discipline and recommendations for change. *The Clearing House: A Journal of Educational Strategies, Issues and Ideas*, 79(1), 45–50.

Morris, M. W. (2016). *Pushout: The criminalization of black girls in schools.* The New Press.

NBC News. (2019, October 7). Michigan third grader denied school picture because of her hair. https://www.nbcnews.com/video/michigan-third-grader-denied-school-picture-because-of-her-hair-70822469817?fbclid=IwAR1Gbu7onUUhZOZqumDUWN52_ys3yxURpZdEN3PtxljD2hITJ8BgGBMNFHg

Ortiz, E. (2019, January 10). N.J. wrestler forced to cut dreadlocks still targeted over hair, lawyer says. *NBC News.* https://www.nbcnews.com/news/nbcblk/n-j-wrestler-forced-cut-dreadlocks-still-targeted-over-hair-n957116

Perry, B. L., & Morris, E. W. (2014). Suspending progress collateral consequences of exclusionary punishment in public schools. *American Sociological Review*, 79(6), 1067–1087.

Project Implicit. (2011). Implicit association test. https://implicit.harvard.edu/implicit/takeatest.html

Rudd, T. (2012). *A quick look at standardized testing and stereotype threat.* Kirwan Institute for the Study of Race and Ethnicity.

Steele, D. M., & Cohn-Vargas, B. E. (2013). *Identity safe classrooms: Places to belong and learn.* Corwin.

Warikoo, N., Sinclair, S., Fei, J., & Jacoby-Senghor, D. (2016). Examining racial bias in education: A new approach. *Educational Researcher*, 45(9), 508–514.

Zion, S.D. & Blanchett, W. (2011). (Re)conceptualizing inclusion: Can critical race theory and interest convergence be utilized to achieve inclusion and equity for African American students? *Teachers College Record*, 113(10), 2186–2205.

References

Anderson, J. (2020, April, 16). *Harvard EdCast: School leadership during crisis.* Harvard School of Education.

National Center on Educational Statistics. (2018). National Teacher and Principal Survey. https://nces.ed.gov/surveys/ntps/tables/ntps1718_19110501_a1s.asp

National Center on Educational Statistics. (May, 2020). The condition of education: Racial and ethnic enrollment in public schools. https://nces.ed.gov

Reardon, S. F. (2011). The widening academic achievement gap between the rich and the poor: New evidence and possible explanations. In Greg J.Duncan, & Richard J. Murnane (Eds.), Whither opportunity (pp. 91). Russell Sage Foundation.

Robinson, O. (2020). *Development through adulthood.* Macmillan Education UK.

WestEd, Learning Policy Institute, & Friday Institute for Educational Innovation at North Carolina State University. (2019). *Sound basic education for all: An action plan for North Carolina: Executive summary.* WestEd.

World Bank. (2020, May). *The COVID-19 pandemic: Shocks to education policy responses.* World Bank.

Index

Introductory Note
When the text is within a table, the number span is in **bold**.
Eg, teacher referrals **85**
When the text is within a figure, the number span is in *italic*.

Eg, purpose statements 115–*16*, 119
8-Step Process for Leading Change
  (Kotter) 96–7

ability to develop 83, 89, 90
academic advising 80, 122, 123, 124–5,
  126–7, 128–9
adaptive challenges 67
adaptive leadership 42, 62, 67, 71, 72, 73
adult development and nonprofit board
  leadership 5–12
adult development theory (Drago-
  Severson & Blum-DeStefano) 180
adult learning and development 77, 118
adult learning theory (andragogy): leadership development 161; leadership
  in an uncertain environment 42, 56–7,
  60, 62; of reflective practice (Schon)
  107; transformational leadership 119;
  visionary and mission-minded school
  leadership 77, 140
African American students 94, 96, 176,
  186, 188–9, 192 *see also* Black students
Alexander Hamilton Junior High School
  (Hamilton JHS) 140, 141–2, 146
Alman, S. W. 62
American Psychological Zero Tolerance
  Task Force Report (2008) 188
andragogy (Knowles) xxii; developmentally appropriate feedback for
  adults 180, 181–2; leadership development 161; leadership in an uncertain environment 57, 61, 62; visionary
  and mission-minded school leadership

142, 145–6 *see also* adult learning
  theory (andragogy)
Anthony, A. B. 78–9
assignments, student 47, 48, 66
associate provosts 170, 171–**2**, 174
authentic leadership theory (Northouse)
  79, 148, 151–2, 153, 155
authoritarian leadership style 170, 173

baby boomers 148–9
Bain, B. 171–**2**
Balkor Elementary Charter School 77,
  176–80, 182–3
Ballou, M. B. 135–6
Barcelona, Tony 190–1
bases of power 71
Bass, B. M. 118–19
Batliwala, S. 80, 134–5
Baxter, Cindy 66, 68
behavioral challenges 112
Belinda, President Susan 149, 150, 155
benchmarks 106, 113
Bernaciak, J. F. 2
Black students 56–7, 76, 84–5, 94, 132,
  185–93 *see also* African American
  students
Blanchard, K. H. 14, 19–20, 60–1
Blum-DeStefano, J. 77, 177–8, 180
board governance 10–11
Board of Directors, Mission Forward 16–17
Board of Trustee's Meeting 150
Bolman, L. G. 1, 14, 17–19
Bourdieu, P. 71
Boydell, T. 119

196　*Index*

Braxton, J. 127
Brion, C. 78, *99*
Broad, M. L. 97
Brodeur, K. 78
Brookfield, S. 71
building a trusting client relationship 16
Burke, W. W. 31
Burns, J. M. 107
Bynoe, T. 77

California 148–9, 151, 154, 191
caring conversations 51
case studies in leadership and adult development: adult development and nonprofit board leadership 5–12; compassionate leadership and school crises 45–53; crisis leadership, time constraints and critical consciousness 65–73; developmentally appropriate feedback for adults 176–83; feminist approach to leadership education 131–8; gap between theory and practice in higher education 167–74; higher education leadership and uncertainty 55–63; leading for transformation 103–10; leading from the middle 23–9; learning transfer 93–101; nonprofit leadership style 14–22; personal growth and leadership development 148–55; professional learning in P-12 schools 158–64; school policing 185–93; servant leadership 122–9; social justice leadership in secondary education 83–91; transformational leadership 31–9, 112–20; visionary and mission-minded school leadership 140–6
cell phones 34, 35, 66, 70
CEOs (Chief Executive Officers) 1, 14–17, 21, 39
Cercone, K. 62
Chait, R. P. 10
Chao, E. L. *et al.* 62
charismatic leadership (idealized influence) 36, 38, 118
Childress, Stephanie 114
Chinese producers 31, 34
Chris (CEO of Second Chances Community Center) 1, 6–12
civil rights organizations 188
climate inventory questionnaires 143
coaching for transformation 107–8
coaching models 103, 104
coaction 80, 135–6, 137, 138

cognitive complexity 89
collaboration: crisis leadership, time constraints and critical consciousness 67; curriculum and pedagogy considerations 148, 150; feminist approach to leadership education 134–5, 136–7; gap between theory and practice in higher education 167, 169, 173; higher education leadership and uncertainty 58, 60; leadership development 79, 158–9, 160, 161–2, 163–4; learning transfer 78, 93; servant leadership 127; transformational leadership 36, 113–14, 115, 117, 119; visionary and mission-minded school leadership 77, 143, 146
collaborative learning process 93, 137
collective purpose 112, 118–19, 120
collective responsibility 25
College of Business and Economics (CBE) 149, 150, 155
College Student Leadership Development Framework 153–*4*
collegiality 76–8, 109, 115, 117–20, 173
Collegiate Cross Country Team 132–4
Collins, J. D. 76
communicating findings to the client 20
community-based organizations 6
compassionate care 49, 50–1, 51–2
compassionate leadership and school crises 45–53
competence: coaching for transformation 107; connecting personal growth and leadership development 148–9, 151–2; and the education system 76–7; gap between theory and practice in higher education 173; higher education leadership and uncertainty 59, 60; leading from the middle 27, 28; nonprofit leadership style 19, 20, 21; social justice leadership in secondary education 88; transformational leadership 37
conceptual frameworks 96, 134, 136, 167, 170–**2**
conflict: adult development and nonprofit board leadership 6–7, 11, 12; coaching for transformation 107, 109; compassionate leadership and school crises 50; crisis leadership, time constraints and critical consciousness 71–2; gap between theory and practice in higher education 169; leading from the middle 23, 26; nonprofit leadership style 18; personal growth and

leadership development 151, 153; transformational leadership 38

conflict resolution 153, 169

Conner, M. 182

constructive development framework (Kegan) 152

constructive developmental theory 5, 8–9, 179

content and materials 98–101, *99*

content reflection 108

Cooper, B. 185

Covid-19 and education 45–53, 55–63, 65–73

Cox, E. 108, 109

Cranton, P. 108

crisis leadership, time constraints and critical consciousness 65–73

crisis planning meetings 66–9, 72–3

critical consciousness 42, 65, 71, 76

critical friends 162

critical reflection 51, 103, 108–9, 109–10, 146, 191–2

critical theory of adult learning (Brookfield) 42, 71

CROWN (Creating a Respectful and Open World for Natural Hair) Act, The (California, 2019) 191, 192

cultivating leadership 132–4

culture: cultural changes 31, 32–3, 35, 89; cultural deficits 185; cultural mismatches 76, 188–9, 192; of the team 17

Cumberland, D. M. 1

Dad's Club 7

Data Team 115

Dawson, Linda 15

Day, Helen 190

Deal, T. E. 1, 14, 17–19

decision-making: coaching for transformation 107, 109; and crisis leadership 41–2, 49, 60; decision-makers 78, 134, 181; gap between theory and practice in higher education 80, 167, 168–9, **172**; leadership development 161; leading from the middle 25–6; personal growth and leadership development 154; visionary and mission-minded school leadership 141, 146

DEEs (Developmentally Effective Experiences) 149–51, 153, 155

deficit theory 185

deficit thinking 42, 77, 177–8

democratic leadership style 60, 87–8, 170, 173

demographic shifts 42, 56–7, 58–9, 60, 63, 76, 94–5

development levels (situational leadership model) 19–20

developmental efficacy 88–9

developmental leadership 152

developmental readiness 76, 83, 87–8, 89–90

developmentally appropriate feedback for adults 77, 176–83

Developmentally Effective Experiences (DEEs) 149–51, 153, 155

differential school discipline 188

directive leadership 15, 20, 60, 109

DiSC® Profile 154

discipline data 83–7, **85–6**

discipline practices 188–90

discussion questions: adult development and nonprofit board leadership 11–12; connecting personal growth and leadership development 154–5; crisis leadership, time constraints and critical consciousness 72–3; feminist approach to leadership education 137–8; leading for transformation 109; nonprofit leadership style 22; professional learning in P-12 schools 162–4; school policing 190, 191–2; social justice leadership in secondary education 91; transformational leadership 38–9 *see also* learning activities

disorienting dilemmas 2, 37, 107–8

disproportionality 61, 75, 76, 83–7, **85–6**, 90, 189

disproportionate impact of Covid-19 on minorities 61

disrespect 84–**5**, 189

distributed leadership 26, 28–9

diverse stakeholders 49, 87

Doe, Dr. John 167–70, 174

dominant conceptualization of leadership 131–2

Drago-Severson, E., 77, 177–8, 180

dress code violations **85**, 186–7, 189

dress codes 67, **85**, 186–7, 187–8, 188–9, 190–1, 192

dropout rates 122, 126

education and Covid-19 45–53, 55–63, 65–73

Education Codes 191

ELA (English Language Arts) 94

Ellis, Principal Jasmine 176–80, 182–3

emerging leaders 2, 35, 132

198 *Index*

emotional exhaustion 49
empathy: compassionate leadership and
   school crises 48, 50; developmentally
   appropriate feedback for adults 181;
   gap between theory and practice in
   higher education 170; racial 185, 188,
   192; servant leadership 126, 128
empowerment 115
English as a Second Language (ESL) 94
English Language Arts (ELA) 94
enrollment decreases 56, 57, 169
entry plans 176–8, 179
epistemological development 152–3
ESL (English as a Second Language) 94
ethics: crisis leadership, time constraints
   and critical consciousness 70–1; gap
   between theory and practice in higher
   education 80, 167, 173–4; personal
   growth and leadership development
   148, 154; servant leadership 122;
   transformational leadership 36
event time 34
explicit biases 189 *see also* implicit biases
external stakeholders 43, 49 *see also*
   internal stakeholders

facilitators 35, 67, 96, 98–9, 101,
   104, 163
fathers 7, 9–10, 11–12
feminist approach to leadership
   education 131–8
feminist leadership diamond 135, 138
feminist pedagogy 80, 81, 132, 134–6,
   136–7
FGCS (First Generation College Students) 122–3, 123–4, 126–7, 128–9
fiduciary responsibilities 10, 12
Fieldstadt, E. 190–1
financial sustainability 5, 11
First Generation College Students
   (FGCS) 122–3, 123–4, 126–7, 128–9
flexible groupings 105–6
flexible working 24, 34
frameworks for change 80, 172–3
Freire, P. 87
Frey, B. A., 62
furloughs 57, 61
Furman, G. 87–8, 91

gap between theory and practice in
   higher education 167–74
generative responsibilities 10, 12
Gibson, B. S. 42
Glickman, M. H. 79

Glickman, R. S. 79
goal orientation 88
Goff, P. A. *et al.* 185
Goodman, J. et al. 61
grading flexibility 68, 69
graduation 57, 69–70, 122, 123,
   126, 129
grant funding 14
grassroots social services 7
Greenleaf, R. 128

habits of mind (assumptions) 2, 37, 53
Hamilton JHS (Alexander Hamilton
   Junior High School) 140, 141–2, 146
Hartley, A. N. 80
Hayes, S. D. 80
Heather (teacher) 103–6, 108, 109
Heifetz, R. 67, 72
Herschel, Max 150
Hersey, P. 14, 19–20, 60–1
Hersey-Blanchard Tridimensional Leader
   Effectiveness Model 60
higher education institutions 55, 79–80,
   122, 126–7, 171
higher education leadership and
   uncertainty 55–63
higher education model of theory and
   practice 172
Hirschy, A. 127
Hispanic students 56, 57 *see also* Latinx
   students
Hoffmann, F. L. 136
Holliway, Janet 114, 117
home schooling 48
human resource frames 18

idealized influence (charismatic
   leadership) 36, 38, 118
immersion teaching 125
implicit biases 76, 89, 185, 188, 189–90,
   191–3 *see also* explicit biases
in-country community support 23–4
individualized consideration (structural
   systems) 36, 38, 118
inequitable discipline practices 188–90
influencers 17, 31, 34, 35, 36, 38, 39
innovation: compassionate leadership 42;
   crisis leadership 60; gap between
   theory and practice in higher education 168; learning transfer 97; personal
   growth and leadership development
   149; transformational leadership 34,
   35, 117
in-school suspensions 90, 187, 190

Index 199

inspirational motivation (collaborative culture) 36, 38, 118
instruction: instructional delivery 56, 69; instructional leadership teams 177–80, 182–3; instructional practices 77, 158–9, 160, 161–2, 163
integration 37, 61, 127, 150
intellectual stimulation (organizational identity) 36, 38, 112, 118–19
internal stakeholders 49, 62 *see also* external stakeholders
international context 24–5, 28
internet, lack of 46, 48
interpersonal leadership skills: compassionate leadership 50, 51; connecting personal growth and leadership development 151–2, 154–5; gap between theory and practice in higher education 169, 171; servant leadership 126, 127; social justice leadership 87 *see also* intrapersonal leadership
interventions 11, 33, 94, 117
intrapersonal leadership 151–2, 154–5 *see also* interpersonal leadership skills

Jamison, James 84–6, 90
Jenny (teacher) 104–7, 108, 109
Jentz, B. C. 176
Jim Higgenbottom 33, 35
Johnson, Rachel 32, 33–5, 37
Jones, J. A. 1
Jones, Jessa 123, 124–5, 128–9
Joseph (philanthropist) 1, 5–12
K-12 schools 45, 66, 75, 83, 103, 108, 191

Kari (NGO policy analyst) 24–6, 26–7, 28–9
Kegan, R. 1, 2, 8–9, 11, 152
Knowles, Ann 113, 120
Knowles, M. S. xxii, 62, 63, 79, 170–1, 181
Komives, S. R. *et al.* 148
Kotter, J. P. 78, 96–7

laissez-faire leadership style 170, 173
Lake University 132
Lasater, C. 41–2
Lasater, K. 41–2
Latinx students 84–**5**, 94, 132, 140, 154, 176 *see also* Hispanic students
LaVenia, K. xi, xii
Lawrence, Mrs. 45, 48, 52
lawsuits 187–8, 191

Le Fevre, D. M. 2
leader behaviors 38
leadership: leadership challenges 41, 67, 72, 75–7, 79–80, 133–4; leadership development 23–4, 26, 28–9, 78–9, 132, 148–55, 159–60; leadership focus 10–11, 107, 151; leadership illustrations 137–8 *see also* adaptive leadership; authentic leadership theory (Northouse); authoritarian leadership style; compassionate leadership and school crises; crisis leadership, time constraints and critical consciousness; democratic leadership style; distributed leadership; feminist approach to leadership education; leadership practices; leadership styles; paternalistic leadership; servant leadership; situational leadership model (Hersey and Blanchard); social justice leadership in secondary education; technical leadership; transformational leadership
leadership practices: feminist approach to leadership education 137; gap between theory and practice in higher education 167, 170–1; leading from the middle 28; personal growth and leadership development 150; social justice leadership in secondary education 83; transformational leadership 2, 38, 112
leadership style levels (situational leadership model) 19–20
leadership styles: gap between theory and practice in higher education 167–8, 170, 174; leadership style analysis (Lestan) 154–5; paternalistic leadership 32; pivoting 1, 14–15, 17–19, 19–20; servant leadership 123; and uncertainty 60; visionary and mission-minded school leadership 145
leading change 96–7, 100, 181–2
leading change model (Kotter) 96–7
leading for transformation 103–10
leading from the middle 23–9
learning activities: compassionate leadership and school crises 51–3; connecting personal growth and leadership development 154–5; leading for transformation 109–10; leading from the middle 28–9; learning transfer 100–1; nonprofit leadership style 21–2; professional learning in P-12 schools 162–3, 164; school policing 192–3; social justice leadership in

200 *Index*

secondary education 90–1; transformational leadership 38–9 *see also* discussion questions
learning organizations 36, 42, 80, 145, 171–**2**, 173, 174
learning organizations versus static organizations 171–**2**
learning outcomes *see* outcomes
learning transfer 93–101
lesson study 162
LHS (Lincoln High School) 84–5, 90
liberal arts higher education institutions 42, 55, 57
life-long learning 141–2, 145
Lincoln High School (LHS) 84–5, 90
Line, J. (Coach Line) 80–1, 132–4
Lingenfelter, P. E. 55
literacy 104–5, 113, 178
Litwin, G. H. 31
living legacies 7
low-income groups 6, 43, 75, 83, 112, 122–3, 126

Magolda, M. B. B. 148, 152
Marcuse, H. 71
marginalized populations 83, 188–9
Martin, J. L. 76
Mary Ann Riley 32, 33–5, 39
Massey, S. L. 78
math: compassionate leadership and school crises 46; developmentally appropriate feedback for adults 178; learning transfer 94; professional learning in P-12 schools 158–9, 163; transformational leadership 115, 117; visionary and mission-minded school leadership 143
Matthews, Dr. Stephen 140–1, 141–2, 142–4, 145
May, J. J. xi, xii
McGregor, D. 170
McNulty, Bryan 32, 33, 39
meaning-making 11, 51, 153, 179
mental maps 8
meta-cognitive ability 89
Mezirow, J. 2, 37, 107, 108
microaggressions 185
middle leadership roles 23–4, 26, 28
Midway Hills Primary School 103
Midwest College 56, 57–8, 60–2
military veterans 14–15, 17
Miller, D. W. 78–9
minoritized identities 81, 131, 136
Mission Forward 14–17, 20, 21

mission statements 77, 116, 140–1, 141–2, 142–4, 145, 146
missions 1, 7, 10, 140–6
MMLT (Multidimensional Model of Learning Transfer) 78, 97–100, *99*, 101
MMS (Murtle Middle School) 93–6
Moore, DeVonte 186–7
Moore family 186–7, 188
motivation to develop 88–9, 90
Mulligan, Mrs. 141
Multidimensional Model of Learning Transfer (MMLT) 78, 97–100, *99*, 101
multiple perspectives 1, 38, 42, 57, 153
multiple stakeholders 119, 160, 176
Murtle Middle School (MMS) 93–6

NACADA (National Academic Advising Association) 123
NALs (Non-traditional Adult Learners) 55–8, 59–60, 61, 62, 63
National Academic Advising Association (NACADA) 123
negative emotions 27, 173
networks of relationships 72
new coaches 78, 102–7
Newstrom, J. W. 97
NGOs (Non-Governmental Organizations) 23–8
Nielsen, G. 1, 14, 15
Non-Governmental Organizations (NGOs) 23–8
nonprofit board leadership 1, 5–12
nonprofit leadership style 14–22
Non-traditional Adult Learners (NALs) 55–8, 59–60, 61, 62, 63
Northouse, P. G. 31, 36, 148, 151
Nutrition Education Group 7

old wounds 11, 12
organizational compassion 50
Ortmann, L. L.
outcomes: adult development and non-profit board leadership 5–6, 9, 11; developmentally appropriate feedback for adults 177, 182; leadership development and adult learning 150, 152–3, 155; leading from the middle 25, 27–8; learning transfer 93, 95, 98; poverty and educational 75–6; professional learning in P-12 schools 158, 161, 163; racial empathy gap 188; servant leadership 126; social justice

leadership in secondary education 83; transformational leadership 38, 113, 119; visionary and mission-minded school leadership 141
Oxford, R. L. 180

Parmigian, G. L. 42
paternalistic leadership 2, 32, 35
Paul, W. *et al.* 128
PBIS (Positive Behavior Interventions and Supports) 94–5
PD (Professional Development) *see* Professional Development (PD)
pedagogy: changing education system 79–81; crisis leadership, time constraints and critical consciousness 71; developmentally appropriate feedback for adults 177, 180, 181–2; feminist approach to leadership education 132, 134–7, 138; higher education leadership and uncertainty 56, 57, 61, 62; personal growth and leadership development 148–55; social justice leadership in secondary education 88
Pepper, M. J. *et al.* 52
perceptions of risk 2, 25–6, 27–8, 29
Perez, Bob 140–1, 142–4
Perry, Dr. Rachel 149, 150
persistence 36, 80, 123, 127
personal growth 35, 79, 136, 148–55
personal growth and leadership development 148–55
perspective transformation 37
Pete Digney 33, 34–5, 39
Peterson, Jeanette 190
philanthropy 1, 5, 7, 11, 14–15
pivoting leadership behaviors 1, 15, 19, 20
plans of action 47, 68, 77, 96, 176, 178–9
PLCs (Professional Learning Communities) 100, 141, 142–4, 146
PLPs (Professional Learning Plans) 158–9, 161, 162–3, 164
political frames 18
Positive Behavior Interventions and Supports (PBIS) 94–5
postsecondary leadership education 149–51
poverty 5, 6, 70, 75, 88, 176
power brokers 18, 72–3
praxis-dimensions-capacities framework (Furman) 87–8, 91
Predominantly White Institutions (PWIs) 57

premise reflection 78, 108
pretraining 98–*9*, 101
problem-centered learning 161
process reflection 108
productive citizenship 140, 142, 144
Professional Development (PD): changing education system 76, 78–9; coaching for transformation 103–4; crisis leadership, time constraints and critical consciousness 69; developmentally appropriate feedback for adults 181–2; leadership development and adult learning 161–2; learning transfer 93–101; racial empathy gap 193; servant leadership 123; visionary and mission-minded school leadership 142, 145–6
professional learning: coaching for transformation 104–5, 108, 109; developmentally appropriate feedback for adults 181; leadership development and adult learning 78, 158–64; learning transfer 100; transformational leadership 112, 116–17, 119, 120; visionary and mission-minded school leadership 141
Professional Learning Communities (PLCs) 100, 141, 142–4, 146
professional learning in P-12 schools 158–64
professional learning instructional strategies 161–2
Professional Learning Plans (PLPs) 158–9, 161, 162–3, 164
project leaders 23–4
PRSSA (Public Relations Student Society of America) 124, 125
Public Relations Student Society of America (PRSSA) 124, 125
purpose statements 115–*16*, 119
PWIs (Predominantly White Institutions) 57

quality for all 140, 142, 144
quality instruction 141

race: changing education system 75; crisis leadership, time constraints and critical consciousness 67; CROWN (Creating a Respectful and Open World for Natural Hair) Act, The (California, 2019) 191–2; explicit biases 189; higher education leadership and uncertainty 57; implicit biases

202 *Index*

185, 192–3; racial tensions 169, 174; social justice leadership in secondary education 84–6, **85**, 91; transformational leadership 39 *see also* racial demographics

racial demographics: changing education system 76; coaching for transformation 94–5; higher education leadership and uncertainty 42, 56–7, 58–9, 60, 63; social justice leadership in secondary education 84, **85–6**, 90

Ramey, Mr. 45–9, 52

reconstruction of schemas 51

recoverable loss 9, 11–12

reduction in staff 2, 31

referrals 83, **85–7**, *86*, 90, 189

reframing (using multiple frames) 14, 16, 17, 18, 50

reframing model (Bolman and Deal) 1, 14, 17–19

reluctant clients 14–17

remote instruction 42–3, 65–73

remote learning 46, 47

remote working 24–5, 28, 48

resistance as perception of risk 29

Reynolds, Tim 32, 33–5, 37, 38, 39

risk perception 2, 25–6, 27–8, 29

risk taking 2, 115, 117

River Run 65–6, 67, 69, 70

River Run High School 69, 70

Riverside Elementary School (RS) 112–14

Roegman, R. 76

role models 36, 134, 137

role of emotion in leadership 2, 23, 24, 26–7, 28, 29

role-play 38–9, 52, 90–1, 174

RS (Riverside Elementary School) 112–14

Rupert, Mr. 94–6, 98, 100–1

Russo, M. R. 167, 172–3

sales staff turnover rate 32, 33

SBA (Susan B. Anthony Elementary School) 112–14, 115–18, *116*, 120

SCCC (Second Chances Community Center) 6–7, 10–11

Schlossberg, N. K. 42, 56–7, 61–2

Schön, D. A. 107

schools: assignments 47–8, 66; crisis 49, 50–1; improvement 77, 115–17, *116*, 119, 181, 182; policing 185–93; school boards 43, 68, 69, 70; transformation 118

Science, Technology, Engineering, and Mathematics (STEM) 94–5

Scranton, Jim 65, 69, 71, 73

Scricca, Dr. Eloise 65–70, 71–3

SCSU (South California State University) 149–50, 151, 155

Second Chances Community Center (SCCC) 6–7, 10–11

self-authoring minds 1, 5–12, 79, 148, 151–3

self-authorship theory (Magolda) 79, 148, 152–3, 155

self-awareness 151, 153

self-directed learning 141, 146

self-sovereign mind 8

self-transforming 8–9

servant leadership 80, 122–9

Sharpie incident 185–93

situational leadership 1, 14, 19–20, 42, 56–7, 60–1, 62

situational leadership model (Hersey and Blanchard) 1, 14, 19–20

SLCs (Small Learning Communities) 104

Small Learning Communities (SLCs) 104

Smalls, Herman 69, 70, 73

Smithville School District 45–9, 49–51, 51–3

social capital 80, 112, 119, 122, 126–7, 128

social distancing 41, 70

social justice leadership in secondary education 76, 83–91

social services 6, 7, 23, 148

socialized mind 8–10

South California State University (SCSU) 149–50, 151, 155

Spanish class 124

Spears, L. 128

Spieler, Martha 140–1, 142–4

Stake, J. E. 136

stakeholders: compassionate leadership and school crises 49–50; crisis leadership, time constraints and critical consciousness 43, 72–3; developmentally appropriate feedback for adults 176–7; gap between theory and practice in higher education 172–3; higher education leadership and uncertainty 55, 56, 58–9, 62; learning transfer 96, 98; nonprofit leadership style 15–16; professional learning in P-12 schools 160, 162, 164; social justice leadership in secondary education 83, 87–8, 89; transformational leadership 38, 119;

visionary and mission-minded school leadership 142, 145–6 *see also* external stakeholders; internal stakeholders
static organizations versus learning organizations 171–**2**
status quo 76, 170
STEM (Science, Technology, Engineering, and Mathematics) 94–5
Stentz, J. E. *et al.* 181
strategic plans: adult development and nonprofit board leadership 10; developmentally appropriate feedback for adults 176, 178; higher education leadership and uncertainty 56; nonprofit leadership style 15–16, 20, 22; personal growth and leadership development 149–50
strategic responsibilities 10–12
structural frames 18
students: accountability 69–70; data 106, 113–14, 116, 159, 163; demographics 57, 59, 94–5, 140; performance data 141, 143–4; self-efficacy 126; student disrespect 84–**5**, 189; support services 57, 61, 122 *see also* students of color
students of color: changing education system 75–7; higher education leadership and uncertainty 56, 57, 59–60; implicit biases 188–9, 192; social justice leadership in secondary education 83–5, 87
subjective misbehavior 83, 85, 90, 188–9
succession plans 15, 20, 21
Susan B. Anthony Elementary School (SBA) 112–14, 115–18, *116*, 120
Suyemoto, K. L. 135–6
symbolic frames 18

Taylor (student) 123–4, 124–5, 128–9
teacher referrals **85**
Teaching and Learning Team (TLT) 115, 117, 118–19
team captains 132, 133, 134
team conflict 2, 38
technical leadership 42, 67, 71, 72, 73
technical situations 72
Teen Club 7
Tell me so I can hear you (Drago-Severson & Blum-DeStefano) 180
ten phases of perspective transformation 37

time constraints 42, 65, 67, 73
Tinto, V. 127
TLT (Teaching and Learning Team) 115, 117, 118–19
top-down management 173
Torrisi-Steele, G. 79–80
transformational leadership 31–9, 112–20
transformational learning 37, 38, 108, 141
transformational learning theory (Mezirow) 37
transition theory (Schlossberg) 42, 56–7, 61–2
Turley, Jenn 113–14, 115–18, *116*, 118–20
Turner, Carole 14–17, 20, 21–2

under-resourced students 122
University of Nashville 122, 123

Valerie (student-athlete) 132–4
Virella, P. M. 77
virtual classrooms 46, 61
virtual environments 25, 46, 56, 57, 61, 155
virtual meetings 25
vision statements 77, 116, 140–1, 141–2, 142–4, 145, 146
visionary and mission-minded school leadership 140–6
Visone, J. D. 77
Voorhees, R. A. 55
Vroom, V. 60
Vroom-Yetton Contingency Model 60
vulnerability 2, 23, 24–6, 27, 45, 50

Wang, V. 79, 167, 171–**2**, 172–3
Warikoo, N. *et al.* 185
Wells, Ruth 83–7, 90–1
white, heteronormative context 134, 135
White students 56, 83, **85**–6, 94, 188–9
Wofford, J. 176
Wooten, L. 72
working from home 24–5, 28, 48
worldviews 19, 97

Yessip, James 114
Yetton, P. 60

zero-tolerance policies 187, 188, 190

Printed in the United States
by Baker & Taylor Publisher Services